# Procurement and Marketing of Minor Forest Produce in Tribal Areas

A Case Study of Andhra Pradesh and Orissa

# Procurement and Marketing of Minor Forest Produce in Tribal Areas

## A Case Study of Andhra Pradesh and Orissa

G. PARTHASARATHY
K. UMA SHANKAR PATNAIK

ATLANTIC
PUBLISHERS & DISTRIBUTORS

*Published by*
**ATLANTIC PUBLISHERS AND DISTRIBUTORS**
B-2, Vishal Enclave, Opp. Rajouri Garden, New Delhi-27
Phones : 25413460, 25429987, 25466842

*Sales Office*
7/22, Ansari Road, Darya Ganj, New Delhi-02
Phones : 23273880, 23285873, 23280451
Fax : 91-11-23285873
web : www.atlanticbooks.com
e-mail : info@atlanticbooks.com



ISBN 81-269-0217-5



*Typeset at*
APD Computer Graphics, Delhi
*Printed in India at*
Nice Printing Press, Delhi

# PREFACE

The title, *Procurement and Marketing of Minor Forest Produce in Tribal Areas*, of this book has been suggested by the Ministry of Rural Employment. It was felt by the Ministry that a comparative study of activities of GCC in Andhra Pradesh and those of TDCC and other organisations in Orissa will be helpful in throwing light on the steps to be taken in Orissa for remedying a bad situation. The functioning of the GCC was considered better by several people. The specific objectives of the study and the hypotheses underlying it have been carefully formulated by us.

The study is based on secondary data as well as primary data. Secondary data on procurement and sales were got from the reports of the GCC for Andhra Pradesh and from the reports of Forest Department, TDCC and other bodies of Orissa. Besides, data for the state as a whole have been obtained from the specific branches in the area of investigation. Data for branches cover month-wise procurement and sales as well as daily procurement and sales for each month. But for the willing cooperation of Branch Managers who have supplied us data from their records, it would not have been possible for us to make an analysis. We are thankful to them for their assistance. We are glad to mention, in particular, the cooperation that we received from the Branch Manager, TDCC, Sunabeda and the Branch Manager, Bhavanipatna and Muniguda in Orissa State. In Andhra Pradesh, we have received cooperation from the Branch

Managers of Rampachodavaram, Addateegala, Paderu and Araku and we are thankful to them for their assistance. The Officers at GCC headquarters have always been helpful in responding to our repeated requests for data on procurement and sales for the latest years.

The collection of field data in tribal areas is not an easy task. Investigators need to have rapport with the tribals before they could collect the data. We appointed local people as investigators. We are thankful to all of them for undertaking the onerous task of investigation. Above all we are grateful to all the tribal respondents who have willingly submitted themselves to our repeated questions. To our staff members who have worked with devotion, we cannot adequately express our thanks.

**G. PARTHASARATHY**
**K. UMA SHANKAR PATNAIK**

# Contents

## LIST OF TABLES

## LIST OF CHARTS



## LIST OF MAPS

# Executive Summary

1. The focus of the study is on procurement and marketing aspects of minor forest produce in a comparative framework between GCC of Andhra Pradesh and TDCC of Orissa.

2. The implicit hypotheses underlying the study are :

(a) The operational differences in terms of the MFP quantities procured and marketed of GCC and TDCC are attributed to the structural differences between the two organisations.

(b) The positive contribution of MFP towards employment, income and living quality differs substantially due to the variability in the operational structure (including practices) between GCC and TDCC.

3. Hypotheses (a) is sought to be tested mainly with secondary data on procurement and marketing, drawn from the documents of GCC in Andhra Pradesh and TDCC and Forest Department in Orissa.

4. Hypotheses (b) is tested mainly through findings of field surveys with a bearing of the impact of MFP on income, employment and quality of life of the tribals.

5. GCC in Andhra Pradesh has monopoly rights over procurement of MFP and has autonomy in fixation of prices. In Orissa there are multiplicity of organisations, of which the most important are TDCC and OFDC. The TDCC is found to suffer from several inadequacies including absence of autonomy in price fixation and lack of liquidity for procurement. The Orissa State appropriates through royalties and other taxes the surplus of the TDCC, while GCC in Andhra Pradesh is exempted from

royalty and purchase tax facilitating GCC to pay higher prices to tribals.

6. Data on procurement by divisions and commodities in Andhra Pradesh and Orissa has shown high concentration of MFP products in certain areas. In Andhra Pradesh, Rampachodavaram, Paderu and Parvathipuram are prominent MFP areas, while in Orissa, Parlakhemundi, Jeypore and Sambalpur are prominent. Commodity-wise concentration in Andhra Pradesh is seen in gum karaya, tamarind, mohwa seed, myrobalans, while in Orissa kendu leaves followed by sal seeds, mohwa flower and tamarind are the most important MFP commodities.

7. There has been a considerable fall in procurement in recent years. Such fall has been at a greater rate in Orissa state.

8. Branch-wise studies and days procured in a year showed the highest values for gum karaya in Addateegala branch, 150 days per year. In other branches, highest number of days procured were only 96 for seeded tamarind in Rampachodavaram and 49 in Araku valley.

9. Comparative procurement prices for the period 1991-92 to 1996 showed that the procurement prices in Orissa lagged behind for several MFP commodities those in Andhra Pradesh. But procurement prices are substantially lower than the labour cost based on prices of IAMR and market prices.

10. Examination of sale price *vis-a-vis* procurement price shows a huge gap between the two prices both for Orissa and Andhra Pradesh. The difference between the two prices much more in the case of Andhra Pradesh though procurement and sale price in Andhra Pradesh are observed to be higher than those in Orissa. The trends in sale and procurement prices showed that the procurement prices lagged behind sale prices both in Orissa and Andhra Pradesh.

11. Marketing margins are studied for hill brooms, salseed, mohwa flower, tamarind, gum of different grades. Margins

between the whole sale prices and prices received by the primary collectors in Orissa are found to be large. In Andhra Pradesh also these are found to be large despite the monopoly power exercised by the GCC.

12. The details collected by us through a field survey on prices received by the tribals for MFP and SAP showed that in respect of all MFP commodities the tribal households in Andhra Pradesh received higher prices than in Orissa, thus, confirming the picture got from the procurement agencies.

13. In the field survey, data are provided on the labour time spent on each commodity by the tribal. Cost of labour time per kg of MFP is calculated by applying market wage. This gave us the labour cost incurred by the tribal on commodity in question. A comparison of the prices paid to tribals with labour cost suggested that the prices paid are invariably lower than the labour cost.

14. One of the objectives of GCC in Andhra Pradesh and TDCC in Orissa is provision of adequate credit for both production and consumption.

15. Institutional financial sources have been faltering both in Andhra Pradesh and Orissa. The comparison between two states shows the performance of GCC in Andhra Pradesh is much better than TDCC in Orissa. The performance of TDCC is not satisfactory because of failure of LAMPS which are expected to provide support at grass-roots level.

16. Judged by the number of DR Depots and advances made, GCC performance in Andhra Pradesh is better. Almost every household is found to participate in PDS both in Andhra Pradesh and Orissa. In both the states, it is the supply factor more than the demand factor that explains the bad functioning of fair price shops.

17. In terms of value addition, GCC has taken several initiatives to add to the values of tribal produce. In Orissa State, a number of forest based industries have been set up in 1960s,

but these are mostly located in towns like Cuttack and their impact on employment and incomes of tribal is negligible.

18. The impact study is based mainly on the field data collected by us in two districts of Andhra Pradesh and two districts of Orissa. In Andhra Pradesh, the two districts namely Visakhapatnam and East Godavari, 8 villages in the purview of four GCC branches, namely : Addateegala, Rampachodavaram, Paderu and Araku are considered for the study. Similarly, in Orissa, the two districts of Koraput and Rayagada, 4 villages in the purview of two TDCC branches, namely : Sunabeda branch of Koraput district, and Muniguda branch of Rayagada district are chosen. These villages both in Andhra Pradesh and Orissa are chosen purposively for their importance in collection of MFP. In total, 200 households in Andhra Pradesh and 100 households in Orissa are chosen on the systematic sampling basis.

19. Per capita income in villages in GCC area of Andhra Pradesh is found to be roughly twice the level observed in TDCC area of Orissa. Per capita income from cultivation and MFP is higher, in absolute terms, in Andhra Pradesh as compared to Orissa. Absolute per capita income for MFP in Andhra Pradesh is Rs. 910 as compared to Rs. 577 in Orissa.

20. Food security as measured by per capita expenditure on food is better in Andhra Pradesh villages as compared to Orissa villages.

21. Per capita monthly consumption of different items also show Andhra Pradesh villages in a better position.

22. The calorie levels are also found to be better in A.P. villages and in villages with higher MFP income than in Orissa.

23. Health status, as seen from number reporting chronic diseases, is also much worse in Orissa villages. Though Orissa, as a whole, shows better literacy levels than A.P.; the selected villages show poor enrollment.

24. The role of primary markets in the development of tribal marketing is examined. Orissa State has undertaken the

development of rural primary markets with partial assistance from Central Government. Auction platforms, trader shops, water supply and sanitary arrangements, resting sheds for buyers and visitors are being proposed. These may provide better infrastructure and attract tribal produce to the market. But the development of primary market provides a necessary condition but not a sufficient condition since the tribals are in the shackles of local moneylenders and traders.

25. The quality of life of Orissa tribals has been poor as compared to Andhra Pradesh because the State in Orissa appropriates the surplus of tribal produce and as a result yields little income for improvement of Forest and Agricultural resources of tribals. The Orissa tribal is caught in Vicious Circle of drain of tribal surplus of the State, non-improvement in the tribals' surpluses (MFP & SAP), low incomes and poor quality of life.

26. GCC in Andhra Pradesh has not been able to improve the lot of tribals despite a favourable state policy. It has not been efficient in increasing the procurement price and reducing the price spread between the market price and procurement price.

# 1

# Organisational Framework for Minor Forest Produce in Orissa and Andhra Pradesh

## INTRODUCTION

The collection of minor-forest produce is one of the important occupations of the tribals in the scheduled areas. The main problem connected with this occupation is the problem of marketing. Hitherto petty traders and merchants from the neighbouring villages used to visit the tribal shandys (weekly markets) or go round the villages and collect the produce at a price favourable to them. Besides, paying a low price they used false weights and measures. Throughout the forest belonging either to the government or private persons, tribesmen used to be employed to collect minor forest produce (MFP). In some localities the forest was leased to contractors while in some the 'sub-lease system' was in vogue. The tribals used to get a wage which was arbitrarily fixed by the contractors.

This chapter presents a description of the institutions governing the marketing of MFP in Orissa in Section I and Girijan Cooperative Corporation Ltd. (GCC) of Andhra Pradesh in Section II. These institutions are intended to free the tribal from the hold of moneylender-cum-trader. In Orissa, the activities are mainly undertaken by the Tribal Development Cooperative Corporation Ltd. (TDCC). Besides the TDCC, a number of other agencies also involved in the procurement of minor forest produce. Of these agencies, the most important are Orissa Forest Development Corporation (OFDC), and Forest Department of Government of Orissa. In recent years, a number of private agencies have been given monopoly rights in specific products. In Andhra Pradesh, G.C.C. has monopoly rights over minor forest produce except in the case of kendu leaves and bamboo which are in the purview of Forest Department.

## SECTION-I

## ORGANISATIONAL FRAMEWORK FOR ORISSA

### 1.1. Categories of Minor Forest Produce

Minor forest produce is also known as non-timber forest produce (NTFP). Forest produce both timber and non-timber has all along being the main stay of tribal economy. Because of the clamping down of a host of government restrictions on timber produce, tribal people and other forest dependent non tribal groups have drifted towards non-timber forest produce (NTFP).

Minor Forest Produce yielded roughly 9 times of revenue obtained from major forest produce as in 1992-93. Production of non wood forest products is given under the following categories in Orissa: (1) Non-wood, (2) Drugs, (3) Lac, (4) Tan stuff and dye stuff, (5) Vegetable and other oil seeds, (6) Gums and resins, (7) Fibre and flosses, (8) Grass and fodders.

Only two items are given under the non-wood forest products (a) Canes and (b) Kendu leaves. Out of the other items, tamarind followed by Mohwa flower is the most prominent. Lac in terms of quantity is not important. Over a period, its production has been declining. Among the items covered under tan stuff, and dye stuff, myrobalan is the most prominent. Its production showed large variation from year to year but it showed an upward trend. Cleaning and marking nuts also showed large variability from year to year. Among the vegetable and oil seeds, sal seed is the most prominent followed by Mohwa seed and mango seed. Among gums and resins, Genduli gum is the most important from the view-point of quality. Among fibres and flosses, siali fibre is the most important followed by mat reed. Both these commodities showed large variations in quantity from year to year. Among grass and fodder, two items are listed namely thatch grass and sabai grass.

Thatch grass is not recorded since 1984-88. Sabai grass procurement shows large variations.

## 1.2. Organisation of Kendu Leaves and the Role of Forest Department

In Orissa, the kendu leaf trade was monopolised by a few merchants who were holding the lease on long-term and short-term basis until it was nationalised in 1972. As part of the scheme nationalisation, Forest Department is in charge of the collection and processing of the kendu leaves and the OFDC Ltd. was entrusted with the task of sale of kendu leaves produced by the department. In 1973, the Government created a separate department for kendu leaf organisation with the Chief Conservator of Forests incharge of it. Government also authorised the appointment of second staff such as Checkers, Head Checkers, Munshis, Moralis, Chowkidars and Watchers every year during the working season for a period of two to eleven months according to the necessity for kendu leaf production.

The work schedule was also prescribed for undertaking preliminary operations such as construction and repair of phadi houses in the month of January. Bush cutting starts from the month of February and the collection of leaves start from the month of April.

## 1.3. Major Activity of Orissa Forest Development Corporation Ltd. (OFDC)

The Orissa Forest Development Corporation (OFDC) Ltd. deals in the marketing of kendu leaves, sal seeds and bamboo. Nationalisation of kendu leaves has not prevented large scale smuggling *via* Sambalpur, the largest producing district to Kolkata. Secondly when the royalty has increased to Rs. 22 crores in 1987-88 to further Rs. 79 crores in 1991, the demand of the pluckers for getting one paise for leaf has gone unheeded. In fact, demand is not unreasonable considering the income obtained by the Forest Department. Kendu leaf also has international demand from countries like Bangladesh, Pakistan and Sri Lanka.

Sal seed is another item which is dealt by OFDC Ltd. Its

use for oil extraction provides a very good marketing. In 1993 it was nationalised and OFDC got the full right over the sal seed trade. Although sal seed was nationalised, the dominance of private traders remained. Due to mismanagement and corruption at OFDC level, there were big losses to the government. The government handed over the sal seed procurement and processing to the private oil companies *viz.* (1) Orissa Oil Industries Limited, Sasan, (2) Orissa Oil Industries Limited, Rairangpur, (3) Utkal Oils, Ambaguda and (4) Orissa Vegetable Oils Complex belongs to Mr. Ajit Samantray.[1]

Under the new arrangement, the OFDC and TDCC remain as the agent of the government as before and they would get a commission of Rs. 150 per m.t. from the affiliated parties. In addition these private promoters could pay the government Rs. 100 per m.t. They would invest their own capital on procurement of sal seed. Government defended the decision on the ground that it was an experimental decision for one year.

Sal seed collection provides sustenance for a number of people. On an average a man collects upto 7 kg. a day and needs 2 to 3 days for primary processing. Unless price offered is remunerative, the primary collectors will have to face hardship. OFDC and TDCC no doubt have failed to deliver the goods. But privatisation does not help the situation. Private people delayed in appointing sub-agents until the primary collector is impatient to sell at whatever price is offered. For example in July 1995, one company was found purchasing at Rs. 1.60 per kg. from Melakai block even when the minimum price fixed was Rs. 1.75 per kg.

Historically, bamboo policy has been to give bamboo forests on long-term lease to paper industries. Prior to 1959, five paper industries were given long-term lease by an agreement in which interest of artisans and villagers were sought to be protected. From mid 70s till the end of 80s, division-wise lease was granted to four paper mills. Accordingly M/s. Bengal Paper Mills got lease in Bolangir division (1977-83), M/s. O.P. Mills in 9 divisions (1977-89), and M/s. M.S. Straw Products Private Limited in 8 divisions (1977-89), M/s. T.P. Mills Private Limited in 11 divisions (1977-89). By a notification in 1993, the Government authorised the private sector paper industries to get into the forests and start auction in connection with bamboo coupes in advance. By this notification the control of bamboo forest passed from OFDC to private industries. A notification reintroduced labour contract system that was earlier abolished in 1960. The notification did not take into account the possibilities of environment hazard. At present the mills are indulging in un-scientific cutting. They are getting a bamboo piece at 15 paise while the communities who live on manufacturing bamboo products need to pay from Rs. 4.30 to Rs. 13.00 at the time of auction. Labourers also were exploited; they get a wage as low as Rs. 4.70 per bundle. Above all, these labourers-cum-cutters are very much likely to be left to the mercy of paper industries with the possible introduction of mechanised cutting of bamboo.

### 1.4. The Tribal Development Cooperative Corporation Ltd.

The TDCC was established in 1973 after winding up the then Forest Produce Cooperative Marketing Society dealing with NTFP. It was given rights of procurement in 11 out of 13 undivided districts. Till December 1990, the TDCC was procuring almost all marketable NTFP except kendu leaves. It functions primarily in 3 sub-divisional offices, 15 branch offices, 130 permanent procurement centres, 74 fair price shops (which also offer act as procument units) and 66 godowns. The actual procurement units are the TDCC depots found at the block headquarters of the districts and the LAMPS procurement units. The objectives of the TDCC were to purchase Surplus Agricultural Produce (SAP) and MFP at fair and reasonable prices, supply essential commodities and other consumer goods at fair prices through its fair price shops under the public distribution system, to arrange for the processing of the procured inputs that could serve the twin purposes of value addition thereby generating additional employment and to advance consumption-cum-production loans to tribals. TDCC is an apex organisation at state level and at present 240 LAMPS and other primary societies, 47 Panchayat Samities, 3 individuals and State Governments are its members. TDCC has been granted lease of MFP in 19 forest divisions since 1991, out of 27 territorial divisions in the state. Besides, with reference to three items, *viz.* tamarind, honey and hillbroom, TDCC has been granted monopoly rights for procurement in some forest divisions of the state. It procures SAP and MFP from the tribals through its own employees in the haats and villages. In addition to the fair price shops which function as procurement centres, temporary centres are also opened in the haats and villages to purchase SAP and MFP from the tribal people. In all around 800 temporary procurement centres are opened in the remote areas for the collection of SAP and MFP every year. LAMPS and other cooperatives are also appointed as agents for the procurement of SAP and MFP.

The private traders are dominating Mohwa flower trade since long. TDCC got the agency right for the procurement and marketing in 1989. It lost its market drastically following the ban on country liquor making. TDCC also did not collect sufficiently. Lakhs and hundred quintals of Mohwa flower collected by common people got wasted. In 1992 Mohwa flower trade was denationalized.

Officially the TDCC and OFDC had agency over many NTFP's until 1990. Agency Marketing Cooperative Society (AMCS) had dominance in some items in Beliguda, Phulbani areas. Later Utkal Forest Products Limited a joint sector company entered into the trade of MFPs. It has exclusive marketing rights over 29 items for 10 years (from 14-1-1990). Recently tamarind in Rayagada division upon which TDCC has the exclusive right has been taken away and is handed over to M/s. Tamarind and Kernel Products of Doki Satyanarayana, a private trader. The controversy is that the right has been given to a party who apparently does not have a processing plant. He collects tamarind at a price ranging from Rs. 2 to Rs. 2.25 per kg. and after removing kernel sells the deseeded tamarind at the rate of Rs. 12.00 per kg. and seeds at Rs. 3.50 per kg. mostly to the one M/s. Mahindra International of Kolkata. Thus, after paying a royalty, he appropriates a net profit of Rs. 2 crores from this trade.

TDCC disposes all its procured articles through tie-up arrangements with national and state level organisations such as Tribal Cooperative Marketing Development of India Ltd. (TRIFED), National Agricultural Cooperative Marketing

Federation of India Ltd. (NAFED), Orissa State Marketing Cooperative Federation, Agro Industries Cooperation, Ordinance Equipment factory of Government of India and through tenders. TDCC has not been a complete success despite its contribution to tribal economy. Its bad performance is due to the following factors.

(1) It has continuously incurred losses thereby leading to the complete erosion of its capital base. Consequently, it has been increasingly depending on loans from banks and other institutions as well as on budgetary support from the State Government. Major reasons for the losses are low business turnover, heavy interest burden on borrowings, high overheads, payment of heavy amount of royalty to Forest Department for procurement of MFP, market fluctuations, and the compulsions for paying higher rate on procurement.

(2) Since 1991, the involvement of LAMPS in procurement has been decreasing. For example, the number has decreased from 50 in 1991-92 to 36 in 1992-93 to 8 in 1993-94.

(3) The tie-up arrangements of the TDCC, although it has the virtue of assuring a stable market, denies the best available price in the market.

(4) TDCC maintains excess staff.

(5) The functioning of its storage department has been found to be inadequate.

(6) The most important reason for the failure of TDCC is its lack of autonomy. The procurement prices for MFP items are fixed by the Price Fixation Committee headed by the District Collector and the TDCC has no say in price fixation. Further, the TDCC has to await the work orders from the government for starting procurement. The work orders of the government are issued much later after the season has commenced. The issue of work order is contingent upon clearance of all earlier royalties to the government. The lease agreement will be renewed every year. Further sales tax clearance certificate should be submitted by the TDCC before starting procurement. For some of the commodities parallel lease is given to private persons.[2]

### 1.5. Orissa Rural Development and Marketing Agency Society (ORMAS)

This society was created in 1989 as an autonomous state agency under the department of Panchayat Raj. Its object is to serve multiple purposes in the value addition and marketing of rural products, especially of the IRDP beneficiaries by establishing a three-tyre marketing network at State, District and Block level. The ORMAS participates in trade fairs, product exhibition, and assists DWACRA groups in the field of marketing, processing etc.

### 1.6. Utkal Forest Products Ltd. (UFP), 1989

Utkal Forest Products (UFP), incorporated in 1989 is a joint venture between Industrial Promotion and Investment Corporation Ltd. (IPICOL), Bhubaneswar and M/s. J.P. Lath and Associates, Bhubaneswar with the agenda of "systematic collection and processing of minor forest products". The Utkal Forest Products Ltd. has been highly profitable. However its performance cannot be so well balanced when social consideration is taken into account for the following reasons:

1. The lease system for a definite period, for a private party, is not a healthy trend from the view-point of perspective planning on forest as the short-term profitability takes precedence over long-term social objectives.
2. Second, the employment of agents to collect forest produce results in the exploitation of tribals by commission agents.
3. Third, the overall government policy of pursuing a multiple objective may be self-defeating as royalty increment of government gets precedence over tribal interest.
4. Linking NTFP with the needs of industrial concerns, which use these as inputs, reflect the interest of the primary collector only if these industries operate in a competitive atmosphere.

Above all, the objectives of UFP are often violated, resulting in demand from the primary collectors for the takeover of UFP by OFDC.

### 1.7. Large Size Multi-Purpose Societies (LAMPS)

LAMPS are based on the recommendations of the Bawa Committee (1977). They were formed in 1977 each covering 10,000 to 20,000 population. Some are attached to TDCC and some are to OFDC and the rest are functioning independently. The objectives of the LAMPS are:

- to meet credit needs of the tribals for their agricultural operation;
- supply fertilizers and insecticides and agricultural implements to the tribals;
- market produce collected or cultivated by the tribals; and extend consumer credit for the tribals for meeting expenses for marriage, education and other important needs.

At present most LAMPS are defunct. However under new revitalization scheme, the government is planning to initiate the process of revamping of LAMPS in a phased manner by providing managerial assistance and working capital.

### 1.8. Agency Marketing Cooperative Society Ltd. (AMCS), Tikabali (1947)[3]

AMCS was primarily a cooperative society for turmeric growers in Phulbani district. In 1950, the society obtained a lease from the Department of Forest, Government of Orissa for other forest produce such as siali plates, tamarind, arrow root, brooms etc. Society is managed by S.C. and S.T. themselves. It is said to be the biggest trader in siali plates in the state. It also has a tamarind powder factory, a turmeric unit, a flower mill, leaf plate — cup unit, a hill broom unit, and a cold storage unit. The business turnover of AMCS in 1994-95 was to the tune of Rs. 268.00 lakhs. The society also gives financial aid to 10 high schools and 4 colleges. It is a profit making concern in comparison with TDCC.

### 1.9. Tassar and Silk Cooperatives

Tassar is produced throughout Orissa. In 1982-83, an inter-state Tassar project under the Indo-Swiss Project was taken up in Keonjhar, Mayurbhanj, Sambalpur and Sundergarh, supporting activities upto 1993-94. This scheme extends support to farmers for Tassar plantation and for rearing tassar worms. The State Tassar and Silk Cooperative Society (STSCS), under which over 60 tribal tassar growers' societies function, has undertaken the implementation of this project. The society has taken up the plantation of arjun trees for tassar growing and the establishment of 13 tassar reeling and spinning centres for yarn production.

The cooperative societies has provided fund to the tribal silk rearers, cooperative societies to procure cocoons. It now intends to involve TRIFED in the marketing of silk. TRIFED has already provided Rs. 10,000 as working capital for the purpose. The Central Silk Board has organised a committee to look into marketing or other problems that may emerge.

### 1.10. Tribal Cooperative Marketing Development Federation of India (TRIFED) Ltd.

Under the Ministry of Social Welfare at the central level, TRIFED was set up in August, 1987 as the Apex Body over the state level tribal development corporations, forest corporations and the forest produce cooperatives under the Multi-State Cooperative Societies Act, 1984.

The members of TRIFED are the Tribal Cooperative Federations, organisations dealing with NTFP, the Government, National Cooperative Development Corporations and the National Agricultural Cooperative Marketing Federation.

One way in which TRIFED has attempted to achieve its objectives is by offering attractive prices to the cooperatives, who are in turn required to pay remunerative prices to the tribals. For example, in 1998, TRIFED offered to purchase sal seed at Rs. 1900 per m.t. if the TDCC would correspondingly offer Rs. 1200 per m.t. for the produce.

## SECTION-II

## ORGANISATIONAL FRAMEWORK FOR MFP IN ANDHRA PRADESH

### 1.11. Girijan Cooperative Corporation, Andhra Pradesh

Credit and marketing are the two problems that beset the tribals. They have a high priority both as a protective and a developmental measure. The policy in relation to the basic structure for credit and marketing has been reasonably settled in the last few years. The Girijan Cooperative Corporation is unique in that it combines both the credit supply and marketing of minor forest produce collected by the Adivasis. Besides, it supplies domestic requirements to the tribal people who were hitherto dependent on local petty traders who very often exploited their ignorance with regard to the quality of the goods and weights and measures used. The government after careful deliberation and discussion thought of establishing one institution which could play the dual role of supplier of credit and agent for marketing both the minor forest and agricultural produce.

### 1.12. Genesis of GCC

In this chapter attention is mainly being focused on the genesis of the Girijan Cooperative Corporation, its aims and objectives, its organisational set up and the working of the Corporation in respect of marketing and credit supply. The pricing policy which has proved to be the Achilles' heel of the whole programme receives special attention.

With a view to improving the conditions and assuring the tribals a fair price and checking leakages in the produce collected in the areas where such a system was in vogue, an experiment was tried in the Rampa Agency (in the East Godavari district) where the government came forward and purchased the tamarind collected by the tribals. The rate to be paid to the tribals was fixed at half the market rate prevailing at Rajahmundry.

This experiment however proved a failure, and the reasons for it are set out in Dr. Baliga's paper on the 'The Agencies and their problems', an extract from which is reproduced below :

> *"This scheme was originally intended to cover the entire Rampa country but it was eventually confined to one depot at Rampa Chodavaram. This naturally resulted in diversion of most of the produce to be sold to the plains sowcars. Moreover, by the time the government opened the depot and made it compulsory for the hillmen to sell the produce*

*to the depot alone, some two months of the season elapsed and during this interval the sowcars with their old established connections gained a long start. Again, since it was known that the scheme would be in operation only for six months, stocks were sold later on to the sowcars. Further, the crop also for the season was poor and the sowcars put their prices in competition. To cap this all, errors were committed in fixing the purchase as well as the depot was able to collect only 4,414 maunds instead of 50,000 maunds anticipated by the Government; it lost Rs. 2,000."*

He concluded that, "these reasons show as plain as chaff that the scheme was not given fair trade. Further, it was not given another tribal in the succeeding year".

Again after independence, the government took keen interest in alleviating the distress of the tribals and appointed a team of experts headed by R.S. Malayappan to formulate plans for the development of Agency areas in Srikakulam, Visakhapatnam, the East and West Godavari districts. The Committee, after a thorough study of the conditions obtaining in the Andhra Agency, suggested, besides many other things, that "if the exploitation by the middlemen is to be eliminated, a network of multipurpose cooperative societies have to be started in the Agency. The functions of these societies will, for the present, be to purchase all minor forest produce collected by hillmen and also their surplus grain and to sell them their daily needs."

By 1955, 70 cooperative societies of different types were started in the scheduled areas in Srikakulam and Visakhapatnam districts. There were 7 multipurpose cooperative societies. The performance of the societies was not satisfactory and they could not touch even the fringe of the problem of providing loans to the tribals and marketing facilities. This compelled the government to set up a special organisation with the responsibility of extending a package of services to the tribals so as to enable them to approach a single agency for credit as well as marketing. Thus, the Andhra Pradesh Scheduled Tribes Cooperative Finance and Development Corporation came into existence with an authorised capital of Rs. two lakhs divided into 20,000 shares of Rs. 10 each.

## 1.13. Functions of GCC and Objectives

The Corporation started functioning in the year 1956 with only two primary marketing societies as its members. In course of time the Corporation expanded its operations both in Andhra and Telangana regions (1969) to cover the entire population of the Scheduled Tribes in the State. At present the activities of the Corporation are carried out through 30 primary marketing societies affiliated to it.

1. to encourage self-help, thrift and cooperation among members;
2. to advance loans to members on the pledge of produce for agricultural and domestic purposes;
3. to purchase outright the produce of hillmen as an owner or an agent;
4. to arrange for the sale of the produce of the members to the best advantage;
5. to rent or own godowns or sale-depots to facilitate the storage of produce purchased or pledged to the Society and sale of domestic requirement of the hillmen;
6. to supply agricultural, domestic and other requirements of the members;
7. to propagate and supply pure seeds;
8. to purchase seeds, manures, implements and other agricultural requirements for sale or distribution to members; and
9. to receive subsidies from the State or the public and to utilise them for the purpose for which they are received.

The functions of the Corporation, as the years rolled on, were given a development orientation. With this there was a change in the approach and objectives of the Corporation and a few more functions were added. The main developmental functions are :

1. to set up forest-based industries in the scheduled areas;
2. to undertake activities such as processing and grading;
3. implement welfare schemes for the economic uplift of the tribals.

### 1.14. Organisational Set-up

The ultimate authority in all matters relating to the administration is the general body which comprises select, non-official directors of the affiliated societies or functional institutions operating in different parts of the State. The executive management of the affairs of the primary society is vested in the board of directors consisting of 9 members as per the by-law (20) of the model by-laws of primary societies. The Board consists of 15 persons of whom 10 are ex-officio directors nominated by the Registrar of Cooperative Societies and the remaining are non-official directors elected by the general body of the Corporation. The first member, Board of Revenue, who is the Commissioner of Tribal Welfare is the ex-officio Chairman of the Board of Directors. The other ex-officio directors are : (1) Managing Director, the Girijan Cooperative Corporation, (2) the Director of Agriculture, (3) the Director of Tribal Welfare, (4) the Registrar of Cooperative Societies, (5) the Collector of the District, (6) the Deputy Secretary Finance, Government of Andhra Pradesh, (7) the Deputy Secretary Industries, Government of Andhra Pradesh and (8) the Chief Conservator of Forests.

The executive administration of the Corporation is the responsibility of the Managing Director, who is assisted by the Divisional Managers. The executive administration of the affiliated societies is in the hands of the manager of the cadre of tahsildar or deputy tahsildar who is under the control of the Managing Director. The manager of the society acts as the ex-officio Secretary of the Society.

### 1.15. Credit-cum-Marketing

One of the two important functions of the Girijan Cooperative Corporation is the supply of credit. The authorities realised that there should be one organisation which would combine both credit and marketing in the tribal areas. This prompted the authorities to convert all the Domestic Requirement Depots into Credit-cum-Marketing Centres.

This set-up ensures the package of services required by the tribals *viz.* credit—both production and consumption, —supply of seeds, fertilizers, pesticides, domestic requirements and marketing of forest produce etc.

The Bawa Committee (1977) recommended that suitable higher level organisations such as land mortgage banks, district cooperative credit banks should be pressed into service to support, supervise, guide and augment the activities of the societies at the primary level.

The Girijan Cooperative Corporation should also approach other institutions like commercial banks, the NCDC for providing the necessary credit for expanding its activities.

### 1.16. Marketing

The procurement of minor forest produce and agricultural produce is one of the important functions of the Corporation. The produce brought by the tribals is generally purchased at shandys, domestic requirements depots and other purchasing points specially set up by the Corporation. The Corporation has monopoly rights for the collection of minor forest produce by the tribals in the scheduled areas for which a fixed amount of rentals is paid to the forest department by the Corporation. (In recent years the corporation is exempted from payment of royalty).

The shandy is a place where the tribals bring their produce for marketing. The operations at the shandys for procurement of different kinds of produce are conducted by a representative of the Corporation known as shandy inspector. At present there are 174 regulated shandys within the area of operation of the Corporation.

In addition to the shandys the Domestic Requirements Depots serve as procurement centres for the purchase of minor forest produce and agricultural produce brought by tribals. This arrangement provided additional facilities for marketing produce on all week days by the tribals. After procurement of produce either at the shandys or other purchasing points the stocks are stored in the nearest godowns maintained by the Corporation.

### 1.17. Domestic Requirements

The tribals sell their produce to the Corporation and in turn purchase their domestic requirements like rice, kerosene, matches, oils, controlled cloth, blankets, pulses etc. from the depots of the Girijan Cooperative Corporation.

There is a large network of 850 (December, 1996) depots all over the tribal areas of the state. Here also the accent is on 'fair price' for the tribals. Earlier, there was a criterion of a minimum turnover of Rs. 3,000 per month for opening a Domestic Requirement Depot. Later, Depots were ordered to be opened in all important centres on the sole consideration that it should be easily accessible to cover 15 to 20 villages and/or a population of 2,000 tribals.

In order to maintain uniformity in the sale-price and ensure quality of the purchase of domestic requirements and other controlled commodities has recently been centralised. The divisional general manager is now responsible for bulk purchases and for adopting procedures to ensure a fair price and good quality.

The line of activity of the corporation is considered to be the most successful and endeared itself to the tribals. By and large it functions as a channel of civil supplies through which rice and consumption articles are supplied at the subsidised rates. Earlier, the petty traders used to exchange these consumption articles for the minor forest produce collected by the tribals without reference to the relative prices of the commodities exchanged. This type of barter worked to the disadvantage of the tribals inasmuch as the prices of minor forest produce bartered and of domestic requirements varied considerably. The Corporation entered the field and tried to eliminate the middlemen in this retail trade.

Though each society played an increasingly important role in supplying good quality consumer goods to the tribals, the Corporation may not be able to totally eliminate middlemen from this retail trade. It could be due to the age-old contact of the tribals with the merchants. The more fundamental reason might be the small price differential (the difference in the price of the Society and of the private dealer) provided by the Corporation and it will prove to be very difficult to eliminate the middlemen unless a stronger price incentive is offered to the tribals.

With a view to developing a sense of self-confidence and initiative among the tribal boys, the Board of Directors of the

Girijan Cooperative Corporation resolved to hand over certain viable domestic requirement depots to tribal salesmen working in the Corporation on self-employment basis. The Girijan Corporation, however, will continue to undertake:

1. to provide cash credit accommodation;
2. supply domestic requirements on credit at the depot point; and
3. subsidise transport and other maintenance costs of the Corporation.

Another feature is that the tribal salesmen will undertake to sell the commodities with 2 per cent profit margin only in lieu of his salary.

Preliminary training under this scheme was imparted to the first batch of the tribal salesmen and they were asked to choose the depots for independent management. It has plans to hand over as many domestic requirements depots possible to the tribal boys.

**1.18. Recent Changes in the Organisational Activities of GCC**

As a major step towards involvement of tribals in the decision making process, GCC currently has facilitated broadly six village development support systems. They are :

(1) Village Tribal Development Associations (VTDA)

(2) Setting of small industrial units

(3) Research and Development

(4) Community Coordination Teams

(5) Tribal Organisations

(6) Commodity Cooperatives

For the purpose of engaging local tribal youth for extension, for imparting training and for providing sustained guidance, GCC facilitates VTDAs with professional support. The VTDAs are informal associations of the residents of one or more habitations on a community basis who undertake group credit, agricultural extension, marketing etc. Specially some of the schemes are gramin banks, village banks, mahila bank, agricultural extension, NTFP extension, agricultural marketing etc. Since such schemes require presence of skilled manpower, the GCC facilitates or supports the VTDAs in the placement of manpower during the initial stages until the tribals are well equipped to take up such tasks by themselves.

The GCC has also set up small industrial units like honey processing, Shikakai and soap nut grinding units at the various places like Rajahmundry, Araku, Vizianagaram and Nirmal etc.

In view of better price for the NTFP of the tribals, GCC is engaged in research and development activity to identify and promote value-added derivatives of the raw produce such as gum karaya, gum olibanum, cleaning nuts, marking nuts etc. It is expected that they would increase the value by 5 to 10 times of the current prices.

GCC has also included the dedicated and talented young professionals as community coordinators to organise the tribals, to engage self-help, thrift and cooperation and to develop the capabilities of the communities for the purpose of creating self-reliance in an area of operation of Community Coordination Teams. So far 12 CCTs are placed in the field and a total of 45 teams are proposed for the next four years.

For the purpose of commercialisation of MFP items, GCC has supported the promotion of tribal organisations, say Girijan Gum Pickers Association under the Kovel Foundation Trust.

GCC has also facilitated the formation of commodity based cooperatives *viz.* Chillies Producers Cooperatives, Niger Seed Producers Marketing Societies etc.

### 1.19. Price Policy of the Girijan Cooperative Corporation

The primary marketing society while fixing the purchase price used to take into consideration the 'Wholesale market rate' and deduct from it the following items:

1. Forest rentals
2. Trading charges
3. Transport costs
4. Establishment charges
5. Dryage and deficients
6. 10 per cent margin for market fluctuations.

The resultant price will be paid to the tribals. The formula was given to the Corporation by Government of India and the State Government approved of it. However, to offer a better price to the tribals, the 10 per cent margin of market fluctuations was subsequently reduced to 5 per cent.

This policy came in for sharp criticism on the obvious ground that the resultant price was very low. In fact, forest rentals and establishment costs alone accounted for 35 per cent of the deductions from the purchase price to be paid to the tribes. This was a disincentive to the tribal to sell his produce to the Corporation. It also afforded a wide margin of maneuverability to the traders to undercut the Corporation, as the trader had few overheads to worry about. Accordingly, the Girijan Cooperative Corporation resolved to pay the ruling market-price in the established markets without making the above deductions. It was assumed that with an efficient system of marketing there would be no loss. However, in case of any loss occasioned by the payment of a fair price to the tribal, the loss would be subsidised by the government. In pursuance of this policy decision the government in its order dated 1-12-1970 ordered that the Corporation should fix the purchase price without making deductions on account of forest rentals and establishment charges. By the same order the government undertook to subsidise the Corporation for its losses on account of non-deduction of the above two items in its costing. Thus the government order represented a major shift in the purchasing policy of the Corporation from a 'fair-price' to that of 'a support price', in which, forest rentals are taken out from the pricing component, as the GCC is exempted from the payment of rentals.

Simultaneously, the Corporation abolished the system of purchasing agents and replaced them with qualified persons fitted into tribal welfare service and formed a nucleus of trained and responsible field personnel. Efforts are also being made to attract the tribals to sell their minor forest produce as and when they collect them to the 'Domestic Requirements Depots' instead of having to wait for the weekly shandy. In course of time, it is hoped that the Domestic Requirements Depots will supplant the weekly shandy as a trading centre for the tribals.

With the shift in policy the Girijan Cooperative Corporation would be in a position to (1) fill the void of absence of marketing facilities for the tribals; (2) at the same time there would be an assurance of 'support price'; (3) in addition, there could be a degree of subsidy inherent in the pricing and costing policy.

The first two factors ensure a certain degree of buoyancy in the prices of the produce for the tribals. The last is in consonance with the social policy of the government which ensures not merely a proper money equivalent, but also, a margin of subsidy in order to progressively improve the economic condition of the tribals. Also inherent in this policy is the concept of price stabilisation to protect the tribals from the adverse effects of the market fluctuations.

The commodities procured by the Corporation range from items of broad based domestic consumption like tamarind and Shikakai to specialised produces such as gum, nuxvomica, rauwolfia serpentina, used in the industrial and pharamaceutical fields. The output of these commodities fluctuates with the season and so also the prices vary sharply and steeply.

In many cases market fluctuations are not easily determined. Consequently the Corporation is continuously faced with the problem of over-stocking, especially in the background of its procurement and price policy which makes procurement an end in itself. The produce of the Girijan Cooperative Corporation has to compete with similar products from other assembly points. Thus the very same factors which determine the purchase price policy present specific problems of marketing.

There is a great need for establishing a grading unit since such processing and grading activity would also generate additional opportunities of employment to the tribals.

## SUMMARY

This Chapter reviewed the organisational framework for MFP in Orissa State. In Orissa State, there is a multiplicity of organisations of which the most important are TDCC and OFDC. The TDCC is found to suffer from several inadequacies including absence of autonomy in price policy and lack of liquidity for procurement. As a result, its procurement and marketing operations have suffered and the tribal is forced to sell to the local traders at non-remunerative prices. OFDC operations have helped the state to obtain huge royalties. But the tribal did not benefit adequately by this operation. In recent years the Orissa State has given monopoly right to private individuals in certain commodities and in specified areas. Monopoly rights to private individuals without the power to enforce their obligations to state and to the tribals has also led to exploitation of the tribal in the product market.

GCC in Andhra Pradesh has monopoly right in the purchase of MFP. It also enjoys exemption from royalty of state and from purchase tax. It has autonomy in price fixation. Its monopoly is exercised in favour of the tribal. In recent years it has moved towards meeting domestic requirements of the tribals by opening a number of domestic requirement depots. It has also involved the tribals in decision making process by setting a number of Village Tribal Development Associations (VTDAs). Yet the GCC has come in for criticism on the obvious ground that the price paid to the tribal is much less than the market price.

## NOTES

1. Council of Professional Social Workers, *Forest Dwellers and Non-timber Forest Marketing in Orissa — A Study and Policy Analysis, Bhubaneswar*, Orissa, 1996, p. 12.
2. Government of Orissa, Department of Forests and Animal Husbandry, work order given by the DFO, Rayagada.
3. A.P. Kansal, "Success Story of the AMCs, Tikabali in Rainbow", Bhubaneswar, Orissa Cooperative Union, Ph.D. thesis submitted to the Berhampur University, 1982.

# 2

# Objectives and Methodology of the Study

## SECTION-I

## OBJECTIVES AND HYPOTHESES

### 2.1. Objectives

The study aims at the procurement and marketing aspects of Minor Forest Produce (MFP) in a comparative framework between the Girijan Cooperative Corporation (GCC) area of Andhra Pradesh and Tribal Development Cooperative Corporation (TDCC) area of Orissa. The specific objectives of the study are :

1. to study the structure and functioning of institutional set-up of both the GCC of Andhra Pradesh and the TDCC of Orissa in relation to their objectives, with particular reference to primary cooperative marketing societies, purchase depots, sale operations, public distribution systems and credit systems;
2. to study the prevailing practices and systems of collection, marketing, processing and utilisation of Minor Forest Produce;
3. to evaluate the policies of GCC and TDCC in relation to procurement, and marketing of MFP and Surplus Agricultural Produce (SAP); and
4. to evaluate the significance of Minor Forest Produce for employment, income and quality of life of tribal people in the GCC area of Andhra Pradesh and in the TDCC area of Orissa.

## 2.2. Hypotheses

In view of the above objectives, the following hypotheses are framed for testing :

1. The operational differences in terms of the MFP quantities procured and marketed of GCC and TDCC are attributed to the structural differences between the two organisations.
2. The positive contribution of MFP towards employment, income and living quality differs substantially due to the variability in the operational structure (including practices) between GCC and TDCC.

## SECTION-II

## DESIGN OF THE SURVEY — ANDHRA PRADESH

The study area is located in Visakhapatnam and East Godavari Districts (see Chart-I). This section provides the profiles of Visakhapatnam District and villages covered by survey followed by East Godavari District.

## 2.3. Profiles of the Study Area — Visakhapatnam, Andhra Pradesh

*Economic Importance*

Visakhapatnam ranks fourth among all the districts in Andhra Pradesh with regard to the area under forests. The area under forests occupies 44.8 per cent of the total geographical area of the district, which is more than 33-1/3 per cent laid down as the desirable minimum in the National Forest Policy of 1952. The average revenue per annum from these forests works out to Rs. 379.48 lakhs as in 1993-94 for the Visakhapatnam forest circle as a whole.

The forests, which are well distributed over the entire district, provide employment to most of the working classes through various forest operations such as felling, logging, plantation, transportation of timber and collection of minor forest produce, and also in forest based industries like basketry, matweaving, toy-making, rope-making, making of leaf plates, saw-mills and tanning of hides and skins. Besides these, other industrial establishments for the manufacture of furniture, toys, paper, packing cases, catamarans (wooden boats) are well supported by the products of these forests. The principal forest products are : (1) timber, (2) fuel, (3) cane, (4) edible and non-edible fruits, (5) fodder, thatch grasses and broom-corn, (6) tamarind, (7) soapnuts, (8) honey, (9) adda leaves, (10) cashewnut and (11) wax. Of the principal products, timber of various species like Teak, *Maddi, Yegisa, Chirumanu, Bandaru* and *Albizzia* is exported to the neighbouring districts. Bamboo, which is abundant in these forests, is mostly supplied to the paper-mills at Rajahmundry. Another species of wood available in these forests, has not only been providing ample scope for the development of toy industry but also supporting a good number of artisan families particularly in Etikoppaka and Darlapudi villages of Yellamanchili taluk. Further, cashewnut, another important produce in the Agency area of this district, is exported to Hyderabad, Chennai, Kolkata and even foreign countries. Besides these products, the forests also bestow some indirect benefits on the district by exerting a wholesome effect on the climate, safeguarding lands from erosion, stabilising underground water and normalising rains.

*Exploitation and Development*

In view of the rich forest potentialities of the district, it is necessary to exploit them in a more scientific and systematic way to get more impressive results. In the beginning, the exploitation of forest produce was carried through licence and voucher system which was later on replaced by the permit system. Under these systems, the licencees or permit holders were allowed to cut trees without much control on the manner or extent of felling. The Forest Conservancy Department was created in A.D. 1856, when the Madras Forest Act was passed. Thereafter, the forests were governed according to the provisions of this Act which was revised from time to time. After the formation of Andhra Pradesh in 1956, the Act was revised in 1967 and renamed as the Andhra Pradesh Forest Act and brought into force from the 15th of April 1967. The total forest area in the district is now managed by the Forest Division, Visakhapatnam, which is in charge of exploitation as well as implementation of developmental plans on sound and scientific

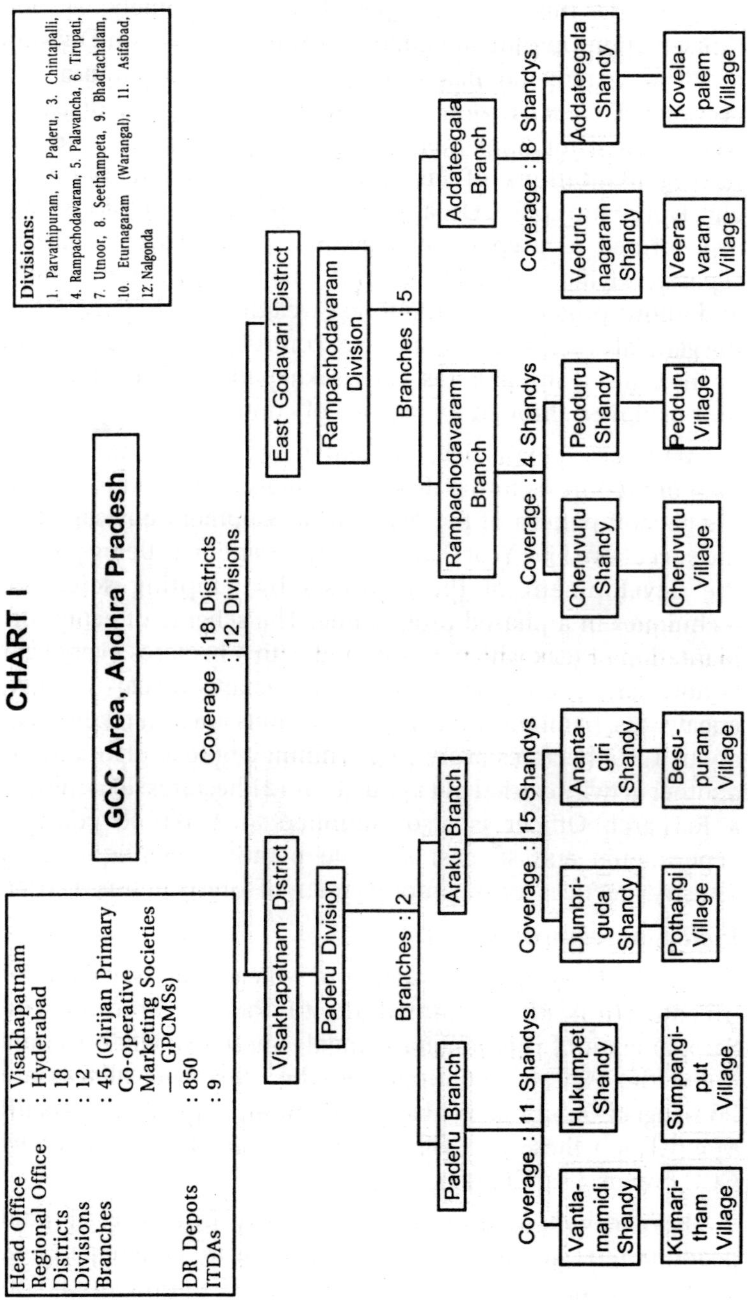
CHART I
GCC Area, Andhra Pradesh
Head Office : Visakhapatnam
Regional Office : Hyderabad
Districts : 18
Divisions : 12
Branches : 45 (Girijan Primary Co-operative Marketing Societies — GPCMSs)
DR Depots : 850
ITDAs : 9
Divisions:
1. Parvathipuram, 2. Paderu, 3. Chintapalli, 4. Rampachodavaram, 5. Palavancha, 6. Tirupati, 7. Utnoor, 8. Seethampeta, 9. Bhadrachalam, 10. Eturnagaram (Warangal), 11. Asifabad, 12. Nalgonda
Coverage : 18 Districts
: 12 Divisions
Visakhapatnam District
Paderu Division
Branches : 2
Paderu Branch
Coverage : 11 Shandys
Vantla-mamidi Shandy
Kumari-tham Village
Hukumpet Shandy
Sumpangi-put Village
Araku Branch
Coverage : 15 Shandys
Dumbri-guda Shandy
Pothangi Village
Ananta-giri Shandy
Besu-puram Village
East Godavari District
Rampachodavaram Division
Branches : 5
Rampachodavaram Branch
Coverage : 4 Shandys
Cheruvuru Shandy
Cheruvuru Village
Pedduru Shandy
Pedduru Village
Addateegala Branch
Coverage : 8 Shandys
Vedurunagaram Shandy
Veeravaram Village
Addateegala Shandy
Kovelapalem Village

lines. Besides this, there are special divisions, namely : (1) Soil Conservation Division at Paderu, (2) Soil Conservation Division at Vizianagaram, (3) Bamboo Division at Narasipatnam and (4) Coffee Project Division at Anakapalle. These special divisions were created for implementing specific programmes such as raising plantations of fast growing species like bamboo, eucalyptus and coffee. Occasionally, working plan divisions were also formed to prepare management plans. There is also a separate Flying Squad Division at Kakinada to conduct raids and afford protection to the forest wealth. All the activities of the general and special divisions are controlled and co-ordinated by the Conservator of Forests at Visakhapatnam. The forests are now exploited through the agency of contractors.

With regard to the development of forests, the management plan of the forests in the district is suitably adjusted to fit into the general pattern of the planned development envisaged by the successive Five Year Plans. Special attention is being paid to the development of these forests by adopting scientific techniques in a phased programme. The scheme of economic plantation of teak which was started with 4 hectares every year is now carried on at the rate of 106 hectares a year. Further, eucalyptus, bamboo and coffee plantations are also taken up in about 1,215 hectares every year. Thinning of teak plantation is another activity carried out annually in 121 hectares. In addition, a Research Officer is also stationed at Araku to conduct experiments and suggest suitable planting techniques and forestry practices for the improvement of forests in this district.

*Profiles of Selected Villages*

In Visakhapatnam district four villages are selected for investigation *viz.* Kumaritham of Paderu Mandal and Sampangiput of Hukumpeta Mandal—these two villages come under the Paderu GCC branches, the other two villages are Pothangi of Dumbriguda Mandal and Besupuram of Ananthagiri Mandal and these two villages come under the Araku valley GCC branch (see Chart I).

Kumaritham village is 25 km. away from the Mandal headquarters *i.e.* Paderu, towards Paderu to Visakhapatnam. Total population of this village is 138 and the entire population of this village belongs to tribes. Kondadora, Valmiki and Primitive Tribal Group (PTG) are the major tribes in this village. The cropped area in this village forms 80.62 acres and the major proportion of the cropped area is covered by irrigation. Tamarind, Adda leaf, Naramamidi bark, Hillbroom, Myrobalans, Marking nuts and Gum Karaya are the major MFP items available in this village. The procured MFP items are sold in the shandy point of Vantalamamidi which is located 5 km. away from this village.

Another village selected in the Paderu GCC branch is Sampangiput village of Hukumpeta Mandal (see Map I). This village is located 5 km. away from the Mandal headquarters. Total population of this village is 186 and the entire population is tribal. Major tribes in this village are Valmiki, Kondadora, Kotias and PTG. Total cropped land in this village is 150.90 acres and out of this total cropped area 32.08 acres has the irrigation facility. Tamarind, Pongam seed, Hillbroom and Adda leaf are the major MFP items available in this village. The villagers sell their procured MFP items in the Hukumpeta shandy which is located 5 km. away from the village.

Pothangi is one of the villages selected for investigation. This is located 3 km. away from the Mandal headquarters. This village comes under Araku valley GCC branch and Dumbriguda Mandal. Total population of this village is 142 and the entire population belongs to Scheduled Tribes. Kotia, PTG, Kondadora and Nookadora are the major tribes in this village. Total cropped area in this village is 120.20 acres and out of this cropped area, 12.35 acres is irrigated. Different types of MFP items available in this village are tamarind, pongam seed, and adda leaf. Procured MFP items are sold in the Dumbriguda shandy which is located 3 km. away from the village.

Besupuram is the other village selected for investigation in Araku Valley GCC branch and Anantagiri Mandal. Total population of this village is 142 and 96.98 per cent of the total population belongs to the Scheduled Tribes. Major types of MFP items available in this village are myrobalans, amlaseed, tamarind, pongam seed and hillbrooms. For the collection of MFP items the villagers usually go upto 19 km. into the forest.

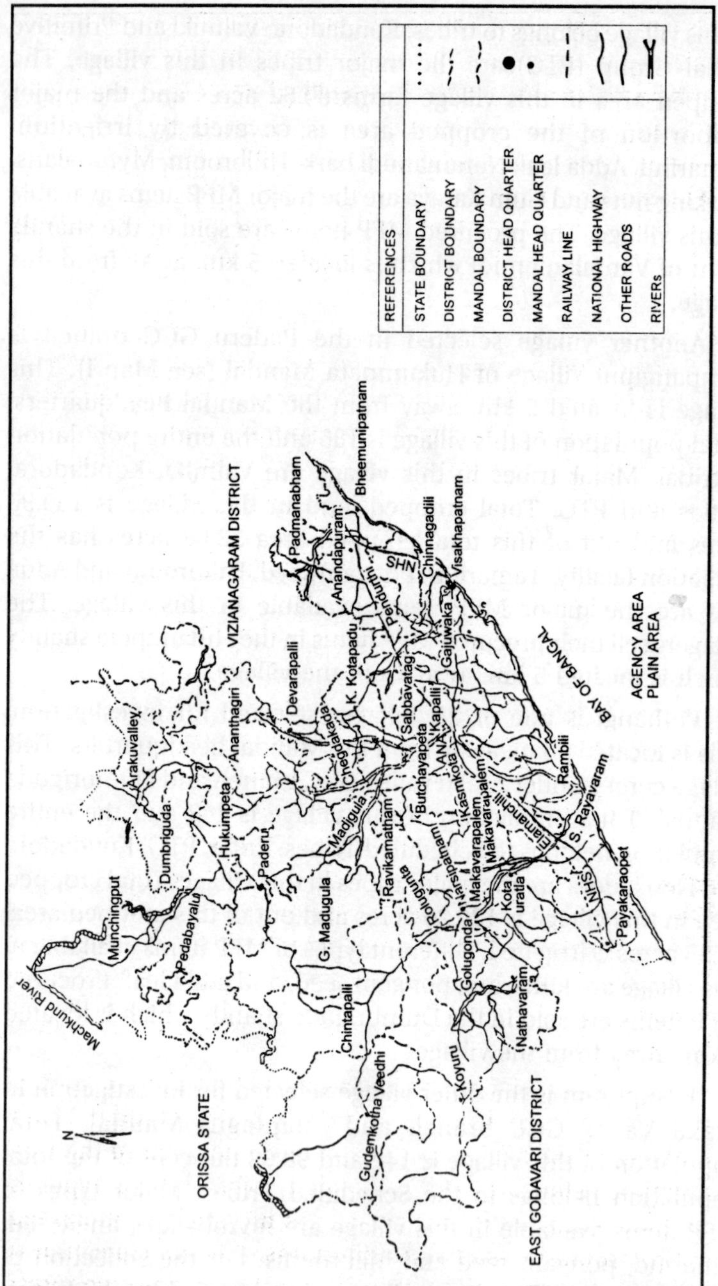


Map I: Visakhapatnam District

The collected MFP items are sold in the shandy at Ananthagiri village which is 15 km. away from this village.

## 2.4. Profile of East Godavari District

East Godavari district is one of the north eastern coastal districts of Andhra Pradesh with 10,807 sq. km. area. It is bounded on north partly by Orissa State and Visakhapatnam district, on the east by Bay of Bengal, on the south and west by West Godavari and Khammam districts. The district is divided into three divisions based on agro-economic conditions *viz.*, delta, upland and agency divisions. Valuable forests with bamboo to the extent of 22,916 hectares are seen in this district. Rivers like Godavari, Yeleru and Pampa traverse through this district.

The population of the district is 45.4 lakhs as per 1991 census and this constituted 6.8 per cent of the population of the State while the geographical area of the district forms only 3.9 per cent of the area of the State. The district has a density of population of 420 per sq. km. Agency area shows lesser density and plain area shows higher density. Around 24 per cent of the population reside in urban settlements while the rest of the population is distributed among 1362 villages. Scheduled Castes constitute 8.28 per cent of the population while Scheduled Tribes accounted for only 1.73 per cent of the population of the district. There are 18.82 lakhs of literates forming 41.4 per cent of total population of the district.

Area under principal crops covers 41 per cent of the total geographical area. Of the cropped area 68 per cent is covered by irrigation. Out of the geographical area of the district 29.91 per cent is under the forest cover. Out of the total forest area, reserved forests cover 83.57 per cent and the rest are unreserved forests. Forest revenue from all forest products accounted for Rs. 713.49 lakhs in 1991-92, out of this Rs. 427.53 lakhs from bamboo; Rs. 147.12 lakhs are accounted for by timber; Rs. 11.52 lakhs from fire wood; Rs. 14.99 lakhs from beedi leaves; and Rs. 112.33 lakhs from other forest products.

*Profiles of Selected Villages*

In East Godavari district 4 villages are selected *viz.*, Cheruvuru from Rampachodavaram Mandal; Pedduru from

Devipatnam Mandal; Veeravaram and Kovelapalem from Addateegala Mandal (see Map II).

Cheruvuru village is 24 km. away from the Mandal headquarters *i.e.* Rampachodavaram. The population of this village is 396 as per 1991 census and the population is distributed in 96 households. Out of the 396 population, 370 belongs to the Konda Dora and Valmiki. The village is approached by Kutcha and Semi Ghati road. For infrastructure, medical and education the villagers have to go from 4 km. to 24 km. Total cropped area in this village is 239.91 acres and out of this cropped area 37.10 acres is irrigated. Different types of minor forest produce available in this village are tamarind, myrobalans and marking nuts. The villagers sell their MFP products in the shandy located in the village itself.

Pedduru village is 24 kms. away from the Mandal headquarters *i.e.* Devipatnam and 11 km. away from the divisional headquarters namely Rampachodavaram. The total population of this village is 338 as per 1991 census and the population is distributed in 86 households out of 338 population, 323 belong to tribal population. Major tribes in this village are Konda Reddy, Konda Kammari. Total cropped area in this village is 165.44 acres and irrigated area is 55.82 acres. Different types of minor forest produce available in this village are myrobalans, tamarind, marking nuts, Gum Karaya, cassia tora. The villagers sell their products in the shandy located in the village itself.

Veeravaram is one of the other villages selected for investigation is 21 km. away from the Mandal headquarters *i.e.* addateegala (see Map II). This village is approached from Mandal headquarters by pucca road and 3 km. long kutcha road. Total population of this village is 285 and the population is distributed in 67 households. Out of the total population, 258 belong to the tribal population. Major tribes in this village are Konda Reddy, Manne Dora, Koya Dora, Konda Kammari. An Ashram school is established by the Government of Andhra Pradesh upto 5th class, but for further studies the students should go to 3 km. For medical treatment, the villagers should go to Duppalapalem, 12 km. away where the primary health centre is located. Total cropped area in this village is 365.60 acres and there is no

Map II: East Godavari District

irrigated area in this village. Major types of minor forest produce available in this village are tamarind, Gum Karaya, kond gogu, marking nuts. The villagers sell their minor forest produce products in the shandy located in Vedurunagaram village, 3 km. away from this village.

Another village selected for investigation is Kovelapalem of Addateegala Mandal. This village has a hamlet called Patapadu. This village is 6 km. away from the Mandal headquarters. It is approached by a kutcha road. Total population of this village is 415 including 54 of the hamlet population. Tribal population of this village is 369 including 54 of the hamlet population. A primary school is established in this village but there are no teachers in this school when the investigator conducted the investigation. For all infrastructure facilities and medical facilities the villager should go to Mandal headquarters, Addateegala. Major tribes in this village are Konda Reddy, Valmiki and Konda Kammari. Total cropped area of this village is 670.11 acres and out of this total cropped area 20.53 acres have irrigation facility. Major minor forest products available in this village are tamarind, Gum Karaya, marking nuts and naramamidi bark. The collected MFP items are sold in the shandy point located in Addateegala, 6 km. away from the village.

## SECTION-III

## DESIGN OF THE SURVEY : ORISSA

For the purpose of enquiry, Sunabeda division in old Koraput district is chosen (see Chart II). This division covers the whole of unified Koraput, Bolangir and Kalahandi districts. It has seven branches. Of which two branches are chosen for enquiry *viz.* Sunabeda branch of Koraput district and Muniguda branch of Rayagada district. The profile of each of the two districts is given below.

### 2.5. Profile of Koraput District

The population of the district is 10.30 lakhs as per 1991 census and this constituted only 3.25 per cent of the population of the state while in the total geographical area of the state, district accounted for 5.37 per cent. The district has a density of population of 123 per sq. km. only. Agency area shows lesser density than plain area. Scheduled Caste population constitute 13.41 per cent of the population while Scheduled Tribes account for 50.67 per cent. The district has a work force of 5.14 lakhs constituting about 49.9 per cent of the population besides the marginal workers to a tune of 0.91 lakh. Among the main workers, cultivators constitute 39.7 per cent, agricultural labourers 25.68 per cent, and the balance of 34.62 per cent are engaged in other occupations.

There are 1.44 lakh literates forming 24.65 per cent of total population of the district. This is only one half of the literacy rate observed for the state. Only two out of 30 districts *viz.*, Malkangiri and Nabarangpur record lower levels of literacy than that of Korapur district. Literates among males constituted 33.99 per cent while among females literacy accounted for 15.16 per cent.

*Profile of Laxmipur Block*

In Sunabeda branch area, Laxmipur and Bandhugaon blocks are chosen for selection of villages on the basis of predominance of MFP. Laxmipur block has a geographical area of 310.33 sq. km. with 101 inhabited villages. The tribal population of the block is about 49,301, of which 33,929 or 68.81 per cent from Scheduled Tribe population. Nearly 50 per cent of the population form as workers. Among these, cultivators accounted for 43.43 per cent and agricultural labourers 24.06 per cent. Among other occupations, trade and commerce and other services are important. Literacy rate in Laxmipur block is only 17.07 per cent as against 24.65 per cent for Koraput district as a whole. The block also has the lowest rate of rainfall with only 831.4 mm. as against 1292.5 mm. for district as a whole during the year 1992-93. Forest area covered only 6.72 per cent of the total geographical area. Barren and uncultivable land accounted for 39.65 per cent. Net sown area formed only 30.36 per cent. There are no medium and major irrigation projects in the block. Even area under minor irrigation projects and lift irrigation projects is minor. Consumption of chemical fertilizers is low, only 42 kg. NPK per hectare. The number of agricultural cooperative credit societies are only two for the entire block and their coverage of membership is 42.33 per cent only. The number of primary schools are 82 while the number of inhabited villages are 101. The total number of ST students in the total students formed only 9.17 per cent while the total population of the ST's is 68.81 per cent.

**CHART II**

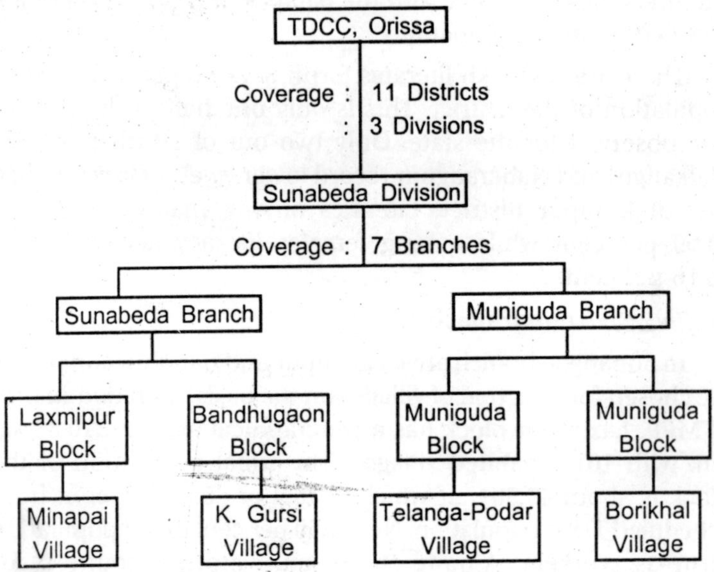


*Profile of Selected Village in Laxmipur Block*

One of the selected villages in Sunabeda TDCC branch is Minapai. This village is 9 km. away from the block headquarters *i.e.* Laxmipur. The population of this village is 560 and out of the population of 560, 528 belongs to tribal population. The major tribe in this village is Kondh. For education, medical and other infrastructure facilities, the villagers should have to cover a distance of 9 km. Total cropped area in this village is 100 acres. Major types of minor forest produce available in this village are siali leaves, tamarind and hillbrooms. The villagers sell their procured minor forest produce items in the Kotinga village, where the shandy point is located (see Map III).

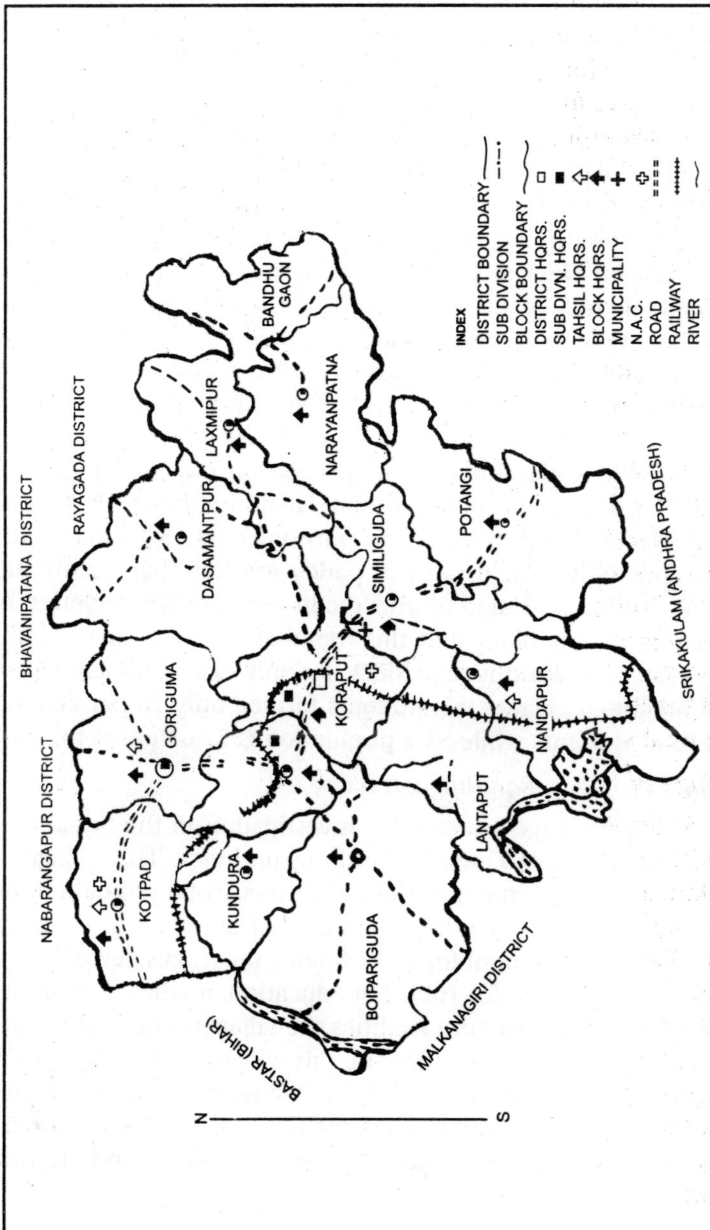


Map III: Koraput District

*Profile of Bandhugaon Block*

Population of the Bandhugaon block is 42,954. Out of this 77.63 per cent were Scheduled Tribes. This is much more than the average for the district which is only 50.67 per cent. The total workers formed 49.16 per cent of the population. As in the case of Laxmipur block, majority of the workers are agriculturists; 40.78 per cent cultivators and 39.57 per cent agricultural labourers. The other major occupations are trade and commerce and household industry. Services are less important in Bandhugaon block as compared to Laxmipur block. As regards literacy, literacy levels are lower at 14.10 per cent as against 17.07 per cent in Laxmipur block. Rainfall is however better in Bandhugaon block as compared to Laxmipur block. Forest coverage in Bandhugaon block is equally bad. Only around 10 per cent of the total area is under forest cover. Barren and uncultivable land formed a lesser proportion, but current fallows formed a higher proportion than Laxmipur block. Net area shown formed slightly higher proportion *i.e.* 34.43 per cent than Laxmipur block. Yield rates of paddy are less than Laxmipur block. Number of agricultural credit cooperative societies is only one in this block and this membership coverage is only 36.61 per cent. Bandhugaon block has only 79 schools as against 149 inhabited villages. ST students formed only 10 per cent of the total students while ST's population is 77.63 per cent.

*Village Profile in Bandhugaon Block*

Another village selected for investigation in the Sunabeda TDCC branch is K. Gursi of Bandhugaon block. This village is 20 km. away from the block headquarters. Total population of the village is 307, including 290 of tribal population. Females per 1000 males account for 1074. Among the tribals, females per 1000 males account for 1071. For education, medical treatment and for the infrastructure facilities the villagers should have to go upto 10 km. Major tribe in this village is Kondh. Total cropped area in this village is 133.38 acres and only 49.4 acres has the irrigation facility. Different types of MFP available in this village are siali leaves, tamarind, Karanja seeds and Mohwa flowers.

## 2.6. Profile of Rayagada District

Rayagada district has the population of 7.14 lakhs. The percentage of ST population in this district is 56.04. Rayagada district has a much higher proportion of population of weaker sections *i.e.* SC, ST's, 70.32 per cent as against 64.08 per cent for Koraput. The percentage of main workers to tribal population is similar to Koraput district *i.e.* 41.25 as against 41.08. The percentage of agriculturists to main workers is also similar to Koraput district *i.e.* around 80 per cent. Among agriculturists, agricultural labourers formed a higher proportion but density of population is low in both the districts *i.e.* 123 in Koraput and 84 in Rayagada. Marginal holdings *i.e.*, below one hectare holdings formed around 30 per cent of the total holdings in Rayagada while in Koraput they formed a lower percentage *i.e.* 22.31. The major crops in Rayagada are rice, jower, bajra, maize, ragi and small millets. In Koraput, small millets accounted for higher proportion than Rayagada. Among commercial crops, oil seeds and vegetables are important both in Koraput and Rayagada districts. Forest coverage is much better in Rayagada as compared to Koraput district. Working of cooperative societies as judged by overdues to outstanding, and profit and loss statements, undivided Koraput district was in a pretty bad position. Number of primary schools in Rayagada district is much less than the corresponding figure for Koraput district. ST's enrolment in primary schools as a percentage of enrolment by all communities is only 36.1 as against the population of ST's which formed 56.04 per cent.

*Profile of Selected Villages in Rayagada District*

Another two villages selected in the Sunabeda TDCC division of Muniguda branch which is located in Rayagada district are Telangapodar and Borikhal. Telangapodar is 17 km. away from the block headquarters *i.e.* Muniguda. Total population of this village is 442. Out of this total population 158 belong to tribes. Major tribe in this village is Kondh. Total cropped area in this village is 943 acres and is mainly dependent on rainfall. Different types of MFP available in this village are Mohwa flower, Mohwa seeds, Naramamidi bark, Tamarind, Hillbrooms, Siali leaves, Myrobalans and Gum.

The other village selected for investigation in Muniguda TDCC branch is Borikhal. It is 15 km. away from the headquarters *i.e.* Muniguda. The population of this village is 178 and out of this population 122 belongs to the Scheduled Tribes. The single largest tribe in this village is Kondh. Around 893 acres of land is cropped in this village, and this area is mainly dependent on rainfall. Mohwa flower, Mohwa seed, Salseed, Naramamidi bark, Tamarind, Hillbroom and Siali leaves are the major items available in this village (see Map IV).

**SECTION-IV**

## 2.7. Design of Field Enquiry

The quantitative assessment in the study is mainly based on the secondary data supplied by the institutions concerned. The impact study is based on field enquiry done by us during 1997-98.

For the purpose of procurement the GCC classifies MFP into two groups *viz.* (1) those which are under the operation of Divisional Manager under decentralised system, (2) others which are of national and international importance which are under the management of GCC headquarters. Based on the data available we identified the divisions in which each of the minor forest produce as an important share. Out of the 12 divisions three divisions *viz.* Paderu, Chintapalli and Rampachodavaram are found to be cover 10 out of 20 specified items of minor forest produce. Among the three divisions two divisions are chosen for study. In each division two Girijan Primary Cooperative Marketing Societies (GPCMS) are chosen for enquiry. In Paderu division, Paderu and Araku branches are chosen and in Rampachodavaram division, Rampachodavaram and Addateegala branches are chosen (see Chart I).

Shandy point in each branch is identified from the view-point of its importance for the minor forest produce. The following shandy points have been selected from each of the branches noted below :

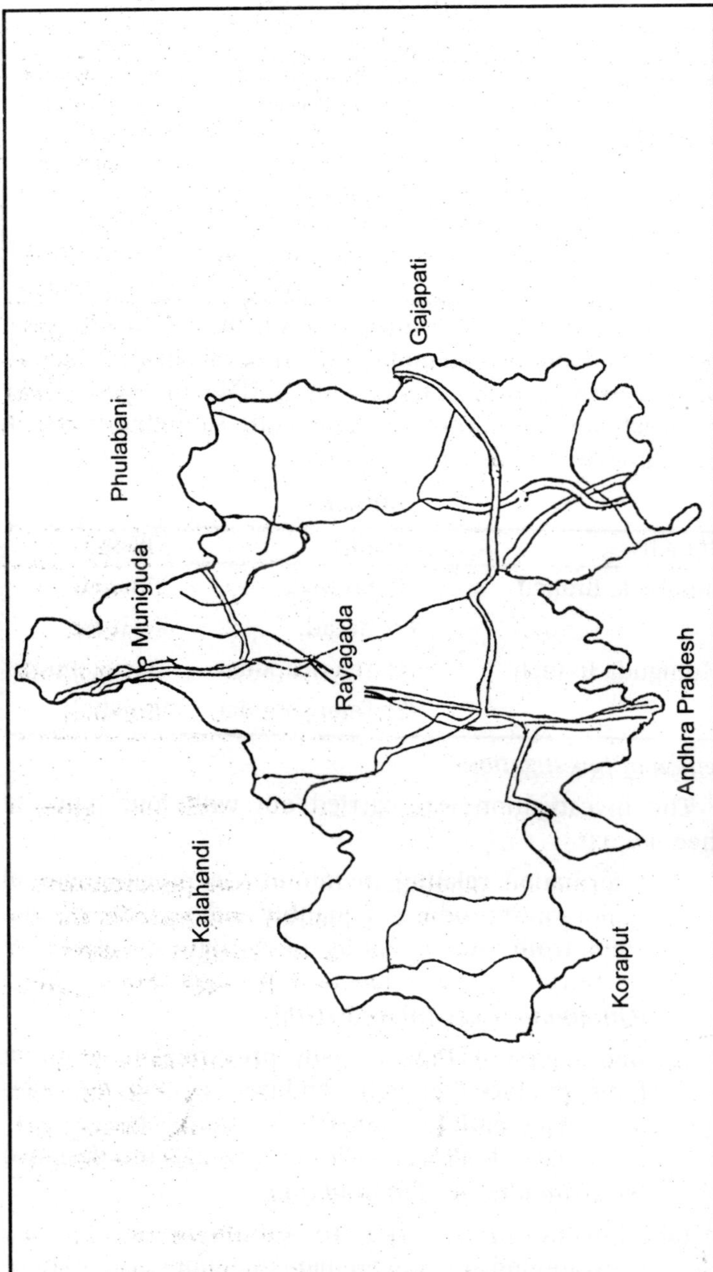


Map IV: Rayagada District

**ANDHRA PRADESH**

| Branch | Shandy | Village |
|---|---|---|
| Paderu Branch | (1) Vantlamamidi | Kumaritham |
| | (2) Hukumpeta | Sampangiput |
| Araku Branch | (1) Dumbriguda | Pothangi |
| | (2) Anantagiri | Besupuram |
| Rampachodavaram Branch | (1) Cheruvuru | Cheruvuru |
| | (2) Pedduru | Pedduru |
| Addateegala Branch | (1) Vedurunagaram | Veeravaram |
| | (2) Addateegala | Kovelapalem |

The villages within the range of 10 km. of each shandy point are identified and two predominantly tribal villages are chosen after discussions with managers of GPCMS. In each village 25 households are chosen on systematic sampling basis. In Orissa also similar method is adopted.

**ORRISA**

| Branch | Shandy | Village |
|---|---|---|
| Sunabeda Branch | (1) Kotinga | Minapai |
| | (2) Garadi | K. Gursi |
| Muniguda Branch | (1) Telengapodar | Telengapodar |
| | (2) Telengapodar | Borikhal |

*Method of Investigation*

The investigation was carried out with four types of schedules, *viz.*

(1) Information relating to monthwise procurement of minor forest produce in quantity and price for the year 1996 from the divisions of Girijan Co-operative Corporation was collected through the designed [***Questionnaires-1(A) and 1(B)***].

(2) Information relating to daily procurement of minor forest produce in quantity and price paid to the tribals once in a month from the GPCMS from February, 1997 to January, 1998 was collected through the designed [***Questionnaires—2 (a) and 2(b)***].

(3) Information relating to employment, income consumption and procurement of minor forest produce

for the year 1996-97 was collected from the selected 300 households (25 from each selected village) was collected by canvassing specially throught the designed [*Questionnaire-3*].

(4) Particulars relating to the village under enquiry also were collected through a proforma of village Schedule.

The details are elicited for single point of time in case of all commodities. There were problems of recall in the case of minor forest produce and also agricultural surplus produce marketed, since the data obtained related to the entire year. Data collected at shorter intervals could have contributed to better accuracy but would have meant higher cost. To get over the problem of recall we have chosen investigators from tribal areas, they are accquainted with the people there and also seasons of minor forest produce.

### 2.8. Chapter Division

The material is organised into the following 9 chapters. Chapter 1 provides organisational framework for MFP in GCC area of Andhra Pradesh and TDCC area of Orissa. Chapter 2 presents objectives and methodology. Chapter 3 analyses the status of procurement of MFP in Andhra Pradesh and Orissa. Chapter 4 examines the marketing of tribal produce in Andhra Pradesh and Orissa. Chapter 5 gives details of loaning performance of GCC in Andhra Pradesh and TDCC and other organisations in Orissa. Chapter 6 throws light on the role of GCC in Andhra Pradesh and TDCC in Orissa in meeting the domestic requirement of tribals and public distribution system. Value addition to tribal produce as a result of operations of GCC in Andhra Pradesh and TDCC and other organisations from the content of Chapter 7. Chapter 8 assesses the impact of MFP on employment, income and quality of life of tribals. The final Chapter 9 provides summary and conclusions of the comparative study of GCC area of Andhra Pradesh and Orissa State and the role of weekly markets in the development of tribal marketing.

A review of earlier studies which throw light on the subject in question precedes the presentation of the results of four field survey in every chapter.

The results are analysed mostly in tabular form, though regressions are fitted wherever relevant.

## SUMMARY

This chapter starts with listing of objectives of the study in Section-I. The hypotheses underlying the study are also spelt out in the same section. Section-II of the chapter provides design of the survey of GCC area of Andhra Pradesh. Similar design is provided for Orissa State in Section-III. Each of the two sections gives the profiles of districts, blocks and villages selected. Section-IV gives a summary of investigation techniques, types of schedules used, techniques of data analysis and methods of investigation. This chapter closes by giving a design of the report and the chapter titles of the Report.

# 3

# Procurement of MFP in Andhra Pradesh and Orissa

One of the important objectives of the institutions like GCC in A.P. and TDCC, Forest Department/OFDC and LAMPS (set-up) in Orissa is to procure the minor forest produce and surplus agricultural produce brought by the tribals to the shandys. In Orissa, the procurement operations of the institutions are oligosponistic in nature. For instance, for a specific commodity of minor forest produce procurement, the LAMPS, TDCC and private agencies do operate simultaneously. However, the competition from LAMPS and TDCC does not seem to be strong due to either malfunctioning or lack of working capital. Hence, the procurement market for MFP in Orissa is undoubtedly a highly exploitative and imperfect one.

In Andhra Pradesh, due to the exercise of monopoly power of GCC in the interests of the tribals, the procurement operations seem to be better than those in Orissa. The performance of the institutions in respect of purchase of MFP and SAP is examined with respect to the trends in quantities and prices. Since the LAMPS are not functioning well and since Forest Department/ OFDC deals with only kendu leaves, a comparative analysis between Orissa and Andhra Pradesh in terms of procurement and prices is made by considering only TDCC of Orissa and GCC of Andhra Pradesh for all procured minor forest produce (MFP).

The chapter is organised into three sections. Section-I covers the procurement of minor forest produce and the importance of commodity in the total procured MFP across divisions of A.P. and Orissa. The seasonality in branch-wise procurement is analysed in Section-II. The last section presents the variability of MFP prices and the trend analysis for the period 1980-81 to 1995-96 for both the States.

Division-wise particulars of minor forest produce are available only for the period upto 1993-94 while commodity-wise particulars are available for the period upto 1995-96.[1] Hence, the latest quinquennium ending with 1993-94 is chosen for analysis, division-wise. While for the commodity-wise analysis last two years *i.e.* 1994-95 and 1995-96 are also included.

Analysis of procurement is done division-wise and commodity-wise for the entire state as per data are available. This is followed by analysis for the selected branches.

## SECTION-I

### 3.1. MFP Share of each Division in Respect of each Commodity : Andhra Pradesh

The division-wise details for the 20 MFP commodities are presented in Table 3.1. There are wide fluctuations from year to year in respect of each commodity. Therefore, the average for a quinquennium ending with 1993-94 is chosen for analysis. The top four divisions in respect of procurement of each commodity are identified and shown in Table 3.2. In respect of Gum Karaya four divisions *viz.* Rampachodavaram, Bhadrachalam, Polancha and Srisailam accounted for 2/3rds of procurement. In respect of Gum tiruman three divisions *viz.* Bhadrachalam, Tirupathi and Rampachodavaram accounted for 82 per cent of the procurement. Similar concentration in procurement is seen in other products like Myrobalans, Nuxvomica etc. The concentration is found to be much more in the case of Tamarind. 91 per cent of seeded tamarind is accounted for by only two divisions *viz.* Parvatipuram and Paderu. The concentration of deseeded tamarind and tamarind seed is found to be equally great. Rampachodavaram alone accounted for 2/3rds of deseeded tamarind and 81 per cent of tamarind seed. As regards Mohwa flower, Utnoor division in Telangana accounted for 2/3rds of procured quantity. Similar concentration is seen in honey and Shikakai.

The divisions are also examined by the number of items in

which their ranks in procurement figure in the first four groups. Rampachodavaram is prominent in figuring in respect of 12 commodities in the first four ranks. Parvatipuram comes second with 9 commodities in the first four ranks. Paderu comes third with 8 commodities.

The division analysis shows high concentration of procurement of certain commodities in certain divisions and also the importance of a few divisions like Rampachodavaram, Parvatipuram and Paderu in procurement of several commodities.

### 3.2. Commodity-wise Procurement

Commodity-wise average value of procurement for the period 1989-90 to 1995-96 is shown in Table 3.3. The average value is Rs. 9.21 crores, out of which Gum Karaya alone accounted for Rs. 4.69 crores. Seeded tamarind accounts for the next highest value of produce, accounting for Rs. 1.37 crores and around 15 per cent of the total value. Mohwa seed comes third in rank with value of Rs. 0.51 crore and accounting for 5.6 per cent. It may be seen that, of 18 items listed Gum Karaya alone accounted for more than 50 per cent.

The table also provides data for the latest year *i.e.* 1995-96. The total value of MFP in 1995-96 is lower than the seven year average suggesting declining procurement value. Gum Karaya in particular, shows sharp decline both in quantity and value as compared to average value for 1989-90 to 1995-96. Similarly, seeded tamarind also shows a decline. Among the no table commodities which show a rise are deseeded tamarind, mohwa seed, mohwa flower, tamarind seed, myrobalans, both types of honey, pungam seed, hillbrooms and marking nuts. The other commodities which show a fall in value are Shikakai, soapnuts, nuxvomica and cleaning nuts. It should be noted that the details covered under MFP procured by GCC do not cover kendu leaves since the operation of kendu leaves is outside the purview of the GCC. However, when we consider the benefits to tribals, it should cover also kendu leaves or beedi leaves. In 1988-89 the quantity of beedi leaves was estimated to be 29,300 tonnes with a worth of Rs. 38.5 crores. Thus, kendu leaves accounted for four times the value of minor forest produce. This is mostly produced in the entire 10 districts of Telangana.

## Table 3.1: Division-wise Quantity Procured during 1989-90 to 1993-94 by each Item of MFP

| DIVISION | 1989-90 | 1990-91 | 1991-92 | 1992-93 | 1993-94 | Total | Average | Percentage |
|---|---|---|---|---|---|---|---|---|
| **1. GUM KARAYA (IN QUINTALS)** | | | | | | | | |
| PARVATIPURAM | 0.00 | 24.00 | 27.00 | 16.00 | 22.00 | 89.00 | 22.25 | 0.12 |
| SEETHAMPETA | 0.00 | 3.00 | 0.55 | 0.62 | 1.92 | 6.09 | 1.52 | 0.01 |
| PADERU | 31.00 | 153.00 | 171.00 | 72.00 | 141.00 | 568.00 | 113.60 | 0.60 |
| CHINTAPALLE | 1851.00 | 1512.00 | 1640.00 | 532.00 | 649.00 | 6184.00 | 1236.80 | 6.51 |
| RAMPA-CHODAVARAM | 5924.00 | 5210.00 | 3147.00 | 1936.00 | 2180.00 | 18397.00 | 2679.40 | 19.37 |
| THIRUPATHI | 3066.00 | 2084.00 | 1060.00 | 526.00 | 344.00 | 7080.00 | 1416.00 | 7.45 |
| SRISAILAM | 4956.00 | 4728.00 | 2220.00 | 1431.00 | 1418.00 | 14753.00 | 2950.60 | 15.53 |
| PALONCHA | 4602.00 | 4795.00 | 4564.00 | 588.00 | 314.00 | 14873.00 | 2972.60 | 15.65 |
| BHADRACHALAM | 3968.00 | 3678.00 | 3763.00 | 2342.00 | 1797.00 | 15538.00 | 3109.60 | 16.37 |
| ETURNAGARAM | 3177.00 | 2157.00 | 1960.00 | 577.00 | 621.00 | 8492.00 | 1698.40 | 8.94 |
| UTNOOR | 425.00 | 440.00 | 271.00 | 58.00 | 56.00 | 1250.00 | 250.00 | 1.32 |
| ASIFABAD | 2914.00 | 2236.00 | 1842.00 | 338.00 | 434.00 | 7864.00 | 1552.80 | 8.17 |
| Grand Total | 30914.00 | 27020.00 | 20665.55 | 8416.62 | 7977.92 | 94994.09 | 18998.82 | 100.00 |
| **2. GUM TIRUMAN (IN QUINTALS)** | | | | | | | | |
| PARVATIPURAM | 0.00 | 0.00 | 0.00 | 0.00 | 0.00 | 0.00 | 0.00 | 0.00 |
| SEETHAMPETA | 0.00 | 0.00 | 0.00 | 0.00 | 0.00 | 0.00 | 0.00 | 0.00 |
| PADERU | 0.00 | 0.00 | 0.00 | 0.00 | 0.00 | 0.00 | 0.00 | 0.00 |
| CHINTAPALLE | 0.00 | 0.00 | 0.00 | 0.00 | 0.00 | 0.00 | 0.00 | 0.00 |
| RAMPA-CHODAVARAM | 13.00 | 73.00 | 88.00 | 46.00 | 118.00 | 338.00 | 67.60 | 11.78 |
| THIRUPATHI | 81.00 | 50.00 | 172.00 | 67.00 | 99.00 | 469.00 | 93.80 | 16.34 |
| SRISAILAM | 17.00 | 25.00 | 27.00 | 8.00 | 17.00 | 94.00 | 18.80 | 3.28 |
| PALONCHA | 53.00 | 0.00 | 0.00 | 6.00 | 13.00 | 73.00 | 18.25 | 3.18 |
| BHADRACHALAM | 106.00 | 7.00 | 8.00 | 404.00 | 1032.00 | 1557.00 | 311.40 | 54.27 |
| ETURNAGARAM | 93.00 | 1.00 | 1.00 | 37.00 | 76.00 | 208.00 | 41.60 | 7.25 |
| UTNOOR | 13.00 | 20.00 | 32.00 | 8.00 | 34.00 | 107.00 | 21.40 | 3.73 |
| ASIFABAD | 10.00 | 2.00 | 0.00 | 0.00 | 11.00 | 23.00 | 4.60 | 0.80 |
| Grand Total | 386.00 | 179.00 | 328.00 | 576.00 | 1400.00 | 2869.00 | 573.80 | 100.00 |

*(Contd.)*

**Table 3.1 (*Contd.*)**

| DIVISION | 1989-90 | 1990-91 | 1991-92 | 1992-93 | 1993-94 | Total | Average | Percentage |
|---|---|---|---|---|---|---|---|---|
| **3. MYROBALANS (IN QUINTALS)** | | | | | | | | |
| PARVATIPURAM | 3669.00 | 9054.00 | 1218.00 | 1340.00 | 2677.00 | 17958.00 | 3591.60 | 24.37 |
| SEETHAMPETA | 215.00 | 56.00 | 83.00 | 8.00 | 65.00 | 427.00 | 85.40 | 0.58 |
| PADERU | 4290.00 | 5932.00 | 2146.00 | 512.00 | 5110.00 | 17990.00 | 3498.00 | 24.41 |
| CHINTAPALLE | 4420.00 | 2905.00 | 426.00 | 115.00 | 585.00 | 8450.00 | 1690.00 | 11.47 |
| RAMPA-CHODAVARAM | 3821.00 | 8547.00 | 3479.00 | 2791.00 | 3191.00 | 21829.00 | 4365.80 | 19.62 |
| THIRUPATHI | 649.00 | 686.00 | 511.00 | 575.00 | 940.00 | 3361.00 | 672.20 | 4.56 |
| SRISAILAM | 97.00 | 413.00 | 565.00 | 73.00 | 12.00 | 1160.00 | 232.00 | 1.57 |
| PALONCHA | 9.00 | 529.00 | 168.00 | 14.00 | 31.00 | 751.00 | 150.10 | 1.03 |
| BHADRACHALAM | 509.00 | 257.00 | 133.00 | 108.00 | 0.00 | 1007.00 | 251.75 | 1.71 |
| ETURNAGARAM | 0.00 | 95.00 | 25.00 | 1.00 | 10.00 | 131.00 | 32.75 | 0.22 |
| UTNOOR | 16.00 | 297.00 | 13.00 | 0.00 | 0.00 | 326.00 | 108.67 | 0.74 |
| ASIFABAD | 0.00 | 155.00 | 101.00 | 33.00 | 20.00 | 309.00 | 77.25 | 0.52 |
| Grand Total | 17695.00 | 28926.00 | 8868.00 | 5570.00 | 12641.00 | 73700.00 | 14740.00 | 100.00 |
| **4. NUXVOMICA (IN QUINTALS)** | | | | | | | | |
| PARVATIPURAM | 269.00 | 63.00 | 10.00 | 331.00 | 326.00 | 999.00 | 199.80 | 4.66 |
| SEETHAMPETA | 128.00 | 33.00 | 42.00 | 156.00 | 102.00 | 461.00 | 92.20 | 2.15 |
| PADERU | 0.00 | 0.00 | 0.00 | 0.00 | 0.00 | 0.00 | 0.00 | 0.00 |
| CHINTAPALLE | 28.00 | 0.00 | 2.00 | 0.00 | 72.00 | 102.00 | 34.00 | 0.79 |
| RAMPA-CHODAVARAM | 1612.00 | 163.00 | 220.00 | 1127.00 | 1634.00 | 4756.00 | 951.20 | 22.20 |
| THIRUPATHI | 174.00 | 224.00 | 464.00 | 393.00 | 138.00 | 1393.00 | 278.60 | 6.50 |
| SRISAILAM | 273.00 | 247.00 | 293.00 | 760.00 | 451.00 | 2024.00 | 404.80 | 9.45 |
| PALONCHA | 2335.00 | 881.00 | 641.00 | 2226.00 | 1515.00 | 7598.00 | 1519.60 | 35.46 |
| BHADRACHALAM | 249.00 | 108.00 | 17.00 | 60.00 | 100.00 | 534.00 | 106.80 | 2.49 |
| ETURNAGARAM | 1267.00 | 571.00 | 372.00 | 610.00 | 572.00 | 3392.00 | 678.40 | 15.83 |
| UTNOOR | 0.00 | 0.00 | 0.00 | 0.00 | 0.00 | 0.00 | 0.00 | 0.00 |
| ASIFABAD | 63.00 | 0.00 | 74.00 | 11.00 | 20.00 | 168.00 | 42.00 | 0.98 |
| Grand Total | 6398.00 | 2290.00 | 2135.00 | 5674.00 | 4930.00 | 21427.00 | 4285.40 | 100.00 |

(*Contd.*)

## Table 3.1 (*Contd.*)

| DIVISION | 1989-90 | 1990-91 | 1991-92 | 1992-93 | 1993-94 | Total | Average | Percentage |
|---|---|---|---|---|---|---|---|---|
| **5. SEEDED TAMARIND (IN QUINTALS)** | | | | | | | | |
| PARVATIPURAM | 21600.00 | 29920.00 | 35656.00 | 35490.00 | 33270.00 | 155936.00 | 31187.20 | 62.85 |
| SEETHAMPETA | 2315.00 | 790.00 | 477.00 | 1615.00 | 4495.00 | 9691.00 | 1938.40 | 3.91 |
| PADERU | 15188.00 | 7263.00 | 12822.00 | 14532.00 | 19911.00 | 69716.00 | 13943.20 | 28.10 |
| CHINTAPALLE | 1551.00 | 242.00 | 1763.00 | 1988.00 | 304.00 | 5858.00 | 1169.60 | 2.36 |
| RAMPA-CHODAVARAM | 894.00 | 67.00 | 548.00 | 380.00 | 382.00 | 2271.00 | 454.20 | 0.92 |
| THIRUPATHI | 311.00 | 125.00 | 170.00 | 593.00 | 1004.00 | 2203.00 | 440.60 | 0.89 |
| SRISAILAM | 265.00 | 218.00 | 142.00 | 27.00 | 3.00 | 655.00 | 131.00 | 0.26 |
| PALONCHA | 473.00 | 257.00 | 25.00 | 0.00 | 35.00 | 790.00 | 197.50 | 0.40 |
| BHADRACHALAM | 13.00 | 0.00 | 0.00 | 0.00 | 0.00 | 13.00 | 13.00 | 0.03 |
| ETURNAGARAM | 387.00 | 454.00 | 134.00 | 0.00 | 12.00 | 987.00 | 246.75 | 0.50 |
| UTNOOR | 0.00 | 0.00 | 0.00 | 0.00 | 0.00 | 0.00 | 0.00 | 0.00 |
| ASIFABAD | 0.00 | 0.00 | 0.00 | 0.00 | 0.00 | 0.00 | 0.00 | 0.00 |
| Grand Total | 42997.00 | 39336.00 | 51737.00 | 54625.00 | 59416.00 | 248111.00 | 49622.20 | 100.00 |
| **6. DS TAMARIND (IN QUINTALS)** | | | | | | | | |
| PARVATIPURAM | 2440.00 | 1183.00 | 1772.00 | 924.00 | 1232.00 | 7551.00 | 1510.00 | 13.70 |
| SEETHAMPETA | 0.00 | 0.00 | 0.00 | 0.00 | 0.00 | 0.00 | 0.00 | 0.00 |
| PADERU | 0.00 | 137.00 | 0.00 | 29.00 | 0.00 | 166.00 | 83.00 | 0.75 |
| CHINTAPALLE | 26.00 | 52.00 | 32.00 | 521.00 | 47.00 | 678.00 | 135.60 | 1.23 |
| RAMPA-CHODAVARAM | 10079.00 | 4483.00 | 1974.00 | 7097.00 | 4128.00 | 27761.00 | 5552.20 | 50.36 |
| THIRUPATHI | 13.00 | 2.00 | 27.00 | 0.00 | 0.00 | 42.00 | 14.00 | 0.13 |
| SRISAILAM | 7003.00 | 331.00 | 0.00 | 0.00 | 0.00 | 7334.00 | 3667.00 | 33.26 |
| PALONCHA | 8.00 | 0.00 | 0.00 | 0.00 | 0.00 | 8.00 | 8.00 | 0.07 |
| BHADRACHALAM | 56.00 | 0.00 | 0.00 | 0.00 | 0.00 | 56.00 | 56.00 | 0.51 |
| ETURNAGARAM | 0.00 | 0.00 | 0.00 | 0.00 | 0.00 | 0.00 | 0.00 | 0.00 |
| UTNOOR | 0.00 | 0.00 | 0.00 | 0.00 | 0.00 | 0.00 | 0.00 | 0.00 |
| ASIFABAD | 0.00 | 0.00 | 0.00 | 0.00 | 0.00 | 0.00 | 0.00 | 0.00 |
| Grand Total | 19625.00 | 6188.00 | 3805.00 | 8571.00 | 5407.00 | 43596.00 | 8719.20 | 100.00 |

(*Contd.*)

## Table 3.1 (*Contd.*)

| DIVISION | 1989-90 | 1990-91 | 1991-92 | 1992-93 | 1993-94 | Total | Average | Percentage |
|---|---|---|---|---|---|---|---|---|
| **7. TAMARIND SEED (IN QUINTALS)** | | | | | | | | |
| PARVATIPURAM | 544.00 | 99.00 | 905.00 | 1174.00 | 429.00 | 3151.00 | 630.20 | 6.62 |
| SEETHAMPETA | 20.00 | 28.00 | 0.00 | 0.00 | 0.00 | 48.00 | 24.00 | 0.25 |
| PADERU | 280.00 | 542.00 | 131.00 | 162.00 | 0.00 | 1115.00 | 278.75 | 2.93 |
| CHINTAPALLE | 305.00 | 362.00 | 633.00 | 801.00 | 550.00 | 2651.00 | 530.00 | 5.57 |
| RAMPA-CHODAVARAM | 11327.00 | 6202.00 | 3621.00 | 11250.00 | 6118.00 | 28518.00 | 6803.60 | 80.88 |
| THIRUPATHI | 0.00 | 0.00 | 0.00 | 0.00 | 0.00 | 0.00 | 0.00 | 0.00 |
| SRISAILAM | 10.00 | 115.00 | 0.00 | 0.00 | 0.00 | 125.00 | 62.50 | 0.66 |
| PALONCHA | 8.00 | 0.00 | 0.00 | 0.00 | 0.00 | 8.00 | 7.00 | 0.09 |
| BHADRACHALAM | 584.00 | 65.00 | 636.00 | 8.00 | 0.00 | 1293.00 | 323.25 | 3.39 |
| ETURNAGARAM | 270.00 | 149.00 | 209.00 | 75.00 | 0.00 | 704.00 | 266.84 | 1.85 |
| UTNOOR | 0.00 | 0.00 | 0.00 | 0.00 | 0.00 | 0.00 | 0.00 | 0.00 |
| ASIFABAD | 14.00 | 0.00 | 0.00 | 0.00 | 0.00 | 14.00 | 14.00 | 0.15 |
| Grand Total | 13362.00 | 7562.00 | 6135.00 | 13470.00 | 7097.00 | 47626.00 | 9525.20 | 100.00 |
| **8. PUNGUM SEED (IN QUINTALS)** | | | | | | | | |
| PARVATIPURAM | 168.00 | 249.00 | 504.00 | 98.00 | 443.00 | 1452.00 | 292.40 | 11.23 |
| SEETHAMPETA | 164.00 | 6.00 | 874.00 | 166.00 | 583.00 | 1793.00 | 358.60 | 13.78 |
| PADERU | 9.00 | 54.00 | 502.00 | 201.00 | 2079.00 | 2845.00 | 569.00 | 21.86 |
| CHINTAPALLE | 128.00 | 10.00 | 232.00 | 202.00 | 870.00 | 1441.00 | 288.40 | 11.08 |
| RAMPA-CHODAVARAM | 568.00 | 109.00 | 354.00 | 224.00 | 1221.00 | 2476.00 | 495.20 | 19.03 |
| THIRUPATHI | 0.00 | 0.00 | 0.00 | 0.00 | 0.00 | 0.00 | 0.00 | 0.00 |
| SRISAILAM | 108.00 | 446.00 | 433.00 | 385.00 | 284.00 | 1656.00 | 331.20 | 12.73 |
| PALONCHA | 233.00 | 15.00 | 441.00 | 15.00 | 388.00 | 1092.00 | 218.40 | 8.39 |
| BHADRACHALAM | 2.00 | 0.00 | 37.00 | 0.00 | 67.00 | 106.00 | 35.33 | 1.36 |
| ETURNAGARAM | 8.00 | 4.00 | 27.00 | 5.00 | 29.00 | 73.00 | 14.60 | 0.56 |
| UTNOOR | 0.00 | 0.00 | 0.00 | 0.00 | 0.00 | 0.00 | 0.00 | 0.00 |
| ASIFABAD | 20.00 | 0.00 | 33.00 | 13.00 | 2.00 | 68.00 | 17.00 | 0.65 |
| Grand Total | 1408.00 | 893.00 | 3437.00 | 1309.00 | 5966.00 | 13013.00 | 2602.60 | 100.00 |

(*Contd.*)

## Table 3.1 (*Contd.*)

| DIVISION | 1989-90 | 1990-91 | 1991-92 | 1992-93 | 1993-94 | Total | Average | Percentage |
|---|---|---|---|---|---|---|---|---|
| **9. CLEANING NUTS (IN QUINTALS)** | | | | | | | | |
| PARVATIPURAM | 76.00 | 19.00 | 367.00 | 1226.00 | 22.00 | 1710.00 | 342.00 | 5.88 |
| SEETHAMPETA | 10.00 | 0.00 | 55.00 | 470.00 | 34.00 | 569.00 | 142.25 | 1.96 |
| PADERU | 44.00 | 66.00 | 79.00 | 515.00 | 73.00 | 777.00 | 155.40 | 2.67 |
| CHINTAPALLE | 17.00 | 41.00 | 0.00 | 144.00 | 29.00 | 231.00 | 57.75 | 0.79 |
| RAMPA-CHODAVARAM | 28.00 | 154.00 | 77.00 | 680.00 | 256.00 | 1195.00 | 239.00 | 4.11 |
| THIRUPATHI | 3.00 | 0.00 | 15.00 | 12.00 | 268.00 | 298.00 | 74.50 | 1.03 |
| SRISAILAM | 16.00 | 93.00 | 361.00 | 583.00 | 976.00 | 2029.00 | 405.80 | 6.98 |
| PALONCHA | 1103.00 | 5230.00 | 399.00 | 1016.00 | 978.00 | 8726.00 | 1745.20 | 30.02 |
| BHADRACHALAM | 355.00 | 1077.00 | 31.00 | 95.00 | 44.00 | 1602.00 | 320.40 | 5.51 |
| ETURNAGARAM | 390.00 | 5835.00 | 1129.00 | 512.00 | 89.00 | 7955.00 | 0692.00 | 27.37 |
| UTNOOR | 0.00 | 198.00 | 7.00 | 19.00 | 4.00 | 228.99 | 57.00 | 0.78 |
| ASIFABAD | 60.00 | 1809.00 | 1338.00 | 283.00 | 256.00 | 3746.00 | 749.10 | 12.89 |
| Grand Total | 2102.00 | 14522.00 | 3858.00 | 5555.00 | 3029.00 | 29066.00 | 5813.20 | 100.00 |
| **10. MARKING NUTS (IN QUINTALS)** | | | | | | | | |
| PARVATIPURAM | 2750.00 | 1539.00 | 596.00 | 96.00 | 169.00 | 5150.00 | 1030.00 | 34.05 |
| SEETHAMPETA | 803.00 | 270.00 | 135.00 | 80.00 | 213.00 | 1501.00 | 300.20 | 9.92 |
| PADERU | 1573.00 | 1187.00 | 318.00 | 116.00 | 182.00 | 2467.00 | 675.20 | 22.32 |
| CHINTAPALLE | 717.00 | 223.00 | 176.00 | 119.00 | 183.00 | 1418.00 | 283.60 | 9.38 |
| RAMPA-CHODAVARAM | 474.00 | 602.00 | 462.00 | 136.00 | 134.00 | 1808.00 | 361.60 | 11.95 |
| THIRUPATHI | 30.00 | 75.00 | 87.00 | 484.00 | 613.00 | 1289.00 | 257.80 | 8.52 |
| SRISAILAM | 0.00 | 0.00 | 17.00 | 37.00 | 0.00 | 54.00 | 27.00 | 0.36 |
| PALONCHA | 0.00 | 5.00 | 3.00 | 0.00 | 0.00 | 8.00 | 4.00 | 0.05 |
| BHADRACHALAM | 2.00 | 0.00 | 1.00 | 0.00 | 0.00 | 3.00 | 1.50 | 0.02 |
| ETURNAGARAM | 0.00 | 8.00 | 0.00 | 0.00 | 0.00 | 8.00 | 8.00 | 0.05 |
| UTNOOR | 12.00 | 18.00 | 52.00 | 10.00 | 0.00 | 92.00 | 23.00 | 0.61 |
| ASIFABAD | 209.00 | 209.00 | 0.00 | 0.00 | 0.00 | 418.00 | 209.00 | 2.76 |
| Grand Total | 6570.00 | 4136.00 | 1847.00 | 1078.00 | 1494.00 | 15125.00 | 3025.00 | 100.00 |

(*Contd.*)

**Table 3.1** *(Contd.)*

| DIVISION | 1989-90 | 1990-91 | 1991-92 | 1992-93 | 1993-94 | Total | Average | Per-centage |
|---|---|---|---|---|---|---|---|---|
| **11. MOHWA SEED (IN QUINTALS)** | | | | | | | | |
| PARVATIPURAM | 190.00 | 434.00 | 1205.00 | 2296.00 | 2222.00 | 6347.00 | 1269.40 | 21.68 |
| SEETHAMPETA | 355.00 | 39.00 | 1137.00 | 480.00 | 1054.00 | 3065.00 | 613.00 | 10.47 |
| PADERU | 0.00 | 0.00 | 0.00 | 0.00 | 0.00 | 0.00 | 0.00 | 0.00 |
| CHINTAPALLE | 0.00 | 0.00 | 0.00 | 0.00 | 0.00 | 0.00 | 0.00 | 0.00 |
| RAMPA-CHODAVARAM | 26.00 | 3.00 | 56.00 | 5.00 | 21.00 | 111.00 | 22.20 | 0.38 |
| THIRUPATHI | 0.00 | 0.00 | 0.00 | 0.00 | 0.00 | 0.00 | 0.00 | 0.00 |
| SRISAILAM | 1547.00 | 1110.00 | 1393.00 | 1468.00 | 1272.00 | 6790.00 | 1358.00 | 23.19 |
| PALONCHA | 318.00 | 57.00 | 434.00 | 26.00 | 118.00 | 954.00 | 190.60 | 3.25 |
| BHADRACHALAM | 1411.00 | 235.00 | 728.00 | 1999.00 | 206.00 | 4579.00 | 915.80 | 15.64 |
| ETURNAGARAM | 192.00 | 135.00 | 477.00 | 81.00 | 164.00 | 1049.00 | 209.80 | 3.58 |
| UTNOOR | 955.00 | 71.00 | 2118.00 | 155.00 | 493.00 | 3792.00 | 758.40 | 12.95 |
| ASIFABAD | 1042.00 | 80.00 | 984.00 | 70.00 | 420.00 | 2596.00 | 519.20 | 8.87 |
| Grand Total | 6036.00 | 2164.00 | 8532.00 | 6580.00 | 5970.00 | 29282.00 | 5856.40 | 100.00 |
| **12. MOHWA FLOWER (IN QUINTALS)** | | | | | | | | |
| PARVATIPURAM | 28.00 | 275.00 | 362.00 | 0.00 | 0.00 | 665.00 | 221.67 | 1.23 |
| SEETHAMPETA | 149.00 | 2.00 | 0.00 | 0.00 | 0.00 | 151.00 | 75.50 | 0.28 |
| PADERU | 0.00 | 0.00 | 0.00 | 0.00 | 0.00 | 0.00 | 0.00 | 0.00 |
| CHINTAPALLE | 0.00 | 0.00 | 0.00 | 0.00 | 0.00 | 0.00 | 0.00 | 0.00 |
| RAMPA-CHODAVARAM | 0.00 | 0.00 | 0.00 | 0.00 | 0.00 | 0.00 | 0.00 | 0.00 |
| THIRUPATHI | 24.00 | 0.00 | 42.00 | 22.00 | 20.00 | 108.00 | 27.00 | 0.20 |
| SRISAILAM | 134.00 | 281.00 | 123.00 | 0.00 | 0.00 | 538.00 | 269.33 | 0.99 |
| PALONCHA | 308.00 | 20.00 | 707.00 | 120.00 | 0.00 | 1164.00 | 288.75 | 2.13 |
| BHADRACHALAM | 246.00 | 4.00 | 435.00 | 200.00 | 11.00 | 996.00 | 179.20 | 1.66 |
| ETURNAGARAM | 564.00 | 44.00 | 176.00 | 136.00 | 251.00 | 1171.00 | 234.20 | 2.16 |
| UTNOOR | 7674.00 | 2609.00 | 11653.00 | 4646.00 | 10524.00 | 37106.00 | 7421.20 | 68.56 |
| ASIFABAD | 2743.00 | 486.00 | 4290.00 | 2036.00 | 2778.00 | 12333.00 | 1466.60 | 22.79 |
| Grand Total | 11870.00 | 3721.00 | 17788.00 | 7160.00 | 13584.00 | 54123.00 | 10824.60 | 100.00 |

*(Contd.)*

**Table 3.1 (*Contd.*)**

| DIVISION | 1989-90 | 1990-91 | 1991-92 | 1992-93 | 1993-94 | Total | Average | Percentage |
|---|---|---|---|---|---|---|---|---|
| **13. ROCK BEE HONEY (IN QUINTALS)** | | | | | | | | |
| PARVATIPURAM | 0.00 | 4.00 | 6.00 | 0.00 | 0.00 | 10.00 | 5.00 | 0.31 |
| SEETHAMPETA | 0.00 | 0.00 | 0.00 | 0.00 | 0.00 | 0.00 | 0.00 | 0.00 |
| PADERU | 0.00 | 1.00 | 38.00 | 9.00 | 1.00 | 49.00 | 12.25 | 1.52 |
| CHINTAPALLE | 257.00 | 246.00 | 276.00 | 525.00 | 293.00 | 1597.00 | 319.40 | 49.47 |
| RAMPA-CHODAVARAM | 11.00 | 46.00 | 83.00 | 217.00 | 41.00 | 398.00 | 79.60 | 12.33 |
| THIRUPATHI | 29.00 | 102.00 | 308.00 | 0.00 | 0.00 | 439.00 | 146.33 | 13.60 |
| SRISAILAM | 17.00 | 104.00 | 198.00 | 266.00 | 126.00 | 711.00 | 142.20 | 22.03 |
| PALONCHA | 1.00 | 2.00 | 6.00 | 6.00 | 9.00 | 24.00 | 4.80 | 0.74 |
| BHADRACHALAM | 0.00 | 0.00 | 0.00 | 0.00 | 0.00 | 0.00 | 0.00 | 0.00 |
| ETURNAGARAM | 0.00 | 0.00 | 0.00 | 0.00 | 0.00 | 0.00 | 0.00 | 0.00 |
| UTNOOR | 0.00 | 0.00 | 0.00 | 0.00 | 0.00 | 0.00 | 0.00 | 0.00 |
| ASIFABAD | 0.00 | 0.00 | 0.00 | 0.00 | 0.00 | 0.00 | 0.00 | 0.00 |
| Grand Total | 315.00 | 505.00 | 915.00 | 1023.00 | 470.00 | 3228.00 | 645.60 | 100.00 |
| **14. APIARY HONEY (IN QUINTALS)** | | | | | | | | |
| PARVATIPURAM | 0.00 | 0.00 | 0.00 | 0.00 | 0.00 | 0.00 | 0.00 | 0.00 |
| SEETHAMPETA | 0.00 | 0.00 | 0.00 | 0.00 | 0.00 | 0.00 | 0.00 | 0.00 |
| PADERU | 0.00 | 0.00 | 0.00 | 0.00 | 0.00 | 0.00 | 0.00 | 0.00 |
| CHINTAPALLE | 12.00 | 33.00 | 39.00 | 39.00 | 65.00 | 188.00 | 37.06 | 19.92 |
| RAMPA-CHODAVARAM | 0.00 | 0.00 | 0.00 | 0.00 | 0.00 | 0.00 | 0.00 | 0.00 |
| THIRUPATHI | 0.00 | 0.00 | 0.00 | 543.00 | 213.00 | 756.00 | 378.00 | 80.08 |
| SRISAILAM | 0.00 | 0.00 | 0.00 | 0.00 | 0.00 | 0.00 | 0.00 | 0.00 |
| PALONCHA | 0.00 | 0.00 | 0.00 | 0.00 | 0.00 | 0.00 | 0.00 | 0.00 |
| BHADRACHALAM | 0.00 | 0.00 | 0.00 | 0.00 | 0.00 | 0.00 | 0.00 | 0.00 |
| ETURNAGARAM | 0.00 | 0.00 | 0.00 | 0.00 | 0.00 | 0.00 | 0.00 | 0.00 |
| UTNOOR | 0.00 | 0.00 | 0.00 | 0.00 | 0.00 | 0.00 | 0.00 | 0.00 |
| ASIFABAD | 0.00 | 0.00 | 0.00 | 0.00 | 0.00 | 0.00 | 0.00 | 0.00 |
| Grand Total | 12.00 | 33.00 | 39.00 | 582.00 | 278.00 | 944.00 | 188.80 | 100.00 |

*(Contd.)*

## Table 3.1 (*Contd.*)

| DIVISION | 1989-90 | 1990-91 | 1991-92 | 1992-93 | 1993-94 | Total | Average | Percentage |
|---|---|---|---|---|---|---|---|---|
| **15. SHIKAKAI (IN QUINTALS)** | | | | | | | | |
| PARVATIPURAM | 0.00 | 0.00 | 0.00 | 0.00 | 0.00 | 0.00 | 0.00 | 0.00 |
| SEETHAMPETA | 0.00 | 0.00 | 0.00 | 0.00 | 0.00 | 0.00 | 0.00 | 0.00 |
| PADERU | 8.00 | 4.00 | 4.00 | 0.00 | 24.00 | 9240.00 | 2380.00 | 0.76 |
| CHINTAPALLE | 1348.00 | 241.00 | 634.00 | 147.00 | 999.00 | 3369.00 | 673.80 | 64.07 |
| RAMPA-CHODAVARAM | 514.00 | 519.00 | 294.00 | 219.00 | 303.00 | 1849.00 | 369.80 | 35.17 |
| THIRUPATHI | 0.00 | 0.00 | 0.00 | 0.00 | 0.00 | 0.00 | 0.00 | 0.00 |
| SRISAILAM | 0.00 | 0.00 | 0.00 | 0.00 | 0.00 | 0.00 | 0.00 | 0.00 |
| PALONCHA | 0.00 | 0.00 | 0.00 | 0.00 | 0.00 | 0.00 | 0.00 | 0.00 |
| BHADRACHALAM | 0.00 | 0.00 | 0.00 | 0.00 | 0.00 | 0.00 | 0.00 | 0.00 |
| ETURNAGARAM | 0.00 | 0.00 | 0.00 | 0.00 | 0.00 | 0.00 | 0.00 | 0.00 |
| UTNOOR | 0.00 | 0.00 | 0.00 | 0.00 | 0.00 | 0.00 | 0.00 | 0.00 |
| ASIFABAD | 0.00 | 0.00 | 0.00 | 0.00 | 0.00 | 0.00 | 0.00 | 0.00 |
| Grand Total | 1870.00 | 764.00 | 932.00 | 366.00 | 1326.00 | 5258.00 | 1051.60 | 100.00 |
| **16. SOAPNUTS (IN QUINTALS)** | | | | | | | | |
| PARVATIPURAM | 536.00 | 30.00 | 179.00 | 106.00 | 355.00 | 1206.00 | 241.20 | 10.93 |
| SEETHAMPETA | 1006.00 | 564.00 | 299.00 | 1051.00 | 752.00 | 3672.00 | 734.40 | 33.27 |
| PADERU | 0.00 | 0.00 | 4.00 | 0.00 | 0.00 | 4.00 | 4.00 | 0.04 |
| CHINTAPALLE | 0.00 | 0.00 | 0.00 | 47.00 | 1.00 | 48.00 | 24.00 | 0.43 |
| RAMPA-CHODAVARAM | 118.00 | 25.00 | 89.00 | 62.00 | 19.00 | 313.00 | 62.60 | 2.84 |
| THIRUPATHI | 0.00 | 0.00 | 0.00 | 0.00 | 0.00 | 0.00 | 0.00 | 0.00 |
| SRISAILAM | 662.00 | 690.00 | 889.00 | 2368.00 | 1186.00 | 5795.00 | 1159.00 | 52.50 |
| PALONCHA | 0.00 | 0.00 | 0.00 | 0.00 | 0.00 | 0.00 | 0.00 | 0.00 |
| BHADRACHALAM | 0.00 | 0.00 | 0.00 | 0.00 | 0.00 | 0.00 | 0.00 | 0.00 |
| ETURNAGARAM | 0.00 | 0.00 | 0.00 | 0.00 | 0.00 | 0.00 | 0.00 | 0.00 |
| UTNOOR | 0.00 | 0.00 | 0.00 | 0.00 | 0.00 | 0.00 | 0.00 | 0.00 |
| ASIFABAD | 0.00 | 0.00 | 0.00 | 0.00 | 0.00 | 0.00 | 0.00 | 0.00 |
| Grand Total | 2322.00 | 1309.00 | 1460.00 | 3634.00 | 2313.00 | 11038.00 | 2207.60 | 100.00 |

(*Contd.*)

## Table 3.1 (*Contd.*)

| DIVISION | 1989-90 | 1990-91 | 1991-92 | 1992-93 | 1993-94 | Total | Average | Percentage |
|---|---|---|---|---|---|---|---|---|
| **17. HILLBROOMS (NOS) (IN QUINTALS)** | | | | | | | | |
| PARVATIPURAM | 2271.00 | 50914.00 | 2747.00 | 43275.00 | 10395.00 | 109602.00 | 21920.40 | 17.09 |
| SEETHAMPETA | 4678.00 | 1986.00 | 1834.00 | 538.00 | 0.00 | 9036.00 | 2259.00 | 1.41 |
| PADERU | 35790.00 | 110866.00 | 18541.00 | 7349.00 | 11638.00 | 193275.00 | 45936.90 | 28.72 |
| CHINTAPALLE | 12923.00 | 7915.00 | 7910.00 | 7550.00 | 3176.00 | 29474.00 | 8793.80 | 6.16 |
| RAMPA-CHODAVARAM | 49989.00 | 127353.00 | 43263.00 | 26261.00 | 40363.00 | 287229.00 | 57445.80 | 44.79 |
| THIRUPATHI | 2035.00 | 458.00 | 325.00 | 436.00 | 335.00 | 3589.00 | 717.80 | 0.56 |
| SRISAILAM | 0.00 | 0.00 | 0.00 | 0.00 | 0.00 | 0.00 | 0.00 | 0.00 |
| PALONCHA | 0.00 | 0.00 | 0.00 | 0.00 | 0.00 | 0.00 | 0.00 | 0.00 |
| BHADRACHALAM | 3250.00 | 0.00 | 612.00 | 3787.00 | 550.00 | 8199.00 | 2049.75 | 1.28 |
| ETURNAGARAM | 0.00 | 0.00 | 0.00 | 0.00 | 0.00 | 0.00 | 0.00 | 0.00 |
| UTNOOR | 0.00 | 0.00 | 0.00 | 0.00 | 0.00 | 0.00 | 0.00 | 0.00 |
| ASIFABAD | 0.00 | 0.00 | 0.00 | 0.00 | 0.00 | 0.00 | 0.00 | 0.00 |
| Grand Total | 110936.00 | 299492.00 | 75232.00 | 89196.00 | 66457.00 | 641313.00 | 128262.60 | 100.00 |
| **18. HILLBROOMS (QTY) (IN QUINTALS)** | | | | | | | | |
| PARVATIPURAM | 212.69 | 604.00 | 769.00 | 416.44 | 528.54 | 2530.64 | 506.13 | 2.97 |
| SEETHAMPETA | 168.50 | 86.00 | 147.00 | 0.00 | 0.00 | 401.50 | 133.80 | 0.47 |
| PADERU | 11306.00 | 15938.00 | 13381.00 | 19480.00 | 20964.00 | 81069.00 | 16213.80 | 95.19 |
| CHINTAPALLE | 0.00 | 0.00 | 0.00 | 0.00 | 0.00 | 00.00 | 00.00 | 0.00 |
| RAMPA-CHODAVARAM | 0.00 | 0.00 | 0.00 | 0.00 | 0.00 | 00.00 | 00.00 | 0.00 |
| THIRUPATHI | 0.00 | 0.00 | 1160.00 | 0.00 | 0.00 | 1160.00 | 1160.00 | 1.36 |
| SRISAILAM | 0.00 | 0.00 | 0.00 | 0.00 | 0.00 | 00.00 | 00.00 | 0.00 |
| PALONCHA | 0.00 | 0.00 | 0.00 | 0.00 | 0.00 | 00.00 | 00.00 | 0.00 |
| BHADRACHALAM | 0.00 | 0.00 | 0.00 | 0.00 | 0.00 | 00.00 | 00.00 | 0.00 |
| ETURNAGARAM | 0.00 | 0.00 | 0.00 | 0.00 | 0.00 | 00.00 | 00.00 | 0.00 |
| UTNOOR | 0.00 | 0.00 | 0.00 | 0.00 | 0.00 | 00.00 | 00.00 | 0.00 |
| ASIFABAD | 0.00 | 0.00 | 0.00 | 0.00 | 0.00 | 00.00 | 00.00 | 0.00 |
| Grand Total | 11687.19 | 16628.00 | 15457.00 | 19896.44 | 21492.54 | 85161.17 | 17032.23 | 100.00 |

(*Contd.*)

## Table 3.1 (*Contd.*)

| DIVISION | 1989-90 | 1990-91 | 1991-92 | 1992-93 | 1993-94 | Total | Average | Percentage |
|---|---|---|---|---|---|---|---|---|
| **19. ADDALEAF (IN QUINTALS)** | | | | | | | | |
| PARVATIPURAM | 13.00 | 38.00 | 0.00 | 0.00 | 0.00 | 51.00 | 25.50 | 1.57 |
| SEETHAMPETA | 0.00 | 0.00 | 0.00 | 0.00 | 0.00 | 0.00 | 0.00 | 0.00 |
| PADERU | 243.00 | 386.00 | 2243.00 | 165.00 | 0.00 | 3037.00 | 759.25 | 46.87 |
| CHINTAPALLE | 151.00 | 1858.00 | 115.00 | 0.00 | 490.00 | 2614.00 | 653.50 | 40.34 |
| RAMPA-CHODAVARAM | 40.00 | 10.00 | 21.00 | 0.00 | 0.00 | 71.00 | 23.67 | 1.46 |
| THIRUPATHI | 0.00 | 4.00 | 0.00 | 0.00 | 0.00 | 4.00 | 4.00 | 0.25 |
| SRISAILAM | 0.00 | 158.00 | 0.00 | 0.00 | 0.00 | 158.00 | 158.00 | 9.75 |
| PALONCHA | 0.00 | 0.00 | 0.00 | 0.00 | 0.00 | 0.00 | 0.00 | 0.00 |
| BHADRACHALAM | 0.00 | 0.00 | 0.00 | 0.00 | 0.00 | 0.00 | 0.00 | 0.00 |
| ETURNAGARAM | 0.00 | 0.00 | 0.00 | 0.00 | 0.00 | 0.00 | 0.00 | 0.00 |
| UTNOOR | 0.00 | 0.00 | 0.00 | 0.00 | 0.00 | 0.00 | 0.00 | 0.00 |
| ASIFABAD | 0.00 | 0.00 | 0.00 | 0.00 | 0.00 | 0.00 | 0.00 | 0.00 |
| Grand Total | 447.00 | 2454.00 | 2379.00 | 165.00 | 490.00 | 5935.00 | 1187.00 | 100.00 |
| **20. NARAMAMIDI BARK (IN QUINTALS)** | | | | | | | | |
| PARVATIPURAM | 0.00 | 0.00 | 0.00 | 0.00 | 0.00 | 0.00 | 0.00 | 0.00 |
| SEETHAMPETA | 0.00 | 0.00 | 0.00 | 0.00 | 0.00 | 0.00 | 0.00 | 0.00 |
| PADERU | 0.00 | 0.00 | 0.00 | 0.00 | 0.00 | 0.00 | 0.00 | 0.00 |
| CHINTAPALLE | 1683.00 | 277.00 | 439.00 | 164.00 | 6.00 | 2569.00 | 513.80 | 33.00 |
| RAMPA-CHODAVARAM | 916.00 | 770.00 | 3064.00 | 261.00 | 204.00 | 5215.00 | 1043.00 | 67.00 |
| THIRUPATHI | 0.00 | 0.00 | 0.00 | 0.00 | 0.00 | 0.00 | 0.00 | 0.00 |
| SRISAILAM | 0.00 | 0.00 | 0.00 | 0.00 | 0.00 | 0.00 | 0.00 | 0.00 |
| PALONCHA | 0.00 | 0.00 | 0.00 | 0.00 | 0.00 | 0.00 | 0.00 | 0.00 |
| BHADRACHALAM | 0.00 | 0.00 | 0.00 | 0.00 | 0.00 | 0.00 | 0.00 | 0.00 |
| ETURNAGARAM | 0.00 | 0.00 | 0.00 | 0.00 | 0.00 | 0.00 | 0.00 | 0.00 |
| UTNOOR | 0.00 | 0.00 | 0.00 | 0.00 | 0.00 | 0.00 | 0.00 | 0.00 |
| ASIFABAD | 0.00 | 0.00 | 0.00 | 0.00 | 0.00 | 0.00 | 0.00 | 0.00 |
| Grand Total | 2599.00 | 1047.00 | 3503.00 | 425.00 | 210.00 | 7784.00 | 1556.80 | 100.00 |

### 3.3. Division-wise Procurement of MFP in Orissa

In Orissa state, out of the three divisions, the details are available only for Sunabeda division. Sunabeda division has 7 branches. These are : Sunabeda, Jeypore, Umerkot, Bhavanipatna, Muniguda, Rayagada and Kashipur. The details of procured quantity branch-wise are given for each commodity for the period 1989-90 to 1995-96.

### 3.4. MFP by Division-wise in Orissa State

Division-wise data on MFP is not available for Orissa State. It is however, possible to present the overall picture of the important divisions from the abstract of scientific management system available from the office of the Chief Conservator of Forests, Bhubaneswar. The details are presented in Table 3.4. Out of 27 forest divisions, MFP area is observed in only 12 divisions. Even out of 12 divisions MFP area covering less than 10 per cent in total forest area of the division concerned is observed only in 3 divisions. Thus MFP area accounts for significant percentage only 9 out of 27 divisions. The divisions more significant in MFP are Parlakhemundi, Jeypore and Sambalpur. In these more than 40 per cent of the forest area is accounted for by MFP. In Phulbani, Rayagada, Bonai and Sundergarh, MFP accounted for more than 20 per cent of the forest area in each of the divisions. When the share of MFP area in the total MFP area of the state is considered, three forest divisions *viz.* Parlakhemundi, Jeypore and Sambalpore accounted for 2/3rd of the total MFP area of the State.

The commodity-wise share of MFP in total MFP value is shown in Table 3.5. Since TDCC did not send the latest available data, we have to use the data available from the publications of the Forest Department. The latest year for which the data available is 1988-89. There are several problems in computing the values. For some of the items, no price data is reported. For other items also, there was a problem in obtaining the price data. For some of the items, we have to use the prices for the nearest years. The total value of MFP in Orissa accounted for Rs. 149 crores. Out of these, kendu leaves accounted for Rs. 131 crores or 87 per cent in the total value. Sal seeds and mohwa flower accounted for Rs. 6 crores each. Both together form 8 per cent of the total value. Tamarind was next in importance to the sal seed and Mohwa flower with Rs. 3 crores and 2 per cent of the total value. All other MFP accounted only for 2 per cent of the total value.

**Table 3.2: Division-wise Share of MFP**
(Summary Table — during 1989-90 to 1993-94)

| Commodity | Division Ranking | | | | Coverage of the Main Division |
|---|---|---|---|---|---|
| | 1 | 2 | 3 | 4 | |
| 1. Gum Karaya | Rampachoda-varam (19.37%) | Bhadra-chalam (16.37%) | Paloncha (15.65%) | Srisailam (15.57) | 66.96% |
| 2. Gum Tiruman | Bhadra-chalam (54.27) | Tirupati (16.35) | Rampachoda-varam (11.78) | — | 82.40% |
| 3. Myrobalans | Rampachoda-varam | Paderu (24.4) (29.62) | Parvati-puram | — (24.37) | 78.35% |
| 4. Nuxvomica | Paloncha (35.46) | Rampacho-davaram (22.20) | Eturnagaram (15.83) | — | 73.49% |
| 5. Seed Tamarind | Parvati-puram (62.85) | Paderu (28.2) | — | — | 90.95% |
| 6. Deseeded Tamarind | Rampachoda-varam (63.68) | Parvati-puram (17.32) | Srisailam (16.82) | — | 97.82% |
| 7. Tamarind seed | Rampachoda-varam (80.88) | Parvati-puram (6.62) | — | — | 87.50% |
| 8. Pungum Seed | Paderu (21.86) | Rampachoda-varam (19.03) | Seethampet (13.78) | Srisailam (12.73) | 67.40% |
| 9. Cleaning Nuts | Paloncha (30.0) | Eturnagaram (27.37) | Asifabad (12.89) | — | 70.28% |
| 10. Marking Nuts | Parvati-puram (34.05) | Paderu (22.32) | Rampachoda-varam (11.95) (10% each) | Seethampet Chintapalle Thirupati | 98.32% |
| 11. Mohwa Seed | Srisailam (23.2) | Parvati-puram (21.7) | Bhadra-chalam (15.6) | Utnoor (13.0) | 73.50% |
| 12. Mohwa Flower | Utnoor (68.56) | Asifabad (27.29) | — | — | 91.4% |
| 13. Rockbee Honey | Chintapalle (50) | Srisailam (22.03) | Thirupati (13.60) | Rampachoda-varam (12.33) | 97.96% |
| 14. Apiary Honey | Thirupati (80.0) | Chintapalli (20.0) | — | — | 100% |
| 15. Shikakai | Chintapalle (64.07%) | Rampachoda-varam (35.17%) | Paderu (0.76) | — | 100% |
| 16. Soapnuts | Srisailam (52.51) | Seethampet (33.27) | Parvati-puram (10.93) | — | 96.71% |

*(Contd.)*

**Table 3.2 (*Contd.*)**

| Commodity | Division Ranking 1 | 2 | 3 | 4 | Coverage of the Main Division |
|---|---|---|---|---|---|
| 17. Hillbrooms (No.) | Rampachoda-varam (44.80) | Paderu (28.7) | Parvati-puram (17.1) | — | 90.60 |
| 18. Hillbrooms (Qty.) | Paderu (90.01) | Thirupati (6.43) | Parvati-puram (2.81) | Seetampet (0.74) | 100% |
| 19. Addaleaf | Paderu (51.2) | Chintapalle (44.8%) | — | — | 100% |
| 20. Naramamidi Bark | Rampachoda-varam (67.00) | Chintapalle (33.0) | — | — | 100% |

**Table 3.3: Commodity-wise Procurement: Average for the 7-Year Period ending with 1995-96**

(Value in Lakhs)

| Sl. No. | Commodity | Average value for the period 1989-90 to 1995-96 | % in total value | Value in 1995-96 | % in total value |
|---|---|---|---|---|---|
| 1. | Gum Karaya[1] | 469.36 | 50.94 | 350.13 | 38.51 |
| 2. | Adda leaf | 29.63 | 3.22 | 47.59 | 5.23 |
| 3. | Seeded tamarind | 137.20 | 14.89 | 130.14 | 14.31 |
| 4. | Deseeded tamarind | 40.73 | 4.42 | 47.78 | 5.26 |
| 5. | Tamarind seed | 10.46 | 1.14 | 23.62 | 2.60 |
| 6. | Mohwa seed | 51.20 | 5.56 | 69.12 | 7.60 |
| 7. | Mohwa flower | 27.43 | 2.98 | 37.71 | 4.15 |
| 8. | Myrobalans | 30.84 | 3.35 | 49.74 | 5.47 |
| 9. | Apiary honey | 1.72 | 0.20 | 3.53 | 0.40 |
| 10. | Rockbee honey | 26.60 | 2.90 | 65.25 | 7.18 |
| 11. | Shikakai | 9.17 | 1.00 | 5.38 | 0.60 |
| 12. | Soapnuts | 16.00 | 1.74 | 10.44 | 1.15 |
| 13. | Pungam seed | 13.22 | 1.43 | 26.02 | 2.86 |
| 14. | Hillbrooms | 7.95 | 0.86 | 19.36 | 2.13 |
| 15. | Wild brooms[2] | 1.96 | 0.21 | N.A. | N.A. |
| 16. | Nuxvomica | 21.03 | 2.30 | 13.73 | 1.50 |
| 17. | Marking nuts | 2.98 | 0.32 | 5.08 | 0.56 |
| 18. | Cleaning nuts | 23.98 | 2.60 | 4.53 | 0.50 |
| | | 921.46 | 100.00 | 909.15 | 100.00 |

1. In the division-wise table, Gum Karaya and gum tiruman are separately given.
2. Average for only two years *i.e.* 1989-90, 1990-91.

Difference between Andhra Pradesh and Orissa may be noted in respect of commodity-wise share. Kendu leaves form the most prominent item in both Orissa and Andhra Pradesh. In Orissa, the share of kendu leaves is much more than the corresponding share in Andhra Pradesh. Gum is the much more important item among MFP in Andhra Pradesh while mohwa flower and sal seeds were the most significant commodities in respect of value in Orissa State. Value of tamarind is much more in Orissa than Andhra Pradesh.

Procurement data for two branches which were intensively studied *viz.* Sunabeda branch of Koraput district and Muniguda branch of Rayagada district are shown for the quinquennium ending with 1993-94 and for the year 1996-97 in Table 3.6. The five year period shows a decline in procurement in items like tamarind in respect of which private persons are given lease. In respect of other items, procurement shows a declining trend. In 1996-97, procurement has been distressingly low in respect of all items both in Sunabeda and Muniguda branches. This is because of the fact that the LAMPS have not been operating and TDCC did not receive the work order in time. When we visited the area in February, 1998, the TDCC complained that they did not receive the work order; though the season had commenced. The lack of autonomy for the TDCC in purchase operations coupled with leases to private individuals is responsible for low procurement.

## SECTION-II

### 3.5. Commodity-wise Share in Total MFP Value in Sunabeda and Muniguda Branches

Commodity-wise share in total MFP value in selected branches is shown in Table 3.7. There was a sharp drop in the value of MFP in 1996-97 both in Sunabeda and Muniguda branches. The highest value was attained in 1994-95 in Sunabeda and 1991-92 in Muniguda. The current value of total procurement (1996-97) in Sunabeda is only 1/16th of the value attained in 1994-95 while in Muniguda which is 1/6th of the value attained in 1991-92. The reasons for the low value of MFP are cited earlier. The value of tamarind procured in 1994-95 was Rs. 38.3 lakhs in Sunabeda division. No procurement of tamarind

## Table 3.4: Share of MFP in Total Forest Area : Division-wise : 1991[1]

(area in sq. km.)

| Sl. No. | Division | Total forest area | MFP area | % share of MFP in the total forest area of the division | % share of MFP in the total MFP area of the state |
|---|---|---|---|---|---|
| 1. | Athamallik | 768.67 | 41.12 | 5.35 | 0.40 |
| 2. | Athagarth | 853.36 | — | — | — |
| 3. | Angul | 1936.31 | — | — | — |
| 4. | Baripada | 1536.55 | 247.80 | 16.13 | 2.22 |
| 5. | Dhenkanal | 1310.43 | — | — | — |
| 6. | Karonjia | 1784.99 | — | — | — |
| 7. | Keonjhar | 1811.89 | — | — | — |
| 8. | Baliguda | 1088.65 | — | — | — |
| 9. | Boudh | 2404.12 | — | — | — |
| 10. | Gh. North | 1698.95 | 22.74 | 1.34 | 0.20 |
| 11. | Gh. South | 821.93 | — | — | — |
| 12. | Nayagarh | 2050.28 | — | — | — |
| 13. | Parlakhemundi | 3506.09 | 2323.00 | 66.26 | 20.80 |
| 14. | Phulbani | 3712.40 | 982.00 | 26.45 | 8.80 |
| 15. | Puri | 3458.79 | 600.38 | 17.36 | 5.40 |
| 16. | Bolangir | 2689.49 | — | — | — |
| 17. | Jeypore | 4967.49 | 2483.86 | 50.00 | 22.25 |
| 18. | Khalahandi | 2494.81 | 167.68 | 6.72 | 1.50 |
| 19. | Khariar | 3654.53 | — | — | — |
| 20. | Nawrangpur | 1470.91 | — | — | — |
| 21. | Rayagada | 2042.42 | 504.17 | 24.68 | 4.5 |
| 22. | Bamra | 2671.78 | — | — | — |
| 23. | Bonai | 2696.73 | 779.32 | 28.90 | 6.98 |
| 24. | Deogarh | 1946.19 | — | — | — |
| 25. | Raikhol | 9401.66 | — | — | — |
| 26. | Sambalpur | 5708.79 | 2515.60 | 44.07 | 22.53 |
| 27. | Sundargarh | 2223.00 | 497.05 | 22.36 | 4.45 |
| | Total | 70711.21 | 11164.74 | 15.78 | |

1. Government of Orissa, Statistical Branch, Office of the Principal Chief Conservator of Forests, Orissa, *A Decade of Forestry in Orissa 1981-90*, Bhubaneswar, p. 74.

**Table 3.5: Commodity-wise Share of MFP in Total MFP Value of the Orissa State : 1988-89**

| | Production in 1988-89 | Price in 1988-89 (in Rs. per Qtl.) | Total value (in Rs. 000') | % Share |
|---|---|---|---|---|
| **1. Non-wood Forest Produce** | | | | |
| (a) Canes (qtl.) | 256.00 | 50.00 | 12.800 | 0.00086 |
| (b) Kendu leaves (lakh qtl.) | 3.90 | 3367.00 | 1313100.00 | 87.94 |
| **2. Drugs** | | | | |
| (a) Tamarind (qtl.) | 149863.00 | 202.00 | 30272.33 | 2.03 |
| (b) Mohwa flower (qtl.) | 394575.00 | 150.00 | 59186.25 | 3.96 |
| (c) Arrow root (qtl.) | 2.00 | 3000.00[1] | 6.00 | 0.0004 |
| (d) Nuxvomica (qtl.) | 173.00 | 166.70 | 28.839 | 0.002 |
| (e) Shikakai (qtl.) | 377.00 | 300.00 | 113.10 | 0.0076 |
| **3. Tan stuff and Dye stuff** | | | | |
| (a) Myrobalans (qtl.) | 45630.00 | 136.00 | 6205.68 | 0.42 |
| (b) Cleaning and marking nuts | 8224.00 | 500.00[2] | 4112.00 | 0.30 |
| **4. Vegetables and other oil seeds** | | | | |
| (a) Sal seeds (qtl.) | 537865.00 | 110.00 | 59165.15 | 3.96 |
| (b) Mohwa seed (qtl.) | 27527.00 | 512.00 | 14093.82 | 0.94 |
| (c) Kusum seed (qtl.) | 4943.00 | 208.00[3] | 1028.144 | 0.07 |
| **5. Gums and resins** | | | | |
| (a) Genduli gum (qtl.) | 3029.00 | 1902.00 | 5761.158 | 0.40 |
| (b) Sal resin (qtl.) | 213.00 | 450.00 | 95.85 | 0.006 |
| Total | | | 1493181.121 | 100.00 |

*Source* : Govt. of Orissa, Statistical Branch, Office of the Principal Chief Conservator of Forests, Bhubaneswar, pp. 79-80.

*Note* : In the previous year sale value per quintal was only Rs. 1434.44. At this rate the value of kendu leaves is Rs. 55.80 crores.

1. Relates to 1991-92.

2. Relates to 1989-90.

3. Relates to 1990-91.

## Table 3.6: Procurement of Different MFP Items in Sunabeda and Muniguda Branches

(In Qtls.)

| | 1989-90 | 1990-91 | 1991-92 | 1992-93 | 1993-94 | Average | 1996-97 |
|---|---|---|---|---|---|---|---|
| **SUNABADA BRANCH** | | | | | | | |
| | QTY | QTY | QTY | QTY | QTY | | |
| SEEDED TAMARIND | 0.00 | 11162.70 | 6074.92 | 9601.21 | 5415.30 | 8063.53 | — |
| DESEED TAMARIND | 0.00 | 1763.04 | 1950.67 | 4629.50 | 2256.00 | 2649.80 | — |
| HARIDA | 0.00 | 39.94 | 0.00 | 0.00 | 0.00 | 39.94 | — |
| HILLBROOMS (L) | 81.72 | 78.48 | 0.00 | 92.00 | 178.00 | 107.55 | 96.21 |
| HILL-BROOMS (B) | 0.00 | 2609.00 | 450.00 | 0.00 | 0.00 | 1529.50 | — |
| NUXVOMICA | 69.60 | 4.80 | 4.52 | 5.12 | 195.70 | 55.95 | 7.00 |
| SIALI LEAVES | 368.00 | 353.00 | 0.00 | 63.00 | 844.80 | 407.2 | 789.25 |
| STITCHED S.P. | 300.00 | 400.00 | 0.00 | 0.00 | 0.00 | 350.00 | — |
| SHIKAKAI | 0.00 | 0.00 | 0.00 | 0.00 | 0.00 | 0.00 | — |
| MOHWA FLOWER | 0.00 | 403.00 | 1157.00 | 0.00 | 0.00 | 1560.00 | — |
| KUSUM SEED | 0.00 | 0.00 | 0.00 | 0.00 | 0.00 | 0.00 | — |
| BAHADA | 0.00 | 0.99 | 0.00 | 0.00 | 0.00 | 0.00 | — |
| AMLA | 0.00 | 0.00 | 0.00 | 0.00 | 0.00 | 0.00 | — |
| BAHADA GUM | 0.00 | 0.00 | 0.00 | 17.47 | 8.94 | 13.21 | — |
| CHAR GUM | 0.00 | 0.00 | 0.00 | 20.00 | 25.00 | 22.50 | — |
| TAMARIND SEED | 0.00 | 0.00 | 34.30 | 650.40 | 199.00 | 294.43 | — |
| CLEANING NUTS | 0.00 | 0.00 | 0.00 | 0.00 | 6.43 | 6.43 | — |
| HONEY | 0.00 | 0.00 | 0.00 | 0.00 | 0.50 | 0.5 | — |
| R.S.ROOT | — | — | — | — | — | — | 9.00 |
| **MUNIGUDA BRANCH** | | | | | | | |
| SEEDED TAMARIND | 105.00 | 6628.59 | 4897.80 | 3282.00 | 2394.00 | 3461.5 | 661.40 |
| DESEED TAMARIND | 65.00 | 0.00 | 0.00 | 0.00 | 0.00 | 0.00 | — |
| HARIDA | 665.00 | 529.88 | 5.00 | 0.00 | 155.00 | 338.72 | 40.25 |
| HILL-BROOMS (L) | 221.00 | 42.61 | 0.90 | 0.00 | 90.00 | 88.62 | 60.98 |
| HILL-BROOMS (B) | 0.00 | 6694.00 | 0.00 | 0.00 | | 6694.00 | — |
| NUXVOMICA | 0.00 | 0.00 | 0.00 | 0.00 | 102.00 | 102.00 | — |
| SIALI LEAVES | 0.00 | 6732.00 | 0.00 | 0.00 | 180.00 | 3456.00 | 25.00 |
| STITCHED S.P. | 0.00 | 0.00 | 0.00 | 0.00 | 0.00 | 0.00 | — |
| SHIKAKAI | 0.00 | 0.00 | 0.00 | 0.00 | 0.00 | 0.00 | — |
| MOHWA FLOWER | 0.00 | 1257.08 | 9724.02 | 0.00 | 0.00 | 5490.55 | — |
| KUSUM SEED | 0.00 | 0.00 | 0.00 | 0.00 | 0.00 | 0.00 | — |
| BAHADA | 0.00 | 0.00 | 0.00 | 60.25 | 53.00 | 56.63 | 307.71 |
| AMLA | 0.00 | 0.00 | 0.00 | 0.00 | 0.00 | 0.00 | — |
| GENGULI GUM | 0.00 | 0.00 | 6.60 | 21.00 | 9.00 | 12.2 | 32.41 |
| THORN BROOMS | 0.00 | 0.00 | 70.00 | 0.00 | 0.00 | 70.00 | — |
| CLEANING NUTS | 0.00 | 0.00 | 0.00 | 0.00 | 15.15 | 15.15 | — |
| CHARGUM | — | — | — | — | — | — | 30.00 |

was reported in 1996-97. The only item of significance in procurement operations was siali leaves, which accounted for 62 per cent of the total MFP value in 1996-97. In Muniguda branch also, tamarind procurement was considerably reduced, though its share in the total MFP value continued to be significant because of the low MFP value. Next to tamarind, bahada gum and genduli gum were prominent in values.

Table 3.8 shows the procured quantity for the selected divisions of Rampachodavaram and Paderu for the quinquennium ending with 1993-94 and also for the year 1996. In almost all the commodities except naramamidi bark in Rampachodavaram, the quantity procured in the year 1996 was less than the quinquennium average. In Paderu, however, myrobalans and adda leaf record a higher procurement level as compared to quinquennium average. New items of procurement are adda leaf plates, cassia tora and kondagogu gum in 1996.

### 3.6. Commodity-wise Share in Total MFP Value in Selected Area of A.P.

In Rampachodavaram, total MFP value is around Rs. 14.3 million and in Paderu Rs. 10.4 million as in 1996 (Table 3.9). Gum Karaya accounted for nearly 50 per cent of the total value in Rampachodavaram division followed by naramamidi bark and deseeded tamarind. In Paderu division, adda leaf accounted for the maximum share followed by tamarind, myrobalans, naramamidi bark and hillbrooms. A few items of the MFP accounted for bulk of the share both in Rampachodavaram and Paderu.

### 3.7. Seasonality in Procurement

Gum is procured during all the months of a year. The procurement is the highest in May and June. Rockbee honey is procured in all the months except in March. May, June, July are the months of highest procurement. Nuxvomica is procured during all the months, except from July to October. The highest procurement of nuxvomica is in the month of January. Myrobalan is also procured in all months except June to October. The highest procurement is in the month of January. Naramamidi bark is procured in all the months. The largest quantity procurement is in the month of December. Cleaning nuts are procured from January to March and again from October to December. Tamarind is procured from January to September. The largest quantities are procured in the month of March to June. Shikakai is procured mostly from February to June. Tamarind seed and pungam seed are procured mostly from April and July. Procurement of wild broom starts from March and ends with August. Most of the procurement takes place between May and June. Procurement of hillbroom starts from February and ends with August. Most of the procurement was done during the months of March and April.

In general, the busy season for procurement is summer season. The period beginning with July is the slack season.

**Table 3.7: Commodity-wise Share in Total MFP Value : 1996-97**

| Name of the Commodity | | Value in Rs. | % share in total value |
|---|---|---|---|
| **Branch: Sunabeda** | | | |
| (1) | Hillbrooms (loose) | 76,968.00 | 30.77 |
| (2) | Nuxvomica | 4,550.00 | 1.82 |
| (3) | R.S. Root | 13,500.00 | 5.40 |
| (4) | Siali leaves | 1,55,105.00 | 62.01 |
| | Total | 2,50,123.00 | 100.00 |
| **Branch: Muniguda** | | | |
| (1) | Seeded tamarind | 2,63,510.00 | 42.27 |
| (2) | Hillbrooms (loose) | 48,784.00 | 7.82 |
| (3) | Harida | 850.00 | 0.14 |
| (4) | Bahada gum | 1,97,315.00 | 31.65 |
| (5) | Char gum | 3,120.00 | 0.50 |
| (6) | Genduli gum | 1,06,140.00 | 17.02 |
| (7) | Siali leaves | 3,750.00 | 0.60 |
| | Total | 6,23,469.00 | 100.00 |

## Table 3.8: Procured Quantity of MFP in the Selected Area for 1996 in Andhra Pradesh

| | Procured Quantity in Qtl. | | | | |
|---|---|---|---|---|---|
| | Name of the Commodity | Rampachoda-varam (1996) | Average for the quin-quennium ending with 1993-94 | Paderu (1996) | Average for the quin-quennium ending with 1993-94 |
| 1. | Gum Karaya-I | 94.95 | | 26.31 | |
| 2. | Gum Karaya-II | 629.54 | 3514.20 | 77.45 | 169.4 |
| 3. | Gum Karaya-III | 376.43 | | 16.52 | |
| 4. | Myrobalans | 2476.15 | 4365.80 | 5529.70 | 3598.00 |
| 5. | Nuxvomica | 107.68 | 952.00 | 8.56 | 0.00 |
| 6. | Naramamidi bark | 2341.30 | 1043.00 | 1145.83 | 0.00 |
| 7. | Cleaning nuts | 24.95 | 239.00 | 56.39 | 155.40 |
| 8. | Bee wax | 2.33 | — | — | — |
| 9. | Deseeded tamarind | 1644.08 | 5552.20 | — | 83.00 |
| 10. | Seeded tamarind | 357.84 | 456.2 | 2582.87 | 13943.20 |
| 11. | Shikakai | 199.79 | 369.80 | 2.81 | 8.00 |
| 12. | Tamarind seed | 5829.19 | 7703.6 | 28.74 | 278.75 |
| 13. | Pungam seed | 200.30 | 495.20 | 286.66 | 569.00 |
| 14. | Teripods | 62.11 | — | — | — |
| 15. | Wildbrooms 1 (No.) | 12580 | — | — | — |
| 16. | Wildbrooms 2 (No.) | 8500 | — | — | — |
| 17. | Marking nuts | 61.22 | 361.60 | 484.75 | 675.20 |
| 18. | Soap nuts | 2.11 | 50.60 | 0.67 | 4.00 |
| 19. | Hillbrooms (No.) | 41759 | 57445 | 136003 | 36836.00 |
| 20. | Mohwa seed | 8.75 | 22.20 | — | — |
| 21. | Amla seed | 5.68 | — | — | — |
| 22. | Rockbee honey | — | 79.60 | 24.91 | 12.25 |
| 23. | Adda leaf | — | 23.67 | 14337.20 | 759.25 |
| 24. | Kondagogu-1 | — | — | 0.06 | — |
| 25. | Kondagogu-2 | — | — | 0.61 | — |
| 26. | Kondagogu-3 | — | — | 1.44 | — |
| 27. | Adda leaf plates | — | — | 9000 | — |
| 28. | Casio tora | — | — | 48.38 | — |

**Table 3.9: Commodity-wise Share in Total MFP Value in Selected Divisions of A.P. in 1996**

| Name of the Commodity | Value in (Rs. 000') | % share in total value |
|---|---|---|
| **Paderu Division:** | | |
| Gum Karaya-1 | 255.996 | 2.47 |
| Gum Karaya-2 | 526.660 | 5.08 |
| Gum Karaya-3 | 80.948 | 0.77 |
| Rockbee honey | 99.640 | 0.96 |
| Nuxvomica | 2.996 | 0.03 |
| Myrobalans | 1658.910 | 16.02 |
| Naramamidi bark | 1197.392 | 11.56 |
| Cleaning nuts | 21.992 | 0.21 |
| Adda leaf | 3154.184 | 30.46 |
| Tamarind seed | 8.047 | 0.08 |
| Seeded tamarind | 1695.262 | 16.37 |
| Shikakai | 1.995 | 0.02 |
| Soapnuts | 0.536 | 0.0052 |
| Marking nuts | 145.425 | 1.40 |
| Pungam seed | 114.664 | 1.10 |
| Hillbrooms | 1088.024 | 10.50 |
| Konda gogu-1 | 0.396 | 0.004 |
| Konda gogu-2 | 2.989 | 0.03 |
| Konda gogu-3 | 6.768 | 0.07 |
| Adda leaf plates | 360.000 | 3.47 |
| Casio tora seed | 14.030 | 0.14 |
| Total | 10436.854 | 100.00 |

(*Contd.*)

Table 3.9 (*Contd.*)

| Name of the Commodity | Value in (Rs. 000') | % share in total value |
|---|---|---|
| **Rampachodavaram Division** | | |
| Gum Karaya-1 | 949.550 | 6.66 |
| Gum Karaya-2 | 4406.791 | 30.91 |
| Gum Karaya-3 | 1882.15 | 13.20 |
| Myrobalans | 792.368 | 5.56 |
| Nuxvomica | 32.306 | 0.27 |
| Naramamidibark | 2809.56 | 19.71 |
| Cleaning nuts | 9.98 | 0.07 |
| Bee Wax | 16.31 | 0.11 |
| Deseeded Tamarind | 1479.62 | 10.38 |
| Seeded Tamarind | 178.920 | 1.26 |
| Shikakai | 189.801 | 1.33 |
| Tamarind seed | 874.379 | 6.13 |
| Pungam seed | 85.128 | 0.60 |
| Teripods | 18.633 | 0.13 |
| Wildbrooms 1 | 22.02 | 0.15 |
| Wildbrooms 2 | 10.625 | 0.075 |
| Marking nuts | 27.549 | 0.19 |
| Soap nuts | 1.68 | 0.01 |
| Hillbrooms | 459.349 | 3.22 |
| Mohwa seed | 6.563 | 0.05 |
| Amla seed | 2.272 | 0.02 |
| Total | 14255.555 | 100.00 |

**Table 3.10: Number of Days Procured by each MFP Item**

| Item | Number of Days Procured | | | | | |
|---|---|---|---|---|---|---|
| | Addateegala (Feb.-March 1997 to December, 1998) | Procured No. of days as a % of total No. of days concerned | Rampachodavaram (Feb.-Mar., 1997 to July-August, 1997 | Procured No. of days as a % of total No. of days concerned | Araku Valley (Feb.-Mar., 1997 to July-August 1997) | Procured No. of days as a % of days concerned |
| 1. Gum-I | 88 | 29.33 | 63 | 42 | — | — |
| 2. Gum-II | 151 | 50.33 | 63 | 42 | — | — |
| 3. Gum-III | 154 | 51.33 | 52 | 34.67 | — | — |
| 4. Myrobalans | 48 | 16.00 | 17 | 11.33 | 12 | 6.7 |
| 5. Naramamidi bark | 71 | 23.67 | 27 | 18.00 | — | — |
| 6. Seeded tamarind | 16 | 5.33 | 76 | 50.66 | 49 | 27.2 |
| 7. Cleaning nuts | 13 | 4.33 | 5 | 3.3 | 8 | 4.4 |
| 8. Rockbee honey | 18 | 6.00 | 6 | 4.00 | 4 | 2.22 |
| 9. Pungam seed | 22 | 7.33 | 20 | 13.33 | 40 | 22.22 |
| 10. Apiary honey | 19 | 6.3 | — | — | — | — |
| 11. Bee wax | 2 | 0.66 | — | — | — | — |
| 12. Nuxvomica | 36 | 12 | 1 | 0.67 | — | — |
| 13. Shikakai | 1 | 0.33 | 6 | 4.00 | — | — |
| 14. Niger seed | 1 | 0.33 | 0 | — | — | — |
| 15. Tantem seed | 4 | 1.33 | 0 | — | — | — |
| 16. Marking nuts | — | — | 16 | 10.67 | 25 | 13.89 |
| 17. Stitched plates | — | — | — | — | 17 | 26.11 (17 and 30 together) |
| 18. Adda leaf | — | — | — | — | 30 | |

## 3.8. Commodity-wise Number of Days Procured in each Selected Branch

Daily procurement of each day of the month in Addateegala, Rampachodavaram, Paderu and Araku Valley are shown in Table 3.10. The data are not available for all the months in a year. For Addateegala March-April, 1997 data are missing and similarly January-February, 1998. However, the data suggest the small number of days during which the procurement is undertaken in a month. Except for gum which is procured for 150 days in a year, all the commodities are procured only for a few days. Even tamarind is procured only for 16 days, out of 300 days considered. Similar picture is seen for other centres also.

Gum and tamarind play an important role in Rampachodavaram and Arakuvally respectively. In Arakuvally, adda leaf and pungam seed are procured in 1/4th to 1/5th of the days considered.

## SECTION-III

### 3.9. Procurement Prices in Andhra Pradesh and Orissa

Procurement prices are important in generating incomes of the tribals. The data on procurement prices are available for Andhra Pradesh in the publications of GCC. The latest year of GCC publications gives quantities and values in respect of each minor forest produce. The prices are derived from the same source. For Orissa, the data are got from the records of the Sunabeda division. These records provide quantities and values as in the case of GCC for which prices were derived. Comparative price data is available for only 12 commodities. These data are presented in Table 3.11. The data shows that, GCC prices are invariably higher as compared to procurement prices in Orissa by TDCC. Moreover the percentage variation in respect of seeded tamarind has been rising. Only in respect of genduli gum prices of Orissa are comparable to those in Andhra Pradesh in 1991-92 and 1992-93. Since 1993-94 even in respect of this commodity, Andhra Pradesh prices exceeded the Orissa prices.

Even though prices in Andhra Pradesh are higher than those in Orissa, the GCC prices are found to be less in local market price and much less than the recommended price of IAMR based on labour cost (See Table 3.12).

*Trend Analysis*

The trend analysis is carried out for some MFP items for the period 1980-81 to 1995-96 for both the States. The trend coefficients and linear growth rates are calculated for both quantities and prices (Tables 3.13 and 3.14). The trend analysis for quantities show that in majority of the items in Orissa, the growth rates are negative indicating depletion of forest resources in Orissa compared to Andhra Pradesh. Orissa also recorded relatively lower growth rates in prices as compared to Andhra Pradesh.

**Table 3.11: Comparative Procurement Prices of Andhra Pradesh and Orissa for Selective Items of Years 1991-92 to 1995-96**

| Item | 1991-92 | | | 1992-93 | | | 1993-94 | | | 1994-95 | | | 1995-96 | | | 1996 (upto 10/96) |
|---|---|---|---|---|---|---|---|---|---|---|---|---|---|---|---|---|
| | Orissa | A.P. | % Variation | Orissa | A.P. | % Variation | Orissa | A.P. | % Variation | Orissa | A.P. | % Variation | Orissa | A.P. | % Variation | |
| Seeded Tamarind | 2.04 | 2.41 | 18.14 | 2.08 | 2.68 | 28.85 | 2.30 | 3.56 | 54.78 | 2.45 | 4.00 | 63.27 | 2.50 | 4.33 | 73.20 | 5.48 |
| D.S. Tamarind | 3.07 | 5.24 | 70.68 | 3.03 | 4.36 | 43.89 | 3.72 | 6.41 | 72.31 | 4.70 | 7.05 | 50.00 | 4.75 | 7.98 | 68.00 | 10.70 |
| Tamarind | 0.40 | 0.80 | 100.00 | 0.40 | 0.84 | 110.00 | 0.40 | 0.96 | 140.00 | 0.40 | 1.00 | 150.00 | 0.50 | 1.70 | 240.00 | 1.50 |
| Hillbroom Seed | 1.75 | 4.51 | 157.71 | 3.75 | 4.01 | 6.93 | 3.95 | 5.91 | 49.62 | 4.66 | 5.86 | 25.75 | — | — | — | 8.18 |
| Nuxvomica | 2.00 | 2.41 | 20.05 | 3.38 | 8.23 | 143.49 | 6.85 | 9.49 | 38.54 | 5.00 | 5.02 | 0.40 | — | — | — | 4.00 |
| Cleaning Nuts | — | — | — | — | — | — | 5.00 | 8.31 | 66.2 | 4.50 | 6.69 | 48.66 | — | — | — | 3.95 |
| Honey | — | — | — | — | — | — | 35.53 | 34.84 | –1.94 | — | — | — | 40.00 | 51.15 | 27.88 | 39.98 |
| Shikakai | — | — | — | — | — | — | 10.00 | 14.34 | 43.34 | — | — | — | 8.00 | 8.00 | 0.00 | 8.63 |
| Siali leaves | — | — | — | 1.00 | 1.20 | 20.00 | 1.00 | 1.55 | 55.00 | 1.00 | 1.90 | 90.00 | 1.25 | 1.81 | 44.8 | 2.50 |
| Genduligum | 25.00 | 22.92 | -8.32 | 25.00 | 25.31 | 1.24 | 25.00 | 37.48 | 49.92 | 25.64 | 48.51 | 89.20 | — | — | — | — |

*Source* : For Andhra Pradesh G.C.C., Note on Activities, Visakhapatnam, December, 1996.
For Orissa TDCC, Records of Sunabeda Division.

**Table 3.12: Average Comparative Prices per Kilogram in the Year 1994-95**

(in Rupees)

| | GCC Price | Local Market Price | IAMR Recommended Price |
|---|---|---|---|
| 1. Adda Leaf | 2.00 | 2.50 | 2.84 |
| 2. Gum Karaya | 58.00 | 62.00 | 66.46 |
| 3. Cleaning Nut | 4.00 | 5.00 | 5.31 |
| 4. Rock Bee Honey | 40.00 | 43.00 | 46.84 |
| 5. Myrobalans | 2.00 | 2.40 | 2.46 |
| 6. Mohwa seed | 7.00 | 7.75 | 9.06 |
| 7. Mohwa Flower | 3.50 | 3.75 | 4.00 |
| 8. Naramamidi Bark | 6.00 | 6.50 | 6.77 |
| 9. Nux vomica | 5.00 | 5.50 | 5.77 |
| 10. Seeded tamarind | 4.00 | 4.70 | 4.75 |
| 11. Hill Brooms | 7.00 | 8.20 | 8.68 |
| 12. Wild Brooms | 8.00 | 8.50 | 8.97 |
| 13. Gum olibanum | 15.00 | 17.00 | 23.45 |
| 14. Shikakai | 16.00 | 17.50 | 19.00 |
| 15. Marking Nuts | 1.50 | 1.75 | 1.91 |
| 16. Pongam seed | 3.50 | 3.75 | 4.07 |
| 17. R.S. Roots | 30.00 | 32.00 | 34.79 |
| 18. Soap Nuts | 8.00 | 9.00 | 9.49 |

*Source* : Institute of Applied Manpower Research, *Pricing of Minor Forest Products Procured by the Girijan Cooperative Corporation, Government of Andhra Pradesh*, New Delhi, September, 1997, p. 12.

**Table 3.13: Trend Coefficients and Linear Growth Rates of Quantities of MFP — Andhra Pradesh and Orissa**

| Minor Forest Produce | Andhra Pradesh (GCC) | | Orissa (TDCC) | |
|---|---|---|---|---|
| | Trend Coefficient | Linear Growth Rate (%) | Trend Coefficient | Linear Growth Rate (%) |
| 1. Gum | 3.30 | 0.022 (4.94) | –4.5 | 0.12 |
| 2. Adda leaf | –786.73 | –3.29 | –3136.45 | –0.72 |
| 3. Mohwa seed | 363.62 | 12.56 | –34313.3 | 0.68 |
| 4. Mohwa Flower | 598.66 | 33.21 | — | 10.90 |
| 5. Apiary Honey | –8.36 | –5.95 | — | — |
| 6. Rock Bee Honey | 69.29 | 14.25 | — | — |
| 7. Pongam seed | 278.14 | 15.90 | — | — |
| 8. Nux vomica | 44.22 | 1.32 | –113.86 | –18.89 |
| 9. Soap Nuts | –49.04 | –4.10 | — | 30.25 |
| 10. Shikakai | 153.79 | 7.59 | — | 35.78 |
| 11. Seeded tamarind | — | 33.48 | — | 7.40 |
| 12. Myrobalan | –264.76 | –1.85 | –1607.00 | –12.76 |
| 13. Cleaning Nuts | 255.46 | 12.17 | –367.97 | –14.29 |
| 14. Marking Nuts | 166.36 | 12.91 | — | 6.96 |
| 15. Seeded tamarind | 1319.0 | 3.33 | — | 7.10 |
| 16. Deseeded tamarind | 112.13 | 0.17 | — | — |
| 17. Tamarind seed | 363.00 | 94.18 | — | — |

**Table 3.14: Trend Coefficients and Liner Growth Rates of Prices of MFP — Andhra Pradesh and Orissa**

| Minor Forest Produce | Andhra Pradesh (GCC) | | Orissa (TDCC) | |
|---|---|---|---|---|
| | Trend Coefficient | Linear Growth Rate (%) | Trend Coefficient | Linear Growth Rate (%) |
| 1. Seeded tamarind | 19.18 | 8.31 | 23.13 | 3.0 |
| 2. Myrobalan | 14.01 | 10.00 | 17.28 | 6.71 |
| 3. Hill Brooms | — | 15.24 | — | 9.22 |
| 4. Gum | 292.86 | 14.23 | — | — |
| 5. Adda Leaf | 9.74 | 9.39 | 38.87 | 8.37 |
| 6. Mohwa Seed | 38.87 | 0.21 | — | — |
| 7. Mohwa Flower | 9.36 | 0.004 | — | — |
| 8. Apiary Honey | 293.74 | 14.20 | — | — |
| 9. Rock Bee Honey | 194.12 | 11.35 | — | — |
| 10. Pongam seed | 22.32 | 9.41 | — | — |
| 11. Nux vomica | 31.56 | 9.91 | — | — |
| 12. Soap Nuts | 71.67 | 13.85 | — | — |
| 13. Shikakai | 40.63 | 10.29 | — | — |
| 14. Marking Nuts | 11.28 | 15.13 | — | — |
| 15. Cleaning Nuts | 45.75 | 15.00 | — | — |
| 16. Deseeded Tamarind | 31.51 | 7.04 | 32.15 | 6.15 |
| 17. Wild Brooms | — | 20.30 | — | — |
| 18. Tamarind seed | 6.63 | 10.38 | — | — |

## SUMMARY

This chapter is presented in three sections. Section-I covered the procurement of MFP division-wise and commodity-wise. Section-II gives the same scenario branch-wise and also seasonality. The final Section-III presents trends in the quantities and prices of MFP procured items for Andhra Pradesh and Orissa. The analysis on the procurement of the divisions in Andhra Pradesh shows concentration of procurement in a few divisions. Division-wise share of MFP and division-ranking has shown that the Rampachodavaram, Paderu and Parvatipuram are prominent.

A commodity-wise procurement for a quinquennium ending with 1993-94 is compared with the procurement for the latest year 1996. This has shown in respect of several MFP commodities, that the procurement has declined. Further, the values of MFP commodities are shown a high concentration in a few commodities like Gum Karaya, tamarind and mohwa seed. The other commodities of importance are myrobalans, both types of honey, pungam seed and marking nuts. Division-wise procurement in Orissa has also shown a similar concentration as in Andhra Pradesh.

Commodity-wise shares showed kendu leaves are the most prominent among MFP items in Orissa, followed by sal seeds, mohwa flowers and tamarind.

Branch-wise data in Orissa has shown a considerable fall in procurement in recent years. Commodity-wise number of days procured for each selected branch for Andhra Pradesh showed a highest value of Gum Karaya (150 days) in Addateegala branch. In Rampachodavaram and Araku branches, the highest days of procurement is in seeded tamarind (49-51 days). A comparative procurement prices has shown that Orissa lags behind Andhra Pradesh in procurement prices in respect of every MFP commodity. Even then, the procurement prices in Andhra Pradesh are substantially lower to the prescribed labour cost based prices of IAMR and market prices.

# 4

# Marketing of Tribal Produce in Andhra Pradesh and Orissa

A market is said to be competitive, if the difference between the sale price and purchase (procurement) price is just exhausted by the operational costs for procurement, storage, transport and processing costs, if any, along with the normal profit margin. In case of tribal produces, particularly minor forest and agricultural produces, the form of product remains the same at the procurement and sale levels in most of the items. Hence, in this case the processing costs do not exist. The Orissa and Andhra Pradesh Governments allow a 5 to 10 per cent price margin on the procured commodities subject to the procured levels of the tribal produce. Thus, the tribal producers face a market, wherein there is no parity between sale and procured prices. The phenomena tends to make the market an imperfect or exploitative one.

Within the above framework, this chapter focuses mainly on : (i) the sale prices in relation to procurement prices, (ii) variability in sale prices, (iii) extent of participation in sales of each of the MFP and SAP commodities by tribals and (iv) price paid to the commodity and labour cost incurred by the tribal households.

The price data used in this study are drawn from the primary as well as secondary sources. The secondary data relate to 1990-91 and 1996-97, the primary data refer to the period 1996-97.

The results are analysed in four sections. A comparative analysis on procurement and sale prices is made in Section-I. Section-II covers the trends in variability of sale prices. Section-III gives the commodity operations by the procurer-sellers and the marketed quantities. The prices are compared with the labour cost and the results are also presented in this section. The analysis on the procurement *Vs.* wholesale prices is presented in Section-IV.

## SECTION-I

### 4.1. Sale Price *Vs.* Procurement Price

For Andhra Pradesh both the procurement data and sales data are derived from GCC publication (December 1996) which provides quantities and values for the period 1990-91 to 1996-97. For Orissa the data are derived from the records on quantities and value of MFP in Sunabeda division. For purpose of comparative analysis, the data for 1996-97 are used both for Andhra Pradesh and Orissa.

The commodity-wise sale prices and procurement prices are compared by considering the proportionate differences with reference to the sale prices. This is for both minor forest products and surplus agricultural items of tribals in Orissa and Andhra Pradesh (Table 4.1). In Andhra Pradesh the difference seems to be quite high for products like Teripods, Cleaning nuts, Gum olibanum (char) followed by Gum Dikmali which have more than 100 per cent gain in sale price over the procured one.

### 4.2. Tribals' Share in the Selling Prices

The ratio of procured price to sale price exhibits that the tribals' share ranges between 11.97 per cent in respect of Apiary Honey to 88.99 per cent in respect of Naramamidi Bark in Andhra Pradesh. Further in respect of 5 commodities *viz.* Gum Tiruman, Cleaning Nuts, Apiary Honey, Nepalam Seed, Teripads the share of tribals in sale price is less than 50 per cent.

In Orissa the sale price was found to be less than the corresponding sale price in Andhra Pradesh in respect of Gum Karaya, Gum Tiruman, Seeded Tamarind, Hill Brooms, but when tribal share is computed as a percentage to sale price is found to be more in Orissa in respect of Gum Tiruman, Gum Karaya, Nux vomica, Adda leaves.

### 4.3. Sale Price *Vs.* Procurement Prices in Andhra Pradesh and Orissa — Surplus Agricultural Produce

The tribals' share varies between 16 per cent to 84 per cent of the sale price in Andhra Pradesh, whereas it is 9 per cent to

**Table 4.1: Sales *Vs.* Procurement Prices — 1996-97**

| Commodity | Andhra Pradesh | | | Orissa | | | % of the Difference to Sale Price | | Tribals' Share | |
|---|---|---|---|---|---|---|---|---|---|---|
| | Procured Price | Sale Price | Differ-ence | Procured Price | Sale Price | Differ-ence | Orissa | A.P. | A.P. | Orissa |
| 1 | 2 | 3 | 4 | 5 | 6 | 7 | 8 | 9 | 10 | 11 |
| 1. Gum karaya (Bahada) | 6825.00 | 11671.70 | 4836.70 (70.87) | 6428.00 | 8781.70 | 2352.80 (36.60) | 26.79 | 41.44 | 58.47 | 73.20 |
| 2. Gum Thiruman | 2375.00 | 5739.10 | 3364.10 (141.65) | 3328.20 | 3656.80 | 328.60 (9.87) | 8.99 | 586.10 | 41.38 | 91.01 |
| 3. Gum Olibnum | 1428.60 | 1977.80 | 549.20 (38.44) | 1134.50 | 2260.00 | 1125.50 (99.21) | 49.80 | 27.77 | 72.23 | 50.19 |
| 4. Gum Dikmali | 500.00 | 1000.00 | 500.00 (100.00) | — | — | — | — | 50.00 | 50.00 | — |
| 5. Myrabolans | 301.10 | 422.70 | 121.60 (40.39) | — | — | — | — | 28.77 | 71.23 | — |
| 6. Nuxvomica Other gum | 400.70 | 484.60 | 83.90 (20.94) | 650.00 | 700.00 | 150.00 (23.08) | 21.43 | 17.31 | 82.59 | 92.96 |
| 7. Seeded Tamarind | 5488.00 | 7039.00 | 1551.00 (28.26) | 3764.50 | 536.38 | 1599.30 (42.48) | 29.82 | 22.03 | 77.97 | 70.18 |
| 8. Deseeded Tamarind | 10698.00 | 13360.00 | 2662.00 (24.88) | — | — | — | — | 19.93 | 80.07 | — |

(*Contd.*)

**Table 4.1 (*Contd.*)**

| 1 | 2 | 3 | 4 | 5 | 6 | 7 | 8 | 9 | 10 | 11 |
|---|---|---|---|---|---|---|---|---|---|---|
| 9. Flower Tamarind | 0 | 0 | 0 | — | — | — | — | — | — | — |
| 10. Tamarind seed | 149.90 | 185.80 | 35.90 (23.95) | — | — | — | — | 19.32 | 80.68 | — |
| 11. Pungum seed | 395.70 | 585.90 | 187.20 (46.95) | — | — | — | — | 31.95 | 67.54 | — |
| 12. Cleaning nuts | 39.57 | 94.19 | 54.62 (138.03) | — | — | — | — | 57.99 | 42.01 | — |
| 13. Marking nuts | 297.60 | 470.60 | 173.00 | — | — | — | — | 36.76 | 63.24 | — |
| 14. Mohwa seed | 748.20 | 959.20 | 211.00 (70.90) | — | — | — | — | 22.00 | 78.00 | — |
| 15. Mohwa Flower | 293.70 | 436.40 | 142.70 (48.59) | — | — | — | — | 32.70 | 67.30 | — |
| 16. Rockbee Honey | 3998.20 | 4826.20 | 828.00 (20.71) | — | — | — | — | 17.16 | 82.84 | — |
| 17. Apiary Honey | 4571.40 | 5469.70 | 898.30 (19.65) | — | — | — | — | 16.42 | 11.97 | — |
| 18. Shikakai | 862.60 | 1588.80 | 726.20 (84.19) | — | — | — | — | 45.71 | 54.29 | — |
| 19. Soap nuts | 758.40 | 918.50 | 160.10 (21.11) | — | — | — | — | 17.43 | 81.65 | — |

| | | | | | | | | | | |
|---|---|---|---|---|---|---|---|---|---|---|
| 20. Hillbrooms | 08.20 | 14.40 | 06.20 (75.61) | 8000.00 | 6677.10 | –1322.90 (16.54) | –198.12 | 43.06 | 56.94 | 11.98 |
| 21. Adda (siali) leaves | 249.90 | 406.50 | 156.60 (62.67) | 1975.20 | 2999.40 | 102.42 (81.85) | 34.15 | 38.52 | 61.48 | 65.83 |
| 22. Nepalam seed | 301.70 | 14134.60 | — | — | — | — | — | — | 21.34 | — |
| 23. Naramamidi bark | 119.30 | 1340.60 | 221.30 (19.77) | — | — | — | — | 16.51 | 88.99 | — |
| 24. Teripods | 306.50 | 1931.40 | 1624.90 (530.15) | — | — | — | — | 84.13 | 15.87 | — |
| 25. Harida | — | — | — | 1929.30 | 2655.30 | 726.00 (37.63) | 27.34 | — | — | 72.66 |
| 26. Bahada | — | — | — | 844.80 | 1500.00 | 655.20 (77.56) | 43.68 | — | — | 56.32 |
| 27. Amla | — | — | — | 3149.50 | 3939.30 | 789.80 (25.08) | 20.50 | — | — | 79.95 |
| 28. R.S. Root | — | — | — | 15000.00 | 20120.00 | 512.00 (34.13) | 25.45 | — | — | 74.55 |

*Note* : Figures in parentheses refer to the percentage difference to procured price.

49.8 per cent in Orissa. In case of agricultural products, the excess of sale price over the procured price seems to be relatively low and to a maximum of 23.72 per cent. In case of Round beans and Mustard seed, sale price is less than the procured price (Table 4.2).

In Orissa the procured price is found to be higher in respect of Niger seed, Jowar and Black Gram but less than the Andhra Pradesh prices in respect of Dry Chillies and Maize. The sale price, however, in Orissa, is lower than the corresponding Andhra Pradesh prices in respect of three out of four commodities for which comparable figures are available.

The excess of sale price over the procured price in Andhra Pradesh compared to Orissa needs an explanation. It is understandable in the case of MFP in respect of which GCC has a monopoly. In Orissa, the absence of monopoly might contribute to a lesser difference between sale price and procured price. Further larger differences in A.P. may be attributed to the value additions by way of processing and better marketing.

### 4.4. Purchase Price, Minimum Support Price and Market Prices of SAP in Orissa and Andhra Pradesh

The difference between the sale price and purchase price may not capture the extent of exploitation of the tribals since the sale price itself may be low because of the inefficiency of the Corporation (see Table 4.3). We sought to get data relating to wholesale prices. Such data are available only for 4 out of 10 commodities in respect of commodities procured in 1995-96 by TDCC. Even in respect of these four commodities prices are not available for the Orissa State. Therefore, we however, are constrained to use the data of the neighbouring States. Such comparisons, however, have shown that procurement prices stand below the market prices by a substantial amount.

For Andhra Pradesh, wholesale prices data are available for 5 out of 9 commodities procured by GCC (see Table 4.4). There is a substantial difference between wholesale price and procurement price, particularly, in respect of cotton. Even in respect of other commodities the difference is not insignificant. The difference should have been more if the data has been compiled for the entire year instead of four months which happens to synchronise with the harvesting season.

**Table 4.2: Sale Price *Vs.* Procurement Price — 1996-97**

| Commodity | Andhra Pradesh | | | Orissa | | |
|---|---|---|---|---|---|---|
| | Procured Price | Sale Price | Difference | Procured Price | Sale Price | Difference |
| 1. Niger seed | 982.06 | 1215.00 | 232.94 (23.72) | 1190.50 | 1214.30 | 23.08 (1.99) |
| 2. Maize | 382.74 | 403.32 | 20.58 (5.38) | 300.00 | 445.00 | 145.00 (48.33) |
| 3. Ragi | 374.39 | 451.55 | 77.16 (20.60) | | | |
| 4. Long Beans | 1754.74 | 1805.19 | 50.45 (2.88) | | | |
| 5. Round Beans | 510.00 | 470.00 | –40.00 (–7.84) | | | |
| 6. Katting | 800.00 | 848.00 | 48.00 (6) | | | |
| 7. Soya beans | 700.00 | 750.00 | 50.00 (7.14) | | | |
| 8. Jhudunga | 1050.00 | 1100.00 | 50.00 (4.76) | | | |
| 9. Blackgram | 1198.44 | 1200.00 | 1.56 (0.13) | 1620.070 | | |
| 10. Dry Chillies | 3800.00 | 3800.00 | 0 | 3308.10 | 3709.07 | 401.06 (12.14) |
| 11. Mustard seed | 1175.35 | 1150.00 | –25.35 (–2.15) | | | |
| 12. Jowar | 301.31 | 350.00 | 48.69 (16.16) | 750.00 | 333.30 | –416.71 |
| 13. Cotton seed | | | | 2155.00 | 5049.60 | 2894.06 (134.32) |
| 14. Redgram | | | | 1526.20 | 1566.70 | 40.50 (2.65) |
| 15. French Beans | | | | 1000.00 | 789.50 | –210.05 (21.05) |
| 16. Paddy | | | | 429.50 | 442.11 | 12.61 (2.94) |
| 17. Turmeric | | | | 1620.010 | 1894.70 | 274.00 (16.91) |
| 18. Cashewnut | | | | 2818.20 | 3000.00 | 181.80 (6.45) |
| 19. Annato seed | | | | 360.00 | 442.11 | 82.11 (17.26) |

*Note* : Figures in brackets pertain to percentage difference between sale price and procurement price.

**Table 4.3: Commodity-wise Procurement Price, Minimum Support Price and Wholesale Price for the Year 1995-96 in Orissa**

| Commodity | Procure-ment Price (Rs./per Qtl.) | Minimum Support Price* (Rs. per Qtl.) | Wholesale Price (Rs. per Qtl.) | % Difference between Whole-sale Price and Procurement Price |
|---|---|---|---|---|
| 1. Niger Seed | 1191.60 | N.A. | 1500.00** | 25.88 |
| 2. Katting | 465.00 | N.A. | N.A. | N.A. |
| 3. Soya Bean | 680.00 | 650.00 | 943.00* | 38.68 |
| 4. Round Bean | 470.00 | N.A. | N.A. | N.A. |
| 5. Long Beans | 1515.00 | N.A. | N.A. | N.A. |
| 6. Blackgram | 1341.20 | N.A. | 1493.75*** | 11.37 |
| 7. Maize | 374.20 | 300.00 | 436.25* | 16.60 |
| 8. Hill-gram | 1600.00 | N.A. | N.A. | N.A. |
| 9. Mustard Seed | 1150.00 | 860.00 | N.A. | N.A. |

*Notes* :* Relates to Madhya Pradesh prices.

** Relates to Maharashtra prices.

*** Relates to Andhra Pradesh.

*Source* : Procurement is derived from the records of the TDCC, Sunabeda division. For minimum support price see Government of Orissa, Directorate of Agriculture and Food Corporation, "Agricultural Statistics of Orissa—at a Glance," Orissa, Bhubaneswar, p. 49. For wholesale prices see Government of India, Department of Agriculture and Cooperation, Ministry of Agriculture, *Commission for Agricultural Costs and Prices for Crops sown in* 1995-96 season and 1996-97 season," pp. 418-429.

## SECTION-II

### 4.5. Trends and Variability in Purchase Price vis-a-vis Sale Price in Andhra Pradesh

The changes in the sale prices of tribal products for the last 7 years, *i.e.*, from 1990-91 to 1996-97 are presented in Table 4.5 for Andhra Pradesh.

Gum Karaya showed a fall between 1991-92 followed by a rise in the succeeding year. It continued to show a rise until 1994-95 and a sharp rise in 1995-96. The procurement price of this commodity has been stagnant between 1989-90 and 1991-92, suggesting that the benefits of the rise in sale price were not derived by the tribals. However, since 1993-94 procurement

**Table 4.4: Commodity-wise Procurement Price, Minimum Support Price and Wholesale Price for the Year 1995-96 in Andhra Pradesh**

| | Commodity | Procurement Price (Rs. per Qtl.) | Minimum Support Price* (Rs. per Qtl.) | Wholesale Price (Rs. per Qtl.) | % Difference between Wholesale Price and Procurement Price |
|---|---|---|---|---|---|
| 1. | Cotton | 2156.00 | 2575.00 | 4800.00 | 122.63 |
| 2. | Niger Seed | 1173.00 | — | 1500.00** | 27.87 |
| 3. | Maize | 300.00 | 290.00 | 360.5 | 20.20 |
| 4. | Redgram | 1526.00 | — | 1705.00 | 11.73 |
| 5. | French Beans | 1237.00 | — | N.A. | N.A. |
| 6. | Jowar | 750.00 | 280.00 | 472.50 | -37.00 |
| 7. | Turmeric | 1600.00 | N.A. | N.A. | N.A. |
| 8. | Dry Chillies | 3168.00 | N.A. | N.A. | N.A. |
| 9. | Cashew Nuts | 2254.00 | N.A. | N.A. | N.A. |

*Notes* :* Relates to 1994-95.

** Relates to Maharashtra Prices.

*Sources* :1. For procurement see AERC, Andhra University, Prospects of Value Addition to Tribal Produce : A Study of Selected Commodities in Tribal Areas of Andhra Pradesh, p. 54.

2. For minimum support prices and whole price see Government of India, Department of Agriculture and Cooperation, Ministry of Agriculture, Commission for Costs and Prices for Crops shown in 1995-96 season and 1996-97 season, pp. 120 and 418 to 433.

price showed a steep rise and kept pace with the trends in sale price. Among various varieties of gum, Grade III gum prices were stagnant and showed only a slight rise as compared to Grade I gum. Grade III gum procurement prices also did not keep pace with the sale prices. As regards other gums, the procurement prices did keep pace with the sale prices. Purchase price has been stagnant since 1990-91 in respect of Gum Tiruman Grade I and Grade II, and Gum Olibanum Grade I and Grade II since 1991-92, even though sale prices showed an increase. In respect of Myrobalans also the purchase prices of the product have lagged behind the sale prices till 1995-96. Purchase prices of Nux Vomica showed a steep rise only in 1993-94, yet there was substantial difference between sale price and purchase price and the difference continued during the subsequent years also, since than there was a sharp fall in the purchase price in 1994-95 and 1995-96. Cleaning Nuts show a wide fluctuation both in purchase price and sale price. The purchase price of Cleaning Nuts has show a rise in 1991-92, 1992-93 and 1993-94. In 1994-95, and 1995-96 the purchase prices were only half the levels of the corresponding prices obtained in 1993-94. Even though sale prices continued to be marked by high levels in 1995-96, purchase prices of Seeded Tamarind was stagnant for the period 1990-91 to 1993-94.

There was a substantial difference between sale price and purchase price of Seeded Tamarind until 1993-94. The difference got reduced in the subsequent years with purchase price showing a steeper rise than sale price. With regard to Deseeded Tamarind, difference between sale price and purchase price continued throughout, since the increase in purchase price did not keep pace with the increase in sale price. As in 1995-96 the difference per quintal of Deseeded Tamarind between purchase price and sale price was of the order of Rs. 2.50. As regard other important minor forest products, Mohwa flower showed steep fluctuations from one year to other in sale prices. Between 1994-95 and 1995-96 sale price of Mohwa flower was more than doubled and in the succeeding year the price level came down to less than half the level. The percentage difference between minimum and maximum in respect of each commodity is noted in the last column of the Table 4.5 during the period 1990-91 to 1996-97. This showed shikakai had the widest range marked by percentage difference of 834.1. This is followed by marking nuts 815 per cent; adda leaves 577.31 per cent; Nux Vomica 459 per cent; and Mohwa flower 402 per cent.

### 4.6. Sale Prices in Orissa

In Orissa, the maintenance of the price data is very poor. The sale prices are made available by the TDCC, OFDC and LAMPS for only a few commodities that too, for the last two years 1995-96 and 1996-97. Based on the available data, it is observed that there is a positive and substantial rise in the sale prices of hillbrooms, tamarind and bahada gum.

**Table 4.5: Variability in Sale Prices in Andhra Pradesh during 1990-91 to 1996-97 (Upto 10/96)**

| Commodity | 1990-91 | 1991-92 | 1992-93 | 1993-94 | 1994-95 | 1995-96 | 1996-97 | Range as a % of minimum price |
|---|---|---|---|---|---|---|---|---|
| 1. Gum Karaya | 4898.83 | 4302.28 | 5277.23 | 5673.44 | 5890.10 | 11154.14 | 11661.72 | 171.10 |
| 2. Gum Thiruman | 3625.00 | 2480.00 | 2227.80 | 3743.75 | 1997.26 | 3735.85 | 5739.13 | 187.34 |
| 3. Gum Olibanum | 1778.28 | 1687.22 | 1697.73 | 2444.44 | 2080.00 | 2145.44 | 1977.78 | 44.90 |
| 4. Gum Dikomali | 685.71 | 515.77 | 554.35 | 525.00 | 777.78 | 666.67 | 1000.00 | 93.88 |
| 5. Myrobalans | 376.27 | 313.97 | 269.38 | 208.04 | 260.03 | 331.82 | 422.74 | 103.03 |
| 6. Nuxvomica | 306.50 | 278.70 | 932.00 | 1280.95 | 1560.06 | 504.30 | 484.65 | 459.95 |
| 7. Seeded Tamarind | 362.20 | 265.90 | 341.70 | 362.00 | 460.20 | 506.23 | 703.90 | 164.72 |
| 8. Deseeded Tamarind | 608.13 | 530.42 | 434.40 | 596.25 | 797.82 | 1015.14 | 1335.97 | 207.54 |
| 9. Tamarind Seed | 104.54 | 99.97 | 151.83 | 163.00 | 178.90 | N.A. | 185.82 | 85.87 |
| 10. Pungam Seed | 335.25 | 436.04 | 714.30 | 379.84 | 440.65 | 179.38 | 585.95 | 298.20 |
| 11. Cleaning Nuts | 479.95 | 648.87 | 747.00 | N.A. | 779.66 | 522.00 | 941.86 | 96.24 |
| 12. Marking Nuts | 165.10 | 121.40 | 103.95 | 181.12 | 166.67 | 951.92 | 470.56 | 815.74 |
| 13. Mohwa Seed | 769.00 | 1030.07 | 902.42 | 794.00 | 957.05 | 326.16 | 959.20 | 215.82 |
| 14. Mohwa Flower | 196.60 | 229.87 | 295.10 | 342.57 | 411.37 | 987.91 | 436.36 | 402.50 |
| 15. Apiary Honey | 5111.00 | N.A. | N.A. | N.A. | N.A. | 4906.91 | N.A. | 4.16 |
| 16. Shikakai | 732.31 | 811.25 | 713.30 | 1333.33 | 2070.56 | 6662.92 | 1588.82 | 834.10 |
| 17. Soap Nuts | 679.69 | 1110.65 | 1009.14 | 935.56 | 741.62 | 996.00 | 918.50 | 63.40 |
| 18. Hill Brooms (Nos.) | 4.48 | 8.52 | 3.70 | 3.36 | 12.45 | N.A. | 14.10 | 319.64 |
| 19. Adda leaves | 60.02 | 160.20 | 167.40 | 190.96 | 254.83 | 10.12 | 406.52 | 577.31 |
| 20. Naramamidi Bark | N.A. | N.A. | N.A. | N.A. | N.A. | 1376.56 | 1931.41 | 40.31 |

*Source* : G.C.C., "Note on Activities," December, 1996, Visakhapatnam.

## 4.7. An Appraisal of the Differences in the Sale Prices of Orissa and Andhra Pradesh

It is observed that the sale prices of MFP in Orissa are substantially less in most of the commodities compared to those in Andhra Pradesh. The causes for such discrepancy between the two States can be attributed in general to: (i) processed MFP items, *i.e.* due to the existence of processing units, the sales of the MFPs must have been in the processed form, thereby, prices quoted at the selling point may be in Andhra Pradesh high; (ii) inclusion of higher transport costs in the selling price in Andhra Pradesh, and (iii) non-existence of transport costs in case of the proximity between the selling and procurement centres in Orissa.

While examining the form of the sale items, it is observed that, due to monopoly power and autonomy in the decision-making process of GCC, *i.e.* non-involvement of Government, the GCC in Andhra Pradesh could facilitate or take up processing of some important commodities. As items after simple processing, grading and packing do command better prices, GCC has set-up small scale processing units at various places, like Rajahmundry, Araku, Vizianagaram, Utnoor, Nirmal, etc. Further, the location of the processing units could benefit in two more ways *i.e.* distance between the procurement — processing/selling points and minimising the problem of transportation, thereby reducing the quality losses, if any (AERC, A.U. Visakhapatnam, November 1996, pp. 60-61).

## 4.8. Variability in Sale Price and Trends in Purchase Price *vis-a-vis* Sale Price during 1990-91 to 1995-96 for SAP in Andhra Pradesh

There is a high year to year variability in both purchase and sale prices in respect of all commodities listed under SAP. In Table 4.6, we noted the purchase price and sale price for the period 1990-91 to 1996-97 *i.e.* for the 7-year period. The maximum price during the 7-year period is compared with the minimum price of the same period and the percentage difference of the maximum over minimum is shown for all commodities in respect of purchase price and sale price respectively. Large variability exceeding 100 per cent is seen in respect of all

**Table 4.6: Variability in Sale Prices and Purchase Prices of Agricultural Produce in Andhra Pradesh during 1990-91 and 1996-97**

(Per Quintal in Rs.)

| Name of the Produce | 1990-91 | | 1991-92 | | 1992-93 | | 1993-94 | | 1994-95 | | 1995-96 | | 1996-97 | | Purchase Price | | Sale Price | | Purchase Price Range as a % of minimum | Sale Price Range as a % of minimum |
|---|---|---|---|---|---|---|---|---|---|---|---|---|---|---|---|---|---|---|---|---|
| | Purchase Price | Sale Price | Purchase Price | Sale Price | Purchase Price | Sale Price | Purchase Price | Sale Price | Purchase Price | Sale Price | Purchase Price | Sale Price | Purchase Price | Sale Price | Minimum | Maximum | Minimum | Maximum | | |
| 1. Cotton | 927 | 929 | 1329 | 1602 | 1050 | 1217 | 1211 | 1646 | 2197 | 2371 | 2156 | 5153 | — | — | 927 | 2156 | 929 | 5153 | 132.60 | 454.68 |
| 2. Niger | 1046 | 711 | 1150 | 1116 | 950 | 1197 | 874 | 1038 | 1202 | 1127 | 1173 | 1214 | 1190 | — | 874 | 1202 | 711 | 1214 | 37.53 | 70.74 |
| 3. Maize | 156 | 153 | 339 | 460 | 334 | 456 | 247 | 284 | 391 | 398 | 300 | 446 | — | 200 | 156 | 391 | 153 | 460 | 150.64 | 200.65 |
| 4. Redgram | 871 | 497 | 958 | 946 | 899 | 757 | 1092 | 969 | 1276 | 1144 | 1526 | 810 | — | 1566 | 871 | 1526 | 497 | 1144 | 75.20 | 130.18 |
| 5. French Beans | 878 | 748 | 605 | 729 | 1038 | 685 | 1092 | 933 | 1371 | 1119 | 1237 | 314 | 1000 | 789 | 605 | 1371 | 314 | 1119 | 126.61 | 256.40 |
| 6. Ground Nut | 847 | 816 | 870 | 886 | 773 | 907 | 685 | 821 | 1250 | 1000 | — | — | — | — | 685 | 1250 | 816 | 1000 | 82.48 | 22.55 |
| 7. Jowar | 182 | 142 | 327 | 271 | 177 | 359 | 240 | 247 | 348 | 214 | 750 | 333 | — | — | 177 | 750 | 142 | 359 | 323.73 | 152.82 |
| 8. Tumeric | 986 | 1553 | 1094 | 1690 | 1513 | 2448 | 466 | 576 | 1962 | 2327 | 1600 | 1500 | 1620 | 1894 | 466 | 1962 | 576 | 2448 | 321.03 | 325.00 |
| 9. Dry Chillies | 891 | 1100 | 1942 | 2848 | 1804 | 1476 | 1287 | 762 | 2194 | 368 | 3168 | 3176 | 3308 | 3709 | 891 | 3308 | 368 | 3709 | 271.27 | 907.46 |
| 10. Cashew Nuts | 1297 | 1543 | 1833 | 1901 | 2521 | 1997 | 1543 | 2204 | 2200 | 2400 | 2254 | 3016 | 2818 | 3000 | 1297 | 2818 | 1543 | 3016 | 117.27 | 95.46 |

*Source* : Agro-Economic Research Centre, Andhra University, Prospects of Value Addition to Tribal Produce (*A Study of Selected Commodities in Tribal Areas of Andhra Pradesh*), Visakhapatnam, p. 54.

commodities, except, Niger Seed, Red Gram and Ground nut. The variability is large in respect of sale price for almost all commodities listed except for Ground nut, Jowar and Cashew nuts. In respect of all other commodities, the trends in purchase price appear to lag behind sale price. This reflects that the benefits of higher sale price are appropriated largely by the intermediaries.

## 4.9. Marketing Margins in Orissa and Andhra Pradesh for Selected MFP Commodities[1]

*Hill Brooms*

The primary collectors of Hill Brooms, sell the broom material to TDCC at Rs. 6.00 per kg. TDCC after taking commission of Rs. 7.00 to Rs. 9.00, sells it on auction to the private businessmen at the rate of Rs. 13.00 to Rs. 15 per kg. The private business people make three brooms from one kg. and per broom their expense is Re. 1 (60 paise labour + 40 paise tying material like rope or plastic). It is assumed, that the retailers are selling at Rs. 15 per broom, for which, they get Rs. 45 per kg. of broom material. TDCC is purchasing Rs. 6 per kg. and taking Rs. 8 on average as their establishment expenses. It is estimated roughly that even under the controlled price system, after giving a fair profit margin to all the traders involved between primary collectors and end users, the farmer should get a minimum of Rs. 18 per kg. if fair play is allowed.

*Sal Seed*

The marketing and trading operation of sal seed is governed by the Sal Seed Nationalisation Act of 1983-84. OFDC and TDCC were the authorised agencies in the matter of procurement from the collectors at a price fixed by the Government from time to time. The present procurement price is Rs. 1.75 per kg. Whereas these two agencies are supposed to collect directly from the collectors, in practice the collectors sell to the local agents.

At present, there are no public sector units worth mentioning in processing of the sal seeds for oil extraction, although, immense opportunities exist in the field. The final processing of oil fat extraction is done by solvent extraction process at the industries level. This traditional method yields as low as 3 per cent which can be increased to as high as 30 per cent if the expeller method of extraction by organic solvent devised by the Regional Research Laboratory, Hyderabad is applied.

It is roughly estimated that, based upon the market price of the highest level of use of sal seed, the primary collectors should get a minimum of Rs. 4 per kg. And as there is the practice that the end product of sal seed commands a still better position in international market, the procurement price per kg. need to be higher than Rs. 4.

***Mohwa Flower***

Mohwa flower is plentily available in Orissa. It is mainly available in the months of March and April for 15 to 20 days hardly. Mohwa flower is very much popular among the people for its alcoholic quality, particularly among the tribals who are used to drink country liquor regularly.

Some people grow Mohwa tree in their own land, from where they collect the flower. Besides, it is available in villages and protected forests. Generally, people cover a distance of maximum 5 to 6 kms., all members of the family men, women and children are engaged during this period in collection. They go for collection early in the morning before sunrise and return before 2 P.M.

After collection, the gatherers sun dry the flowers for 2 to 3 days on the floor. The raw flower which is faint green in colour after sun dry becomes reddish and becomes almost 1/3 both in size and weight. The raw flowers contain 60 to 65 per cent of water. After sun dry people hammer it with a stick to separate the petals and the remnant is the bud, which is used for sale or manufacturing liquor.

Many people sell the dry flowers to the local shopkeepers, vendors and petty traders. A few of them go for manufacturing liquor. A particular caste known as Sundhi makes liquor which is one of their traditional occupation. In some places, another caste, Pana (SC) also manufactures liquor. The higher caste people however, prefer to drink the liquor made by Sundhi.

Unofficially many private traders and liquor-lords are purchasing Mohwa flower from the people in the months of March and April at Rs. 2.50 or Rs. 3.00 per kg. Except a few rich, all other people sell whatever amount they collect because they need money to purchase their daily requirements like dal, rice, oil, and salt etc. Just after one month *i.e.* from the month of May onwards people purchase the same flower at Rs. 10 to Rs. 15 per kg. from the same trader for preparing liquor. The liquor preparation goes throughout the year. As one proceeds in the calendar from May onwards, the price rise continues and at times it reaches a peak of Rs. 20 to Rs. 22. In remote villages the traders collect the Mohwa Flower even at Rs. 1 per kg.

Many traders use local weights and cheat the tribals. For instance, the traders use *gauni* (equivalent to 4 kgs.) but calculate as *mana* (equivalent to 2 kgs.) and similarly use *mana* and calculate it as *sera/ada* (equivalent to 1 kg.). At the time of weighing, they pour the flower to the *tambi.* They use various types of pots made of wood to measure the mohwa flower, locally known as *tambi* with high pressure by hand, by which they take more.

### *Tamarind*

The whole process of purchase, processing and marketing of tamarind is fully dominated by private business men, petty traders and middlemen. TDCC, AMCS like few government agencies and Doki Satyanarayana (a private businessman) of Rayagada and Koraput are the lease holders of tamarind. The following gives a picture of tamarind at various stages and the price at each stage.

| | Sale Made by Whom/to Whom | Price | Remark |
|---|---|---|---|
| Stage-1 | Sale made by people to agents, moneylenders and petty traders | at Rs. 1.25 to Rs. 1.50 | Fixed price by Govt. is Rs. 2.50 to Rs. 3.00. |
| Stage-2 | Sale made by agents/ moneylenders/petty traders to Govt. agencies/private lease holders | at Rs. 5 to Rs. 6 per kg. (deseeded) | Fixed price by Govt. is Rs. 5 per kg. (deseeded). |
| Stage-3 | Lease holders sell to wholesalers/businessmen who export it to other states and overseas countries | Rs. 12 to Rs. 15 per kg. (deseeded) Rs. 20 at Cuttack and Bhubaneswar. Rs. 40 at other metro cities of India. | In most of the cases the lease holers are whole-salers. |

Thus a kg. of tamarind for which the primary producers are getting Rs. 1.25 is being sold at a price of Rs. 20 inside Orissa and at Rs. 40 in metro cities, which is 15 to 30 times higher than the ground level price.

## GCC in Andhra Pradesh

### *Gum Karaya*

GCC has the monopoly rights over purchase of MFP. It purchases gums in 3 grades. Grade I is pure white and translucent colour, Grade II is slightly brownish or amber white, Grade III is brown and contains impurities.

Besides these, other type of gums are also available. We give below, four types of gum with their botanical names alongwith the prices fixed by GCC.

| Name of the Gum | Grade | Price fixed by GCC in 1994-95 (Rs./Kg.) |
|---|---|---|
| Gum Karaya | Special | 120.00 |
| | Grade-I | 90.00 |
| | Grade-II | 60.00 |
| | Grade-III | 40.00 |
| Gum Kondagogu | Grade-I | 72.00 |
| | Grade-II | 56.00 |
| | Grade-III | 40.00 |
| Gum Tiruman | Grade-I | 30.00 |
| | Grade-II | 20.00 |
| | Grade-III | 15.00 |
| Gum Olibanum | Grade-I | 15.00 |
| | Grade-II | 12.00 |

After a visit to many places and consulting with the tribals, it is felt that the people were both exploited and cheated in many ways. First of all, people were complaining that GCC was giving less price than the market price. Many business people purchased gum from the tribals by paying a higher price than GCC, though GCC has a monopoly. Secondly, GCC people are not fair in grading and weighing. They often under-weigh the gums by which the people loose 15-20 per cent of their original price. Again at the time of gradation, they cheat the tribals, by assigning a lower grade, though, it belongs to a higher grade.

## SECTION-III

### 4.10. Participation of Households in Collection of MFP — Field Survey

It may be recalled that the household survey is conducted in 12 villages *i.e.* 8 in Andhra Pradesh and 4 in Orissa. Some of the questions in the schedule related to the sale of MFP by the household. In respect of each commodity, number of households selling the particular commodity in each of the village are listed in Table 4.7. In Table 4.8, village-wise number of sellers by the frequency of commodity sold is shown and the amount of sale of each commodity in each of the villages is listed in Table 4.9. Out of the four villages in Orissa, the participation in procurement of MFP in two villages of Sunabeda division is meagre. In this division, the participation is high in respect of Adda leaf and Tamarind seed in one of the four villages. For the division, as a whole, participation is low. In Orissa, Muniguda branch presents higher rate of participation, the two villages in the branch, participation rate is high in Adda leaf, Naramamidi Bark, Myrobalans, Hill Brooms, Tamarind Seed, Sal Seed, Mohwa Seed and Mohwa Flower. It may be recalled that the Rayagada district in which Muniguda block is located, has a dense forest area as compared to Koraput district in which Sunabeda branch is covered.

In Andhra Pradesh out of the 8 villages under survey, 4 villages are in Paderu division and an equal number in Rampachodavaram division. The participation rate is high in Paderu division, in respect of Adda leaf, Naramamidi Bark and Amla seed. In Rampachodavaram division there is a variation between Addateegala branch and Rampachodavaram branch with respect of MFP collection. In Rampachodavaram branch, Deseeded Tamarind, Tamarind, Marking Nuts and Myrobalans are the prominent Minor Forest Produce collected by households while in Addateegala branch Gum Karaya, of all grades, Marking Nuts and Naramamidi Bark are prominent.

## Table 4.7: Commodity-wise Distribution of Sellers — Village-wise

| Commodity Code | | Villages | | | | | | | | | | | |
|---|---|---|---|---|---|---|---|---|---|---|---|---|---|
| | | 1 | 2 | 3 | 4 | 5 | 6 | 7 | 8 | 9 | 10 | 11 | 12 |
| 1. | Pungam seed | 11 | 2 | 14 | — | 1 | — | — | — | — | — | — | 1 |
| 2. | Seeded tamarind | 21 | 25 | 25 | — | — | — | — | — | — | — | — | — |
| 3. | Adda leaf | 24 | 25 | 24 | 25 | 1 | — | — | — | 21 | 21 | 9 | 23 |
| 4. | Naramamidi bark | 18 | — | — | 2 | — | — | 7 | 13 | 18 | 23 | — | — |
| 5. | Myrobalans | 18 | — | — | 25 | 24 | 1 | — | 2 | 25 | 24 | — | — |
| 6. | Hillbrooms | 11 | — | 7 | 2 | — | — | — | — | 25 | 25 | — | — |
| 7. | Marking nuts | 9 | — | 1 | — | 1 | 14 | 2 | 15 | — | — | — | — |
| 8. | Neem seed | 1 | — | — | — | — | — | — | — | — | — | — | — |
| 9. | Soap nuts | 1 | — | — | — | — | — | — | — | — | — | — | — |
| 10. | Gum Kariya G-II | 3 | — | — | — | — | — | 13 | 20 | 24 | — | — | — |
| 11. | Gum Kariya G-I | 2 | — | — | — | — | — | 8 | 20 | 2 | — | — | — |
| 12. | Amla seed | — | — | — | 25 | — | — | — | — | — | — | — | — |
| 13. | Deseeded tamarind | — | — | — | — | 23 | 25 | 9 | 8 | 1 | — | — | — |
| 14. | Cassiolara seed | — | — | — | — | — | 9 | — | — | — | — | — | — |
| 15. | Tamarind seed | — | — | — | — | — | 15 | — | — | 24 | 23 | 7 | 16 |
| 16. | GKG III | — | — | — | — | — | — | 10 | 20 | — | 25 | — | — |
| 17. | Sal seed | — | — | — | — | — | — | — | — | 25 | 24 | — | — |
| 18. | Mohwa seed | — | — | — | — | — | — | — | — | 23 | 25 | — | — |
| 19. | Mohwa flower | — | — | — | — | — | — | — | — | 23 | 25 | — | 3 |
| 20. | Kondagogu I | — | — | — | — | — | — | — | — | 1 | — | — | — |
| 21. | Kusumoil seeds | — | — | — | — | — | — | — | — | 1 | 7 | — | — |
| 22. | Rockbee Honey | — | — | — | — | — | — | — | — | — | 3 | — | — |
| 23. | Nux Vomica | — | — | — | — | — | — | — | — | — | 2 | — | — |
| 24. | R.S. Roots | 11 | 3 | 5 | 5 | 6 | 5 | 6 | 7 | 13 | 13 | 3 | 4 |
| | Total | | 52 | 72 | 79 | 51 | 64 | 49 | 98 | 213 | 230 | 17 | 43 |

**Village Names**

Andhra Pradesh :

1. Kumaritham, 2. Sumpangiput, 3. Pothangi, 4. Besupuram, 5. Cheruvuru, 6. Pedduru, 7. Veeravaran, 8. Kovelapalem.

Orissa :

9. Telengapodar, 10. Borikhal, 11. Minapai, 12. K. Gursi.

**Table 4.8: Number of Sellers by Frequency of Commodities — Village-wise**

| No. of Commodities | Villages | | | | | | | | | | | | | | |
|---|---|---|---|---|---|---|---|---|---|---|---|---|---|---|---|
| | 1 | 2 | 3 | 4 | 5 | 6 | 7 | 8 | 9 | 10 | 11 | 12 | AP | Orissa | Sample |
| 1. | 0 | 0 | 0 | 0 | 2 | 7 | 8 | 3 | 0 | 0 | 15 | 10 | 20 | 25 | 45 |
| 2. | 0 | 23 | 9 | 1 | 22 | 3 | 9 | 0 | 0 | 0 | 1 | 12 | 67 | 13 | 80 |
| 3. | 2 | 2 | 10 | 20 | 1 | 8 | 6 | 7 | 0 | 0 | 0 | 3 | 56 | 3 | 59 |
| 4. | 9 | 0 | 6 | 4 | 0 | 7 | 1 | 2 | 0 | 0 | 0 | 0 | 29 | 0 | 29 |
| 5. | 10 | 0 | 0 | 0 | 0 | 0 | 0 | 10 | 0 | 0 | 0 | 0 | 20 | 0 | 20 |
| 6. | 2 | 0 | 0 | 0 | 0 | 0 | 0 | 3 | 0 | 0 | 0 | 0 | 5 | 0 | 5 |
| 7. | 2 | 0 | 0 | 0 | 0 | 0 | 0 | 0 | 2 | 0 | 0 | 0 | 2 | 2 | 4 |
| 8. | 0 | 0 | 0 | 0 | 0 | 0 | 0 | 0 | 11 | 4 | 0 | 0 | 0 | 15 | 15 |
| 9. | 0 | 0 | 0 | 0 | 0 | 0 | 0 | 0 | 10 | 13 | 0 | 0 | 0 | 23 | 23 |
| 10. | 0 | 0 | 0 | 0 | 0 | 0 | 0 | 0 | 0 | 1 | 7 | 0 | 0 | 8 | 8 |
| 11. | 0 | 0 | 0 | 0 | 0 | 0 | 0 | 0 | 1 | 1 | 0 | 0 | 0 | 2 | 2 |
| Total | 25 | 25 | 25 | 25 | 25 | 25 | 24 | 25 | 25 | 25 | 16 | 25 | 199 | 91 | 290 |

**Village Names**

Andhra Pradesh : 1. Kumaritham, 2. Sumpangiput, 3. Pothangi, 4. Besupuram, 5. Cheruvuru, 6. Pedduru, 7. Veeravaram, 8. Kovelapalem.

Orissa : 9. Telengapodar, 10. Borikhal, 11. Minapai, 12. K. Gursi.

The total number of households by frequency of commodities in 8 villages of Andhra Pradesh and in 4 villages of Orissa are shown separately. In Andhra Pradesh, the single maximum percentage *i.e.* 33 per cent sell only two commodities, while as a maximum number of commodities sold *i.e.* 7 is only by 1 per cent of the households. In Orissa, 27 per cent sell only one commodity, at the other end 52.7 per cent sell more than 8 commodities. This is because of extremely divergent conditions with respect to forest cover among the villages chosen in Orissa.

**Table 4.9: Commodity-wise Distribution of Procurement — Village-wise**

(quantities in kgs.)

| Commodity Code | Village | | | | | | | | | | | |
|---|---|---|---|---|---|---|---|---|---|---|---|---|
| | 1 | 2 | 3 | 4 | 5 | 6 | 7 | 8 | 9 | 10 | 11 | 12 |
| 1. Pungum seed | 405 | 230 | 130 | — | — | — | — | — | — | — | — | 200 |
| 2. Seeded tamarind | 16010 | 10220 | 5540 | — | — | — | — | — | — | — | — | — |
| 3. Adda leaf | 19980 | 26650 | 31100 | 22800 | 100 | — | — | — | 562 | 1022 | 4100 | 1970 |
| 4. Naramamidi bark | 343 | — | — | — | — | — | — | — | — | — | — | — |
| 5. Myrobalans | 490 | 29100 | 4500 | 50 | — | 250 | 2430 | 2210 | — | — | — | — |
| 6. Hillbrooms | 55 | — | 40 | 10 | — | — | — | — | 462 | 500 | — | — |
| 7. Marking nuts | 265 | — | 50 | — | 50 | 1025 | 420 | 1910 | — | — | — | — |
| 8. Neem seed | 500 | — | — | — | — | — | — | — | — | — | — | — |
| 9. Soap nuts | 10 | — | — | — | — | — | — | — | — | — | — | — |
| 10. Gum Kariya G-II | 55 | — | — | — | — | — | 345 | 438 | 434 | — | — | — |
| 11. Gum Kariya G-I | 7 | — | — | — | — | — | 275 | 431 | 3 | — | — | — |
| 12. Amla seed | — | — | — | 38900 | — | — | — | — | — | — | — | — |
| 13. Deseeded tamarind | — | — | — | — | 2075 | 3925 | 540 | 680 | 0 | — | — | — |
| 14. Cassiolara seed | — | — | — | — | — | 1650 | — | — | — | — | — | — |
| 15. Tamarind seed | — | — | — | — | — | 3200 | — | — | 1220 | 1160 | 1925 | 2555 |
| 16. GKG III | — | — | — | — | — | — | 220 | 481 | — | 383 | — | — |
| 17. Sal seed | — | — | — | — | — | — | — | — | 2395 | 2718 | — | — |
| 18. Mohwa seed | — | — | — | — | — | — | — | — | 2865 | 2787 | — | — |
| 19. Mohwa flower | — | — | — | — | — | — | — | — | 5762 | 5704 | — | 120 |
| 20. Kondagogu I | — | — | — | — | — | — | — | — | 50 | — | — | — |
| 21. Kusumoil seeds | — | — | — | — | — | — | — | — | 5 | 79 | — | — |
| 22. Rockbee Honey | — | — | — | — | — | — | — | — | 6 | — | — | — |
| 23. Nuxvomica | — | — | — | — | — | — | — | — | 150 | — | — | — |
| 24. R.S. Roots | — | — | — | — | — | — | — | — | 113 | — | — | — |

**Village Names**

Andhra Pradesh : 1. Kumaritham, 2. Sumpangiput, 3. Pothangi, 4. Besupuram, 5. Cheruvuru, 6. Pedduru , 7. Veeravaram, 8. Kovelapalem.

Orissa : 9. Telangapodar, 10. Borikhal, 11. Minapai, 12. K. Gursi.

In A.P., the sale of Seeded Tamarind, Adda leaf, Myrobalans are much more than other commodities. Whereas in Orissa, Tamarind Seed, Seeded Tamarind, Sal Seed, Mohwa Flower are sold more than other commodities.

The value figures (Table 4.10) also show the superiority of Andhra Pradesh in respect of all commodities except Tamarind

Seed and Hill Brooms, Kondagogu, Mohwa Flower and Mohwa Seed.

The comparison of Orissa and Andhra Pradesh in respect of prices received by households, shows that in almost all commodities, Andhra Pradesh prices are higher than that of Orissa. This confirms the earlier picture regarding the procurement agency, that the prices paid by GCC are higher than those paid by TDCC in Orissa (Table 4.11).

We sought to examine whether the price paid by agents meets at least the labour cost. Each household was asked about number of members engaged in the collection of MFP, procurement, total days spent, total procured quantity. Average procured quantity per day, per person, was derived from such data. Labour required for 1 kg. of MFP is computed from the preceding data. It is assumed that the labourer engaged in the collection of MFP must obtain at least the market wage prevailing in the village. The market wage rate per man-day is Rs. 25. The price of that needs to be paid of 1 kg. of MFP is derived by applying the wage rate to the labour required for one kg. Finally, the actual price is compared with the price based on labour cost.

We find from the data presented (Table 4.12), that in all the villages of Andhra Pradesh, the price paid is not equivalent to the labour cost, and the tribals are being exploited. It may be noted that in Paderu, in respect of some items, more than the labour cost is reported. This is due to the fact that in these villages the sellers have their own trees close to the residency and no rental is allowed on the trees their own. In Orissa, there is a wide variation between villages in Muniguda branch and those in Sunabeda branch in respect of difference between price paid and the labour cost. The villages in Muniguda branch show larger difference between labour cost and actual price paid, the former being higher. In Sunabeda branch, however, the villages show the price paid is higher than labour cost in respect of commodities such as tamarind, mohwa flower and adda leaf (Table 4.13). These commodities are got from areas very close to the residence and since no rental is allowed in our calculations, labour cost tends to be less.

## Table 4.10: Marketed Value by each Commodity and by Village : Orissa and Andhra Pradesh

| | Village Commodity | Kumari-tham | Sumpan-giput | Pothangi | Besu-puram | Cheru-vuru | Ped-duru | Veera-varam | Kovela-palem | A.P. Total | T. Poduru | Borikhal | Minapai | K. Gursi | Orissa Total | Grand Total |
|---|---|---|---|---|---|---|---|---|---|---|---|---|---|---|---|---|
| 1. | Gum Karaya-I | 700 | 0 | 0 | 0 | 0 | 0 | 27500 | 43100 | 71300 | 27.5 | 0 | 0 | 0 | 27.5 | 71327.5 |
| 2. | Gum Karaya-II | 3850 | 0 | 0 | 0 | 0 | 0 | 241500 | 30705 | 276055 | 2821 | 0 | 0 | 0 | 2821 | 278876 |
| 3. | Gum Karaya-III | 0 | 0 | 0 | 0 | 0 | 0 | 11000 | 21550 | 32550 | | 2489 | 0 | 0 | 2489 | 35039 |
| 4. | Rockbee Honey | 0 | 0 | 0 | 0 | 0 | 0 | 0 | 0 | 0 | 0 | 240 | 0 | 0 | 240 | 240 |
| 5. | Nux Vomica | 0 | 0 | 0 | 0 | 0 | 0 | 0 | 0 | 0 | 0 | 300 | 0 | 0 | 300 | 300 |
| 6. | Myrobalans | 1568 | 0 | 0 | 93120 | 14400 | 160 | 0 | 800 | 110048 | 4860 | 4520 | 0 | 0 | 9380 | 119428 |
| 7. | Naramamidi Bark | 4116 | 0 | 0 | 480 | 0 | 0 | 3960 | 25560 | 34116 | 24885 | 21615 | 0 | 0 | 46500 | 80616 |
| 8. | R.S. Roots | 0 | 0 | 0 | 0 | 0 | 0 | 0 | 0 | 0 | 0 | 0 | 1695 | 0 | 1695 | 1695 |
| 9. | Kusum Oil Seeds | 0 | 0 | 0 | 0 | 0 | 0 | 0 | 0 | 0 | 20 | 292 | 0 | 0 | 312 | 312 |
| 10. | Gum Oliganum | 0 | 0 | 0 | 0 | 0 | 0 | 0 | 0 | 0 | 0 | 2 | 0 | 0 | 2 | 2 |
| 11. | Adda Leaf | 39960 | 53300 | 62200 | 45600 | 200 | 0 | 0 | 0 | 201260 | 1124 | 2594 | 8200 | 3940 | 15858 | 217118 |
| 12. | Seeded Tamarind | 80050 | 51100 | 24700 | 0 | 0 | 0 | 0 | 0 | 155850 | 5490 | 0 | 0 | 0 | 5490 | 161340 |
| 13. | Deseeded Tamarind | 0 | 0 | 0 | 0 | 181710 | 39250 | 540 | 6800 | 65300 | 0 | 0 | 0 | 0 | 0 | 65300 |
| 14. | Tamarind Seed | 0 | 0 | 0 | 0 | 0 | 14400 | 0 | 0 | 14400 | 0 | 6300 | 8662 | 0 | 14962 | 29362 |
| 15. | Mohwa Flower | 0 | 0 | 0 | 0 | 0 | 0 | 0 | 0 | 0 | 18798 | 18012 | 0 | 11497 | 48307 | 48307 |
| 16. | Mohwa Seed | 0 | 0 | 0 | 0 | 0 | 0 | 0 | 0 | 0 | 12892 | 15961 | 0 | 480 | 29333 | 29333 |
| 17. | Soap Nuts | 0 | 0 | 0 | 0 | 0 | 0 | 0 | 0 | 0 | 0 | 0 | 0 | 0 | 0 | 0 |
| 18. | Amla Seed | 0 | 0 | 0 | 77800 | 0 | 0 | 0 | 0 | 77800 | 0 | 0 | 0 | 0 | 0 | 77800 |
| 19. | Marking Nuts | 1192 | 0 | 200 | 0 | 225 | 4612 | 1890 | 8595 | 16714 | 0 | 0 | 0 | 0 | 0 | 16714 |
| 20. | Pungam Seed | 1620 | 520 | 1320 | 0 | 160 | 0 | 0 | 0 | 3620 | 0 | 0 | 0 | 800 | 800 | 4420 |
| 21. | Hill Brooms | 440 | 0 | 320 | 80 | 0 | 0 | 0 | 0 | 840 | 3696 | 4000 | 0 | 0 | 7696 | 8536 |
| 22. | Kondagogu-I | 0 | 0 | 0 | 0 | 0 | 0 | 0 | 0 | 0 | 375 | 0 | 0 | 0 | 375 | 375 |
| 23. | Cassiotora Seed | 0 | 0 | 0 | 0 | 0 | 5200 | 0 | 0 | 5200 | 0 | 0 | 0 | 0 | 0 | 5200 |
| 24. | Sal Seeds | 0 | 0 | 0 | 0 | 0 | 0 | 0 | 0 | 0 | 4147.5 | 5299 | 0 | 0 | 9446.5 | 9446.5 |
| | | 134496 | 104920 | 88740 | 217080 | 33695 | 63622 | 286390 | 137110 | 1066053 | 79136 | 81624 | 18557 | 16717 | 196034 | |

**Table 4.11: Village Level Prices**

| | Commodity | Reported Procured Price 1996-97 | |
|---|---|---|---|
| | | Andhra Pradesh | Orissa |
| 1. | Gum Karaya-I | 100.00 | 9.50 |
| 2. | Gum Karaya-II | 70.00 | 6.50 |
| 3. | Gum Karaya-III | 50.00 | 6.50 |
| 4. | Rockbee Honey | — | 40.00 |
| 5. | Nux vomica | — | 2.00 |
| 6. | Myrobalans | 3.20 | 2.00 |
| 7. | Naramamidi Bark | 12.00 | 7.00 |
| 8. | Adda Leaf | 2.00 | 2.10 |
| 9. | Seeded Tamarind | 4.80 | — |
| 10. | Deseeded Tamarind | 9.72 | — |
| 11. | Tamarind Seed | 4.50 | 4.70 |
| 12. | Mohwa Flower | — | 3.21 |
| 13. | Mohwa Seed | 2.00 | — |
| 14. | Marking Nuts | 4.50 | — |
| 15. | Pungam Seed | 4.00 | 4.00 |
| 16. | Hill Brooms | 8.00 | 8.00 |
| 17. | Cassiotora Seed | 3.15 | — |
| 18. | Sal Seed | — | 1.90 |

## SECTION-IV

### 4.11. Procurement Price *Vs.* Whole Sale Price

A comparison of procurement price to the nearest whole-sale market price shows the procurement price formed 23.60 per cent in the case of marking nuts and 82.2 per cent in the case of adda leaf in whole sale price. For seeded tamarind, deseeded tamarind and adda leaf the competition among the traders is much more than the case of other products which are not locally consumed (Table 4.14). A large difference between price paid to the tribal and the whole sale market price suggests the nature of the market is not competitive and indicates the exploitation of the tribals particularly when no processing is done by the trader.

**Table 4.12: Prices as per the Labour Cost *vis-a-vis* Actual Price : Andhra Pradesh**

| Item/Village | Procured Qty. per day per person (in kg.) | Labour required per one kg. | Market Wage per day | Price to be paid for kg. of MFP of market wage is to be derived by the labour | Actual Price paid per kg. | Percentage difference between price according to labour cost and actual price |
|---|---|---|---|---|---|---|
| 1 | 2 | 3 | 4 | 5 | 6 | 7 |
| **1. Pedduru** | | | | | | |
| (a) Tamarind | 1.6247 | 0.62 | 25 | 15.50 | 10.00 | 55.00 |
| (b) Marking Nuts | 3.4942 | 0.29 | 25 | 7.25 | 4.50 | 61.00 |
| (c) Tentanga Seed (Cassiotora) | 4.2746 | 0.23 | 25 | 5.75 | 3.00 | 91.67 |
| (d) Tamarind Seed | 9.9322 | 0.10 | 25 | 2.50 | 1.50 | 66.67 |
| (e) Myrobalans | 3.3333 | 0.30 | 25 | 7.50 | 3.20 | 134.38 |
| **2. Cheruvuru** | | | | | | |
| (a) Tamarind | 1.56 | 0.64 | 25 | 16.00 | 10.00 | 60.00 |
| (b) Myrobalans | 4.00 | 0.25 | 25 | 6.25 | 3.20 | 95.31 |
| (c) Marking Nuts | 3.33 | 0.30 | 25 | 7.50 | 4.50 | 66.67 |
| (d) Pungam Seed | 4.00 | 0.25 | 25 | 6.25 | 4.00 | 56.25 |

(*Contd.*)

Table 4.12 (*Contd.*)

| 1 | 2 | 3 | 4 | 5 | 6 | 7 |
|---|---|---|---|---|---|---|
| **3. Kovelapalem** | | | | | | |
| (a) Gum Karaya | 0.318 | 3.14 | 25 | 78.5 | 70.00 | 12.14 |
| (b) Naramamidi Bark | 2.028 | 0.49 | 25 | 12.25 | 12.00 | 2.08 |
| (c) Tamarind | 1.60 | 0.625 | 25 | 15.63 | 10.00 | 56.3 |
| (d) Marking Nuts | 3.32 | 0.30 | 25 | 7.50 | 4.50 | 66.67 |
| (e) Myrobalans | 3.71 | 0.27 | 25 | 6.75 | 3.20 | 110.94 |
| **4. Veeravaram** | | | | | | |
| (a) Gum Karaya | 0.3084 | 3.24 | 25 | 81.00 | 70.00 | 15.71 |
| (b) Naramamidi Bark | 1.70 | 0.59 | 25 | 14.75 | 12.00 | 22.91 |
| (c) Tamarind | 1.55 | 0.65 | 25 | 16.25 | 10.00 | 62.5 |
| (d) Marking Nuts | 3.36 | 0.30 | 25 | 7.50 | 4.50 | 66.7 |
| **5. Pothangi** | | | | | | |
| (a) Adda Leaf | 10.90 | 0.09 | 25 | 2.25 | 2.00 | 12.5 |
| (b) Seeded Tamarind | 9.95 | 0.10 | 25 | 2.50 | 5.00 | –50.00 |
| (c) Pungam Seed | 7.84 | 0.13 | 25 | 3.25 | 4.00 | –18.75 |
| (d) Hill Broom | 3.64 | .27 | 25 | 6.75 | 10.00 | –32.5 |

| | | | | | | |
|---|---|---|---|---|---|---|
| **6. Besupuram** | | | | | | |
| (a) Myrobalans | 10.51 | .095 | 30.00 | 2.85 | 3.2 | –10.94 |
| (b) Adda Leaf | 10.88 | .092 | 30.00 | 2.76 | 2.00 | 38.00 |
| (c) Amla Seed | 13.63 | .073 | 30.00 | 2.19 | 2.00 | 9.50 |
| (d) Naramamidi Bark | 2.10 | .48 | 30.00 | 14.40 | 12.00 | 20.00 |
| (e) Hill Broom | 2.5 | .40 | 30.00 | 12.00 | 10.00 | 20.00 |
| **7. Sumpangiput** | | | | | | |
| (a) Adda Leaf | 11.93 | .083 | 30.00 | 2.49 | 2.00 | 24.5 |
| (b) Deseeded Tamarind | 12.45 | .08 | 30.00 | 2.4 | 5.00 | –52.80 |
| (c) Pungam Seed | 4.81 | .21 | 30.00 | 6.30 | 4.00 | 57.5 |
| **8. Kumaritham** | | | | | | |
| (a) Adda Leaf | 9.83 | .1 | 25.00 | 2.50 | 2.00 | 25.00 |
| (b) Seeded Tamarind | 12.49 | 0.08 | 25.00 | 2.00 | 5.00 | –60.00 |
| (c) Pungam Seed | 5.99 | .17 | 25 | 4.25 | 4.00 | 6.25 |
| (d) Naramamidi Bark | 1.68 | .6 | 25 | 15.00 | 12.00 | 25.00 |
| (e) Myrobalans | 6.38 | .16 | 25 | 4.00 | 3.20 | 25.00 |
| (f) Hill Brooms | 2.86 | .35 | 25 | 8.75 | 10.00 | –12.5 |
| (g) Marking Nuts | 6.28 | .16 | 25 | 21.00 | 21.00 | 0.00 |
| (h) Soap Nuts | 5.00 | .20 | 25 | 5.00 | 5.00 | 0.00 |

**Table 4.13: Prices as per the Labour Cost *vis-a-vis* Actual Price : Orissa**

| Item/Village | Procured Qty. per day per person (in kg.) | Labour required per one kg. | Market Wage per day | Price to be paid for kg. of MFP of market wage is to be derived by the labour | Actual Price paid per kg. | Percentage difference between price according to labour cost and actual price |
|---|---|---|---|---|---|---|
| 1 | 2 | 3 | 4 | 5 | 6 | 7 |
| **1. Telangapodar** | | | | | | |
| (a) Adda Leaf | 1.25 | 0.8 | 20 | 16 | 2.00 | 700.00 |
| (b) Tamarind | 1.97 | 0.51 | 20 | 10.20 | 7.50 | 36.00 |
| (c) Gum-I | 0.2 | 5.00 | 20 | 100.00 | 6.50 | 1438.46 |
| (d) Hill Brooms | 0.81 | 1.23 | 20 | 24.6 | 8.00 | 207.5 |
| (e) Myrobalans | 3.57 | 0.28 | 20 | 5.60 | 2.00 | 180.00 |
| (f) Mohwa flower | 5.26 | 0.19 | 20 | 3.80 | 3.00 | 26.66 |
| (g) Mohwa seed | 2.30 | 0.43 | 20 | 8.60 | 7.50 | 14.66 |
| (h) Sal seed | 2.21 | 0.45 | 20 | 9.00 | 1.75 | 414.30 |
| (i) Naramamidi Bark | 6.05 | 0.17 | 20 | 3.40 | 7.00 | –51.42 |
| **2. Borikhal** | | | | | | |
| (a) Gum-III | 0.47 | 2.13 | 20 | 42.60 | 4.00 | 965.00 |
| (b) Myrobalans | 3.23 | 0.31 | 20 | 6.20 | 2.00 | 210.00 |

| | | | | | | |
|---|---|---|---|---|---|---|
| (c) Naramamidi Bark | 4.04 | 0.25 | 20 | 5.00 | 7.00 | –28.57 |
| (d) Tamarind | 1.42 | 0.70 | 20 | 14.00 | 7.50 | 86.67 |
| (e) Hill Brooms | 0.63 | 1.59 | 20 | 31.80 | 8.00 | 297.05 |
| (f) Mohwa seed | 2.92 | 0.34 | 20 | 6.80 | 7.50 | –9.33 |
| (g) Sal seed | 2.81 | 0.36 | 20 | 7.20 | 1.75 | 311.43 |
| (h) Kusum Oil seed | 1.03 | 0.97 | 20 | 19.40 | 2.00 | 870.00 |
| (i) Rockbee Honey | 0.43 | 2.33 | 20 | 46.60 | 20.00 | 133.00 |
| (j) Mohwa flower | 5.10 | 0.20 | 20 | 4.00 | 3.00 | 33.33 |
| (k) Nux vomica | 3.00 | 0.33 | 20 | 6.60 | 2.00 | 230.00 |
| **3. Minapai** | | | | | | |
| (a) R.S. Roots | 20.00 | 0.05 | 20 | 1.00 | 15.00 | –93.33 |
| (b) Adda Leaf (Siali Leaves) | 25.89 | 0.04 | 20 | 0.80 | 2.00 | –60.00 |
| (c) Tamarind | 26.38 | 0.038 | 20 | 0.76 | 5.00 | –84.80 |
| **4. K. Gursi** | | | | | | |
| (a) Adda Leaf (Siali Leaves) | 13.22 | 0.07 | 20 | 1.40 | 2.50 | –44.00 |
| (b) Tamarind | 24.13 | 0.04 | 20 | 0.80 | 5.00 | –84.00 |
| (c) Mohwa flower | 7.19 | 0.14 | 20 | 2.8 | 4.00 | –30.00 |
| (d) Pungam Seed | 40.00 | 0.025 | 20 | 0.50 | 2.00 | –75.75 |

**Table 4.14: Procurement Price as a Percentage of Wholesale Price**

| Sl. No. | Commodity | Procurement Price Per Quintal (in Rs.) | Whole Sale Price Per Quintal (in Rs.) | Procurement as a Percentage in Wholesale Price |
|---|---|---|---|---|
| 1. | Myrobalans | 400.00 | 800.00 | 50.00 |
| 2. | Nuxvomica | 375.00 | 600.00 | 46.87 |
| 3. | Marking Nuts | 189.00 | 800.00 | 23.60 |
| 4. | Shikakai | 425.00 | 1000.00 | 42.50 |
| 5. | Soap Nuts | 756.00 | 1600.00 | 47.25 |
| 6. | Seeded Tamarind | 551.00 | 750.00 | 73.00 |
| 7. | Deseeded Tamarind | 971.00 | 1400.00 | 69.35 |
| 8. | Adda Leaf | 411.00 | 500.00 | 82.20 |

*Source* : Procurement prices are collected from the GCC Headquarters for the month of March, 1998.

Wholesale prices are collected from the wholesale traders at Visakhapatnam.

We also sought to know the procurement price paid to the tribal during the season and off-season. For each commodity, the season of marketing is noted. The average price during the season and during the off-season are noted (Table 4.15). Except in the case of marking nuts, Shikakai and Deseeded tamarind, the off-season procurement price is less than the price during the season. We expected off-season price to be higher since this price should cover the cost of storage, interest rate and driage. It is surprising that the off-season price is fixed at a lower level and acts as a disincentive to the tribal in staggering the arrivals of the market produce. This itself will push down the market price during the season.

It will be noted that more than 90 per cent of the quantity in respect of myrobalans, nuxvomica, marking nuts, seeded tamarind, D.S. tamarind, adda leaf, cleaning nuts and pungam seed are procured during the season covering less than 6 months. Only Shikakai is an exception to this practice. In respect of this commodity 70 per cent is procured during the off season and the price paid also is higher.

In the case of agricultural produce, only a few commodities are procured by GC. These are niger seed, french beans, turmeric, dry chillies and annatto seed. The marketing season is also much shorter *i.e.* not more than three months in many cases, as compared to minor forest produce. Except turmeric and dry chillies, more than 90 per cent of the quantities is procured during the season (Table 4.16).

In the case of agricultural commodities, tribals' share is generally better than the minor forest produce. The market prices are got from the Business Line, a newspaper published from Chennai, and these are cited for different centres. Chennai for niger seed; Hyderabad for turmeric, red gram, dry chillies and jowar and Cochin for black gram, green gram. Market prices are found to vary largely from one month to another. But we have ensured that the month for which the prices are cited are same as the prices for which the procurement prices are cited. This method of comparison allows mainly for transport cost between the producing centres and marketing centres. The difference between the procurement price and wholesale price per quintal ranges from around Rs. 200 for niger seed to Rs. 1200 for green gram (Table 4.17). The difference cannot be attributed to transportation, loading, unloading and local taxes only. There must be a large element of monopoly in the price at the wholesale market which amounts the exploitation of the tribals.

## SUMMARY

This chapter focuses mainly on:

(i) sale price *vis-a-vis* procurement price;

(ii) extent variability in sale price;

(iii) participation in sales of each of the MFP & SAP commodities by tribal households; and

(iv) price paid to the commodity and labour cost incurred by the tribals.

Examination of sale price *vis-a-vis* procurement price shows huge gap between the two. The procurement price is lower. The difference between the two prices is much more in case of Andhra Pradesh. Yet, in Orissa, the sale prices are found to be less

**Table 4.15: Details of Procurement Season in 1997**

| Commodity | Season | Procured Qty. in season (in quintals) | Procured Qty. in Off-season (in (quintals) | Total Qty. | Average Procure-ment Price per Qtl. in Season (in Rupees) | Average Procure-ment Price per Qtl. in Off-Season (in Rupees) |
|---|---|---|---|---|---|---|
| 1 | 2 | 3 | 4 | 5 | 6 | 7 |
| 1. Myrobalans | October to April | 11467.15<br>(94.19) | 707.61<br>(5.81) | 12174.76<br>(100.00) | 383.70 | 321.40 |
| 2. Nuxvomica | November to March | 4825.93<br>(98.96) | 55.64<br>(1.14) | 4881.57<br>(100.00) | 366.40 | 327.40 |
| 3. Marking Nuts | January to May | 3443.79<br>(93.88) | 224.60<br>(6.12) | 3668.39<br>(100.00) | 274.20 | 349.33 |
| 4. Shikakai | January to March | 308.82<br>(26.88) | 890.03<br>(73.12) | 1148.85<br>(100.00) | 453.60 | 767.11 |

| | | | | | | |
|---|---|---|---|---|---|---|
| 5. Soap Nuts | March to May | 524.29<br>(85.91) | 85.99<br>(14.09) | 610.28<br>(100.00) | 675.00 | N.A. |
| 6. Seeded Tamarind | January to June | 48595.45<br>(99.70) | 147.13<br>(0.30) | 48742.58<br>(100.00) | 505.30 | 519.00 |
| 7. Deseeded Tamarind | January to June | 11464.11<br>(99.29) | 82.08<br>(0.71) | 11546.19<br>(100.00) | 982.4 | 935.25 |
| 8. Adda Leaf | April to July | 16345.94<br>(98.49) | 251.30<br>(1.51) | 16597.24<br>(100.00) | 308.66 | 289.4 |
| 9. Cleaning Nuts | November to March | 238.03<br>(93.78) | 15.78<br>(6.22) | 253.81<br>(100.00) | 398.80 | 398.83 |
| 10. Pungam Seed | February to June | 4399.64<br>(96.20) | 173.58<br>(3.80) | 4573.22<br>(100.00) | 371.4 | 349.57 |

**Table 4.16: Procurement on Season and Off-Season : 1997-98 : Surplus Agricultural Produce**

| Commodity | Season | Procured Qty. in season (in quintals) | Procured Qty. in Off-season (in (quintals) | Total Qty. | Average Procure-ment Price per Qtl. in Season (in Rupees) | Average Procure-ment Price per Qtl. in Off-Season (in Rupees) |
|---|---|---|---|---|---|---|
| 1. Niger Seed | December to February | 8067.22 (90.66) | 831.26 (9.34) | 8898.48 (100.00) | 1160.60 | 1197.00 |
| 2. French Beans | December to February | 529.80 (95.97) | 22.27 (4.03) | 552.07 (100.00) | 1639.30 | 1559.50 |
| 3. Turmeric | December to April | 7.46 (41.15) | 10.67 (58.85) | 18.13 (100.00) | 1829.50 | 1500.00 |
| 4. Dry chillies | February to April | 97.49 (63.07) | 57.09 (36.93) | 154.58 (100.00) | 2493.50 | 1854.00 |
| 5. Annatto Seed | January to March | 21.51 (99.08) | 0.20 (0.92) | 21.71 (100.00) | 944.30 | 2000.00 |

**Table 4.17: Procurement Price as a Percentage of Wholesale Price (Surplus Agricultural Price)**

| Sl. No. | Commodity | Procurement Price Per Quintal (in Rupees) (March, 1998) | Whole Sale Price Per Quintal (in Rupees) (March, 1998) | Procurement Price as a % of Whole-sale Price |
|---|---|---|---|---|
| 1. | Niger Seed | 1197.00 | 1415.00 (Chennai) | 84.60 |
| 2. | Turmeric | 2000.00 | 2900.00 (Hyderabad) | 68.97 |
| 3. | Dry Chillies | 3000.00 | 3800.00 (Hyderabad) | 78.95 |
| 4. | Red Gram | 1000.00 | 1700.00* (Hyderabad) | 58.82 |
| 5. | Jowar | 300.00 | 740.00 (Hyderabad) | 40.55 |
| 6. | Block Gram | 900.00 | 1500.00 (Cochin) | 60.00 |
| 7. | Green Gram | 900.00 | 2100.00 (Cochin) | 42.87 |

*Relates to May, 1998.

compared to those in Andhra Pradesh in most of the commodities. As between MFP & SAP, SAP shows lesser difference between the sale and procurement prices. There is a substantial difference between the wholesale and procurement price particularly in respect of cotton.

The trends in sale and procurement prices show the procurement prices lag behing the sale prices both in Orissa and Andhra Pradesh. GCC in Andhra Pradesh is found to be better than TDCC in Orissa in fixing the procurement prices; the latter did not have autonomy.

Marketing margins are studied for industrial commodities such as hill brooms, sal seed, mohwa flower, tamarind and gum of different grades. In all these, the marketing margins in Orissa between the wholesale prices and the prices received by the primary collector are found to be quite large. In Andhra Pradesh, these are also found to be large despite the monopoly power exercised by the GCC.

From the field survey, we collected details relating to prices received by households for MFP & SAP. A comparison between Andhra Pradesh and Orissa shows in respect of almost in all commodities, the tribal households in Andhra Pradesh receive higher prices than that in Orissa, thus, confirming the picture got from the procurement agencies.

A comparison of prices paid by agents to the tribal households, with the labour cost incurred by them for the commodity showed invariably the price is less than the labour cost, thus suggesting exploitation of the tribals.

## NOTE

1. This is drawn from "Forest Dwellers and Non-timber Forest Produce Marketing in Orissa — A Study and Policy Analysis" Commissioned by Orissa Drought Forum — Advocacy Cell, Bhubaneswar, Orissa, India.

# 5

# Loaning Performance by GCC in Andhra Pradesh and TDCC in Orissa

GCC of Andhra Pradesh was provided with a separate line of credit to give loans to tribals with effect from 1990. Consequently, GCC has introduced a loaning programme in 1991. Until 1996, it has disbursed Rs. 40.91 crores. The overall recovery is 72 per cent, much higher than the cooperatives in the plains. GCC has extended unique facility to tribals of accepting repayment in kind.

## 5.1. Loaning Performance of GCC

For short-term/seasonal agricultural operations loans disbursed are shown in Table 5.1 (year wise). Number of loanees have increased between 1990-91 to 1992-93 remarkably. There was a ten-fold increase in these two years but in subsequent years there was a drop. In 1996-97 the number of loanees was slightly better than the position in 1990-91. The recovery performance which was 100 per cent earlier shows a gradual deterioration.

## 5.2. Performance of Cooperatives in Orissa and A.P.

For the purpose of comparison with Orissa state, we show the performance of PACS's in predominantly tribal districts, defined as those with more than 50 per cent of population as tribals. The position of eight districts is compared with the position in A.P. Per loanee advances amounted to Rs. 2256.40 in 1993-94 in A.P. while in Orissa per member advances amounted to only Rs. 214.85 (Table 5.2). Even if we assume that only a fraction of members are loanees, Andhra performance appears to be better.

**Table 5.1: Loaning Performance in Andhra Pradesh by GCC**

| Year | No. of Loanees | Amount Disbursed (in lakhs) | Recovery (in lakhs) | Percentage |
|---|---|---|---|---|
| 1990-91 | 8064 | 158.75 | 158.75 | 100.00 |
| 1991-92 | 40132 | 538.84 | 538.84 | 100.00 |
| 1992-93 | 84819 | 1232.28 | 992.03 | 81.00 |
| 1993-94 | 39522 | 891.27 | 462.48 | 52.00 |
| 1994-95 | 24777 | 590.92 | 381.77 | 65.00 |
| 1995-96 | 16687 | 471.37 | 269.22 | 57.00 |
| 1996-97 | 8918 | 207.97 | 0.24 | 0.12 |
| Total | 222919 | 4091.40 | 2803.33 | 69 |
| Per Loanee in 1993-94 | | 2256.40 | 1170.80 | 69 |

*Source* : Girijan Cooperative Corporation Limited, Visakhapatnam, *Note on Activities*, December, 1996.

The performance of Central Cooperative Banks in the tribal areas of A.P. and tribal areas of Orissa also could be compared. Performance of Central Cooperative Banks (overall), is much worse in Orissa as compared to A.P. Overdues in Orissa formed 52.80 per cent of outstanding, while in A.P. it formed only 34.5 per cent (Table 5.3). In the tribal areas of Orissa except two banks *viz.* Sundargarh and Sambalpur, all other recorded losses. The overdues in Koraput district as percentage of outstanding was at the order of 63 per cent. An examination of the performance of Primary Agricultural Credit Societies shows that the loans advanced per member in tribal areas is higher as compared to overall. This superior performance of the tribal areas must be attributed to the loaning functions of GCC. As against this, the Primary Agricultural Cooperative Credit Societies in Orissa loan advances per member is only of Rs. 215.00. It is less than one-half of the loan advances per member in A.P. (Table 5.4). The poor position in Orissa could also be seen in the performance indicators of credit delivery systems of different districts compiled by the evaluation study of NABARD.[1] Percentage of overdues to demand in RRB's and commercial

## Table 5.2: Performance of Primary Agricultural Credit Cooperative Societies in Predominantly Tribal Districts of Orissa, 1993-94

| Predominantly Tribal | No. of Societies | Membership (000's) | Working Capital (Rs. in lakhs) | Loans Advanced (Rs. in Lakhs) | | | Loans Outstanding (Rs. in lakhs) |
|---|---|---|---|---|---|---|---|
| | | | | Short-term | Medium term | Total | |
| Khandhamal | 24 | 86 | 358 | 18 | — | 18 | 48 |
| Koraput | 20 | 86 | 675 | 135 | 51 | 186 | 285 |
| Malkangiri | 10 | 34 | 228 | 43 | 25 | 68 | 71 |
| Mayurbanj | 55 | 228 | 1146 | 216 | — | 216 | 380 |
| Nabarangpur | 14 | 64 | 493 | 79 | 30 | 109 | 485 |
| Rayagada | 15 | 61 | 449 | 103 | 15 | 118 | 129 |
| Sambalpur | 48 | 82 | 1004 | 360 | 35 | 395 | 474 |
| Sundargarh | 47 | 140 | 1759 | 293 | 275 | 568 | 736 |
| Total | 233 | 781 | 6112 | 1247 | 431 | 1678 | 2608 |
| Per member values | | | 782.60 | 159.66 | 55.18 | 214.85 | 333.93 |
| Per member values for all areas (tribal + non-tribal) | 2805 | 3370 | 948.34 | 200.90 | 20.35 | 221.25 | 395.73 |

*Source* : Govt. of Orissa, Directorate of Economics and Statistics, *Statistical Abstract of Orissa*, 1996, p. 61.

## Table 5.3: Performance of Central Cooperative Banks in Predominantly Tribal Districts of Orissa, 1993-94

(Rs. in lakhs)

| Name of the Bank | Loans Advanced | Loans Outstanding | Overdues | Overdues as a % of outstanding | Profit (+) Loss (–) |
|---|---|---|---|---|---|
| Bhawanipatna | 431 | 871 | 403 | 46.27 | (–)101 |
| Koraput | 770 | 954 | 602 | 63.10 | (–)7 |
| Mayurbanj | 290 | 623 | 338 | 54.25 | (–)109 |
| Sambalpur | 3414 | 4298 | 1881 | 43.76 | (+)1 |
| Sundargarh | 889 | 1243 | 348 | 28.00 | (+)1 |
| Total | 5794 | 7989 | 3572 | 44.71 | (–)215 |
| All Banks | 12862 | 20070 | 10587 | 52.75 | (–)1178 |
| Andhra Pradesh | 111572 | 163713 | 56431 | 34.50 | |

*Source* : Govt. of Orissa, Directorate of Economics and Statistics, *Statistical Abstract of Orissa*, p. 66. For Andhra Pradesh, Directorate of Economics and Statistics, *Statistical Abstract*, 1993, p. 325.

**Table 5.4: Performance of PACS's in Predominantly Tribal Districts of Andhra Pradesh as on 31-3-1992**

(Rs. in lakhas)

| District | No. of Socie-ties | Mem-bership ('000) | Working Capital | Loans | | | |
|---|---|---|---|---|---|---|---|
| | | | | Advanced | Outstand-ing | Overdues | Overdues as a % of Outstand-ing |
| Visakhapatnam | 111 | 375 | 2919 | 3884 | 8431 | 1066 | 12.64 |
| Warangal | 169 | 232 | 2366 | 359 | 1724 | 1148 | 66.60 |
| Khammam | 203 | 401 | 5900 | 1263 | 5777 | 3703 | 64.10 |
| Adilabad | 191 | 159 | 1997 | 533 | 1066 | 546 | 51.02 |
| Total | 674 | 1167 | 13180 | 6039 | 16998 | 6463 | 38.00 |
| Per member values | | | 1129.40 | 517.50 | 1456.55 | 553.81 | |
| Andhra | 4605 | 11047 | 124797 | 52630 | 125592 | 41296 | 32.88 |
| Per member values | | | 1129.704 | 76.04 | 1136.90 | 373.82 | |

*Source* : Govt. of Andhra Pradesh, Directorate of Economic and Statistics, *Andhra Pradesh Statistical Abstract*, 1993, Hyderabad, p. 227.

banks reaches a high figure of 80 per cent. The recovery percentage is as low as 20 per cent among the commercial banks. Cooperatives fared better as compared to commercial banks and RRB's (Table 5.5).

## 5.3. Household Surveys: NSS 44th Round (July 1988-June 1989)

The NSS 44th Round (July 1988-June 1989) collected data on assets and liabilities of the tribal households state-wise. In A.P. average amount of dues outstanding per household was Rs. 1330.00, while in Orissa the corresponding figure was Rs. 361.00. The percentage of households reporting outstanding dues is also much less in Orissa as compared to Andhra Pradesh. It appears, debt follows credit worthiness of the tribal households and not poverty as such. Percentage of households reporting loans in cash was also much more in Andhra Pradesh as compared to Orissa. 41.2 per cent of the households report loans in cash out of 43.5 per cent of the individual households, while in Orissa the corresponding percentages are 15.2 and 21.6 respectively. Non-institutional loans figured much more

## Table 5.5: Performance Indicators of the Credit Delivery System in Different Districts of Orissa

| Sl. No. | Particulars | Bargarh | | | | | Deogarh | | | | | Jharsuguda | | | | | Sambalpur | | | | |
|---|---|---|---|---|---|---|---|---|---|---|---|---|---|---|---|---|---|---|---|---|---|
| | | Cooperatives | | RRB | CB | Total | Cooperatives | | RRB | CB | Total | Cooperatives | | RRB | CB | Total | Cooperatives | | RRB | CB | Total |
| | | ST | LT | | | | ST | LT | | | | ST | LT | | | | ST | LT | | | |
| 1. | Total Loan Outstanding on 30-6-1994 (Rs. in crores) | 20.74 | 3.14 | 11.89 | 51.19 | 86.96 | 442.16 | 122.2 | 195.01 | 16590.51 | N.A. | 85.65 | 135.85 | 271.45 | N.A. | N.A. | 10.58 | 4.58 | 75.70 | 2.96 | 93.82 |
| 2. | Recovery Percentage | 58 | 25 | 12 | 30 | 20 | 44 | 42 | 43 | N.A. | N.A. | 67 | 51 | 48 | N.A. | N.A. | 31 | 21 | 30 | 19 | 23 |
| 3. | % of overdues to demand | 42 | 75 | 88 | 70 | 80 | 56 | 58 | N.A. | N.A. | N.A. | N.A. | 49 | 52@ | N.A. | N.A. | 69 | 79 | 70 | 81 | 77 |
| 4. | % of overdues to loan D/S | 56 | 45 | 10 | 18 | 27 | 6 | 32 | 35 | N.A. | N.A. | N.A. | 30 | N.A. | N.A. | N.A. | 64 | 11 | 12 | 63 | 37 |

*Notes* :

1. Data pertains to undivided Sambalpur District.
2. Figuries retate to March 1996.

@ Figures relate to June 1995.

*Source* : NABARD Ex-post Evaluation Study, Evaluation Sense to Bhabaneswar RO 5, Regional Office, Bhubaneswar, 1997, pp. 13-14.

prominently in A.P. as compared to Orissa. Non-institutional loans formed 3 times of the institutional loans in A.P., while in Orissa non-institutional loans formed only a minor proportion. We suggest that even private moneylenders avoid non-credit worthy tribal households.[2]

### 5.4. Household Survey : Berhampur University (1993)

The results of the NSS Survey are confirmed by recent survey undertaken by Berhampur University in November 1992.[3] According to this Survey non-borrowers formed 42 per cent of the sample; 47 per cent are institutional borrowers; 7 per cent are non-institutional borrowers and 4 per cent are bonded labourer borrowers. Maximum number of families borrowed for domestic consumption and social expenditure. Marriages accounted for 47 per cent of the loan incurred. Rate of interest exceeded 25 per cent or more in 49 out of 60 cases borrowed from moneylenders. In no case the written agreement was signed by the lender and borrower. An extra rate of interest was charged in the case of default. Out of 862 sample households 33 households or 4 per cent are bonded labourers. In the case of 52 per cent of these families, the present head of the household has incurred loan for the family requirement and in about 45 per cent of the cases loan was incurred by the parents for which the present head was working as a bonded labourer. In the case of 3 per cent of families the grandfather had incurred the loan for which in the third generation the present head still was in bonded fold. The families have been in the bondage continuously for generations for an amount of Rs. 500 on an average. The purpose of borrowing is mainly household consumption. Out of 33 households 6 have borrowed outside the village mainly from the big farmers or businessmen. The rest of the families borrowed from the big farmers in the village. At the time of survey 30 families were released from bondage and rehabilitated.

Institutional borrowers numbering 411 borrowed from different financial institutions of the locality. The tribals get credit from different income generating schemes. These are as follows: (1) IRDP, (2) ERRP, (3) ITDP, (4) Cooperative Sector including LAMPS. Around 30 per cent of the institutional credit was provided in cash while the rest of the money was supplied in the form of assets to the beneficiary. APGP and the LAMPS together supplied more than 75 per cent of the total credit. Maximum percentage of loans were given for purchase of plough bullocks and small business. The transaction cost on institutional loans appear to be high. The borrowers had to run several times to contact the bank official and block officials for getting the loan and for approval of the loan application. Out of 459 institutional borrowers only 42 have fully paid their dues. 181 have not paid anything. Non-repayment is attributed to low earnings and poverty and crop failures. Only 252 borrowers retained the assets given to them. Two-third of the beneficiaries complained about huge loss and the rest one-third could not operate due to lack of working capital.

The non-borrowers numbered 42 per cent of the total sample households. Daily wage form the single major source of income of the non-borrowers. Festivals accounted for lesser share of expenditure among non-borrowers as compared to borrowers. In fact festivals accounted for half of the loans from money-lenders.

Institutional borrowers recorded the maximum deficit since the creation of assets from this loans did not contribute to income of the family adequately. The debt burden in the case of such borrowers is attributable to the diversion of loans to unproductive purposes.

## 5.5. Household Survey (1996-97)

### *Credit Structure*

The differences between A.P. and Orissa in respect of credit structure are striking (Table 5.6). In the 8 villages together 40 per cent of the households are found to be borrowers in A.P., the corresponding figure for Orissa is only 11 per cent. The variation among villages in A.P. is quite large, 20 per cent in Pothangi and Cheruvuru villages and 84 per cent in Veeravaram village. In Orissa villages also variations among the villages are large, 0 per cent in Borikhal village and 20 per cent in Telangapodar. It appears that the percentage of borrowers in village is much influence by the capacity to borrow rather than by its need. Low capacity to borrow in Orissa tribal villages is

## Table 5.6: Distribution of Households by Institutional Borrowers and Non-Institutional Borrowers in Andhra Pradesh and Orissa in 1996

| Sl. No. | Name of the Village | Total House-holds | Total Borrow-ers | Total indebtors | Amount Borrowed (In Rupees) | | Total Borrowed Amount (in Rupees) | Borrowed Amount per Borrowed Household (in Rupees) | Total Out-standing Debt (in Rupees) | Out-standing Debt | Per House-hold Income | Value of Marketed Output MFP Income | Per House-hold Income |
|---|---|---|---|---|---|---|---|---|---|---|---|---|---|
| | | | | | Institu-tional | Non-institu-tional | | | | | | | |
| 1 | 2 | 3 | 4 | 5 | 6 | 7 | 8 | 9 | 10 | 11 | 12 | 13 | 14 |
| 1. | Kumaritham | 25 | 13 (52.00) | 8 (32.00) | 0 | 12300.00 (100.00) | 12300.00 | 946.15 | 5400.00 | 675.00 | 17879.80 | 310995.00 | 12439.5 (7.61) |
| 2. | Sampangiput | 25 | 6 (24.00) | 9 (36.00) | 30000.00 | 0 (100.00) | 30000.00 | 5000.00 | 33500.00 | 3722.20 | 19700.80 | 319360.00 | 12974.4 (40.00) |
| 3. | Pothangi | 25 | 4 (15.00) | 5 (20.00) | 7200.00 (100.00) | 0 | 7200.00 | 1800.00 | 7400.00 | 1450.00 | 11525.60 | 131000.00 | 5240.00 (34.40) |
| 4. | Besupuram | 25 | 9 (36.00) | 6 (24.00) | 4500.00 (60.40) | 2950.00 (39.60) | 7450.00 | 827.78 | 6200.00 | 1033.30 | 1929.20 | 363250.00 | 14530.00 (5.70) |
| 5. | Cheruvuru | 25 | 5 (20.00) | 5 (20.00) | 0 | 5050.00 (100.00) | 5050.00 | 1010.00 | 6025.00 | 1205.00 | 8748.24 | 64665.00 | 2586.85 (39.10) |
| 6. | Pedduru | 25 | 9 (36.00) | 11 (44.00) | 5000.00 (26.67) | 13750.00 (73.33) | 18750.00 | 2083.33 | 20450.00 | 1859.10 | 10947.56 | 85872.00 | 3434.86 (60.67) |
| 7. | Veeravaram | 25 | 21 (84.00) | 21 (84.00) | 25100.00 (72.02) | 9750.00 (27.98) | 34850.00 | 1659.52 | 34850.00 | 1659.52 | 15050.4 | 191990.00 | 7679.6 (21.61) |
| 8. | Kovelapalem | 24 | 16 (66.7) | 16 (66.7) | 42700.00 (92.42) | 3500.00 (7.58) | 46200.00 | 2717.65 | 46200.00 | 2717.65 | 15508.75 | 204895.00 | 8537.29 (31.83) |
| | Andhra Pradesh | 199 | 83 (41.70) | 81 (40.20) | 114500.00 (70.77) | 47300.00 (29.23) | 161800.00 | 1949.40 | 160025.00 | 1975.61 | 14826.63 | 1675027.00 | 8417.22 (22.90) |

*(Contd.)*

| 1 | 2 | 3 | 4 | 5 | 6 | 7 | 8 | 9 | 10 | 11 | 12 | 13 | 14 |
|---|---|---|---|---|---|---|---|---|---|---|---|---|---|
| 9. | Telangapodar | 25 | 2 | 4 | 8000.00 | 0 | 8000.00 | 4000.00 | 29500.00 | 5900.00 | 9013.64 | 125769.00 | 5030.76 |
| | | | (8.00) | (20.00) | (100.00) | | | | | | | | (80.52) |
| 10. | Borikhal | 25 | 1 | 0 | 3500.00 | 0 | 3500.00 | 3500.00 | 0 | 0 | 9005.44 | 90277.00 | 3611.10 |
| | | | (4.0) | (0.00) | (100.00) | | | | | | | | (96.92) |
| 11. | Minapai | 25 | 4 | 4 | 12400.00 | 0 | 12400.00 | 3100.00 | 6700.00 | 1675.00 | 5700.28 | 21557.00 | 862.28 |
| | | | (16.00) | (16.00) | (100.00) | | | | | | | | (360.00) |
| 12. | K. Gursi | 25 | 2 | 3 | 1200.00 | 1000.00 | 2200.00 | 1100.00 | 2700.00 | 900.00 | 4795.80 | 62367.00 | 2494.68 |
| | | | (8.00) | (12.00) | (100.00) | | | | | | | | (44.10) |
| | Orissa | 100 | 9 | 11 | 25100.00 | 1000.00 | 26100.00 | 3262.50 | 38900.00 | 3536.36 | 7128.8 | 299970.00 | 2999.70 |
| | | | (8.00) | (11.00) | (100.00) | | | | | | | | (96.68) |

*Notes* :

1. Figures in brackets of column 3 and column 4 relates to No. of borrowers, total indebtors as a percentage of total No. of households in the village concerned

2. Figures in brackets of column 5 and column 6 relates to the Institutional area as percentage of amount borrowed.

not only revealed in our survey but also in NSS survey and Berhampur survey as seen earlier. Surprisingly in all Orissa villages except in one village there is no borrowing reported from non-institutional sources. Lesser importance of non-institutional source is also seen from other studies. Even in A.P. tribal areas, non-institutional sources have less importance than institutional source of credit; around 70 per cent of borrowings from institutional sources and 30 per cent from non-institutional sources. Amount borrowed per borrowing household in all the A.P. villages together is not adequate even to meet the cost of cultivation of crops. As a share of income, from cultivation and MFP, borrowing accounted only for 1/5th of the income of the borrowing members in A.P. villages. In Orissa villages in which incomes of household are low borrowings accounted for a large percentage of total income. But borrowers in these villages formed only 11 per cent of the total household. Much larger percentage do not have access to either institutional or non-institutional finance.

### *Purpose of Loans*

Distribution of borrowers by purpose is shown in Table 5.7. In the 8 villages of Andhra Pradesh 63.90 per cent of the borrowing households are found to have borrowed for the purpose of cultivation/agriculture and the corresponding figure for Orissa is 50.00.

For agriculture purpose institutional credit is the single largest source. Institutional credit is also found to be used for social function (1.73 per cent), house loan (22.34 per cent), living expenses (4.42 per cent), and purchasing of agricultural implements and cattle (3.46 per cent). Out of the total institutional credit, 28.50 per cent of the credit is for the non-productive purpose. In Orissa all borrowings are from the institutional sources except one and for the purposes of agriculture/cultivation and purchasing cattle. Out of the total borrowed amount from institutions 50.60 per cent was for the purpose of agriculture and the rest is used for purchasing agricultural implements and cattle. It is seen earlier that the large percentage of households do not have access to either institutional or non-institutional finance.

**Table 5.7: Distribution of Borrowers by Purpose, Institutional and Non-Institutional in Andhra Pradesh and Orissa in 1996**

| Purpose | Total Borrowers | | Amount Borrowed (Andhra Pradesh) | | Amount Borrowed (Orissa) | |
|---|---|---|---|---|---|---|
| | A.P. | Orissa | Institutional | Non-Institutional | Institutional | Non-Institutional |
| Agriculture/ cultivation | 53 (63.86) | 4 (50.00) | 77600.00 (68.05) | 22100.00 (45.57) | 12700.00 (50.60) | 1000.00 (100.00) |
| Social Function | 5 (6.02) | 0 | 2000.00 (1.73) | 3550.00 (7.67) | 0 | 0 |
| House Loan | 6 (7.23) | 0 | 25800.00 (22.34) | 1500.00 (3.24) | 0 | 0 |
| Travel | 1 (1.20) | 0 | 0 | 3000.00 (6.48) | 0 | 0 |
| Living expenses | 13 (15.68) | 0 | 6100.00 (4.42) | 9650.00 (20.84) | 0 | 0 |
| Purchasing of agricultural implements/ cattle | 1 (1.20) | 4 (50.00) | 4000.00 (3.46) | 0 | 12400.00 (49.40) | 0 |
| Medical | 4 (4.82) | 0 | 0 | 7500.00 (16.20) | 0 | 0 |
| Total | 83 | 8 | 114500.00 (100.00) | 47300.00 (100.00) | 25100.00 (100.00) | 1000.00 (100.00) |

In Andhra Pradesh out of the total credit borrowed from the non-institutional sources, 45.60 per cent was for the purpose of agriculture, the rest for unproductive purposes. Among the unproductive purposes, social functions, medical and living expenses together constituted 44.7 per cent of the total non-institutional credit. So, non-institutional credit is the single largest source for the family maintenance of tribals in A.P. during the slack seasons.

The maximum number of institutional borrowers belonged to the category of marginal and small farmers. The households with more than two acres constituted only 12.5 per cent of the total borrowers (Table 5.8). In Orissa the total number of borrowers are far less. They are drawn mostly from holdings less than one acre.

## Table 5.8: Distribution of Borrowers by Per Capita Cultivable Land and Interest Rate

| Per Capita Cultivable Land (in acres) | No. of Borrowers | | | | Amount Borrowed (in Ruppes) | | | | Interest Rate Range A.P. | | Interest Rate Range Orissa | |
|---|---|---|---|---|---|---|---|---|---|---|---|---|
| | Institutional | | Non-institutional | | Institutional | | Non-institutional | | Institutional | Institutional | Institutional | Non-institutional |
| | A.P. | Orissa | A.P. | Orissa | A.P. | Orissa | A.P. | Orissa | | | | |
| Nil | 4<br>(10.00) | 2<br>(28.57) | 7<br>(16.28) | 0 | 5300.00<br>(4.63) | 6000.00<br>(23.90) | 7800.00<br>(16.50) | 0 | 0.00 to 12% | 48% to 50% | 11% | |
| 0.00-1.00 | 21<br>(52.5) | 4<br>(57.14) | 31<br>(72.10) | 1 | 52400.00<br>(45.76) | 17900.00<br>(71.31) | 35200.00<br>(74.42) | 1000.00 | 0.00 to 12% | 18% to 120% | 11% to 12% | 60% |
| 1.00-2.00 | 10<br>(25) | 1<br>(14.29) | 5<br>(11.63) | 0 | 39900.00<br>(34.85) | 1200.00<br>(4.78) | 4300.00<br>(9.19) | 0 | 11 to 12% | 14% to 48% | 12% | |
| Above 2.00 | 5<br>(12.5) | | 0 | | 16900.00<br>(14.76) | | | | 11 to 12% | 24% to 36% | | |
| | 40<br>(100.00) | 7<br>(100.00) | 43<br>(100.00) | 1 | 11450.00<br>(100.00) | 25100.00<br>(100.00) | 27300.00<br>(100.00) | 1000.00 | | | | |

Non-institutional borrowers in A.P. exceeded slightly the institutional borrowers. The much larger percentage of non-institutional borrowers are drawn from landless or less than one acre holdings. The sole non-institutional borrower from Orissa also belonged to the group of marginal holding. When the amount borrowed is related to size of holding, the share of landless and marginal holdings is much less in A.P. But within the category of non-institutional credit the share of amount taken corresponded closely the share in numbers.

### *Rate of Interests*

The highest rates of interest from the non-institutional sources are paid by landless and least by above two acres. Even the landowners paid double or triple the rate of interest to the non-institutional sources as compared to institutional sources. Surprisingly, linkages of credit with marketing is found to be absent both in Orissa and Andhra Pradesh.

### GCC and TDCC: A Comparison

The preceding analysis shows that the institutional sources of financing have been faltering both in A.P. and Orissa. Yet, a comparison between the two states, shows A.P. performance is much better. The GCC in A.P. lent about Rs. 41 crores during the period 1990-91 to 1996-97 for short-term seasonal agricultural operations. Besides it has also advanced Rs. 6.9 crores for medium-term/long-term loans for land improvement, irrigation sources, etc.

Since 1990-91 it has also advanced consumption credit to the landless tribals who are mainly dependent on collection of MFP for their sustenance during lean season, from its own funds augmented by A.P. Tribal Development Project for this purpose. The loans are advanced amounted to Rs. 1.51 crores in 1990-91.

On the other hand the performance of TDCC has not been satisfactory, mainly due to the failure of LAMPS which provide support to the grass-roots level. According to declared objectives, the LAMPS have to meet credit needs of tribals, supply pesticides and fertilisers; collect market produce, collected/cultivated by tribal; and extend consumer credit to them for meeting expenses

**Table 5.9: Target and Achievement of Surplus Agricultural Produce and Minor Forest Produce during 1994-95 to 1997-98 (Upto 8/97) in Sunabeda Division**

| | Year | Target (Rs. in lakhs) | Achievement (Rs. in lakhs) | Achievement as a % of target |
|---|---|---|---|---|
| Procurement of SAP | 1994-95 | 491.05 | 36.08 | 7.35 |
| | 1995-96 | 652.75 | 506.72 | 77.05 |
| | 1996-97 | 1100.30 | 210.64 | 19.14 |
| | 1997-98 (upto 8/97) | 974.15 | 0.32 | 0.03 |
| Procurement of MFP | 1994-95 | 260.93 | 128.60 | 49.30 |
| | 1995-96 | 317.60 | 122.65 | 38.62 |
| | 1996-97 | 315.37 | 65.38 | 20.73 |
| | 1997-98 (upto 8/97) | 254.82 | 24.95 | 9.80 |

*Source* : Information Sheet of TDCC Ltd., Orissa, Sunabeda division for the Committee on welfare of SC/ST.

**Table 5.10: Performance of GCC for the Past Five Years**

| Item | | 1991-92 | 1992-93 | 1993-94 | 1994-95 | 1995-96 |
|---|---|---|---|---|---|---|
| 1. Procurement | NTEP | 1020.00 | 790.00 | 1020.00 | 820.00 | 989.00 |
| | A.P. | 670.00 | 490.00 | 250.00 | 210.00 | 279.00 |
| | Total | 1690.00 | 1280.00 | 1270.00 | 1030.00 | 1268.00 |
| 2. Sales | NTFP | 1200.00 | 970.00 | 1250.00 | 990.00 | 1375.00 |
| | A.P. | 790.00 | 340.00 | 420.00 | 130.00 | 109.00 |
| | Total | 1990.00 | 1310.00 | 1670.00 | 1120.00 | 1484.00 |
| 3. Supply of Agricultural Inputs | | 260.00 | 640.00 | 600.00 | 310.00 | 235.00 |
| 4. Turnover (commercial) 2+3 | | 2250 | 1950 | 2270 | 1430 | 1719 |
| 5. Credit (SAO/ Consumption/ MT/group) | | 700.00 | 1330.00 | 930.00 | 790.00 | 471.37 |
| 6. Grand Total (Including supply of DRs) | | 6990.00 | 7570.00 | 7880.00 | 6990.00 | 5872.82 |

*Source* : GCC, *Note on Activities*. December 1998, Visakhapatnam.

for marriage, education and other important needs. Although LAMP have begun as part of the great cooperative movement at present most LAMPS are defunct. The reasons cited are shortage of funds for day-to-day operations, lack of managerial abilities and of infrastructural facilities like, storage and transportation. As a result of this, the gap between achievement and targeting of procurement of MFP and SAP has been widening and the details of Sunabeda division are illustrative (Table 5.9). It may be seen the procurement of MFP falls below that of SAP in Orissa State while in Andhra Pradesh the procurement of MFP exceeds that of SAP by several times (Table 5.10).

## SUMMARY

This chapter reviewed the loan performance of GCC in Andhra Pradesh and TDCC in Orissa. Besides, it also throws light on the status of debt in Andhra Pradesh and Orissa, drawing from several household surveys, *viz.*, NSSO 44th Round (July 1988-June 1989), Berhampur University Survey, 1993 and the Field Survey of the Study, 1996-97.

The loaning performance of GCC is found to be much better than that of TDCC in Orissa. GCC has distributed Rs. 41 crores to the tribals until 1996. The overall recovery performance of GCC area is also much better than that in Orissa State and also in comparison with the plains of Andhra Pradesh. The performance of the cooperatives in predominantly tribal districts of Orissa State compared very poorly with the position of Andhra Pradesh. The performance of Central Cooperative Banks is much worse in Orissa compared to Andhra Pradesh.

All the household surveys confirmed the poor status of the credit in Orissa State as compared to Andhra Pradesh. Even the access to credit to non-institutional sources is found to be limited in Orissa. As per our field survey, 1996-97, the borrowers in Orissa villages formed only 11.0 per cent of the total households, as against 40.0 per cent in Andhra Pradesh villages.

Institutional financial sources have been faltering both in Andhra Pradesh and Orissa. Yet, a comparison between two States, shows Andhra Pradesh performance is much better. Since 1991, GCC has also advanced credit to landless tribals who are mainly dependent upon collection of MFP for their sustenance. The performance of TDCC has not been satisfactory because of the failure of LAMPS which are supposed to provide support at gross-roots level.

## NOTES

1. NABARD (1997), *Expost Evaluation Study,* Evaluation Series No. 5, Regional Office, Bhubaneswar.
2. Government of India, NSSO, *Sarvekshana,* 59th Issue, Vol. XXII, No. 4, April-June 1994, NSS 44th Round, Section XI, pp. 74-80.
3. R.P. Sarma and N.C. Sahu (1993), *Tribal Indebtedness in Koraput District, Orissa,* The survey was conducted in Koraput district. It covered 31 blocks and 206 villages and 862 sample households.

# 6

# Domestic Requirements and Public Distribution System : The Role of GCC and TDCC

## Introduction

One of the objectives of GCC in Andhra Pradesh is, supply of essential commodities under PDS through DR Depots to the tribals at fair and reasonable prices. Efforts are made to place all items by 14th of every month. In addition to this, GCC also supplies food provisions to all tribal welfare hostels. List of daily requirements handled include — (1) cereals : rice and wheat; (2) pulses : (a) redgram dal, (b) bengal gram dal, (c) green gram dal; (3) sugar; (4) edible oils : (a) palmolive oil, (b) ground nut oil, (c) cotton seed oil, (d) other edible oils; (5) coconut oil; (6) kerosene oil; (7) salt; (8) soaps; (9) condiments: (a) chillies, (b) turmeric, (c) jaggery and (10) others : (a) matches, (b) tea packets and (c) dry fish.

GCC provides consumption credit to the landless tribals who are mainly dependent on collection of MFP for their sustenance during the lean season. Since 1990-91, GCC has advanced Rs. 150.78 lakhs to 29,624 landless tribals and recovered a sum of Rs. 98.98 lakhs by the end of October, 1996.

Similarly, TDCC also engaged in catering to domestic requirements of tribals in Orissa. These operations are performed through the PDS in both the States. There are 850 DR depots in GCC area of Andhra Pradesh and only 74 fair price shops in TDCC area of Orissa.

## 6.1. Findings of NSS 42nd Round (July 1986–June 1987) in Orissa and Andhra Pradesh

NSSO 42nd Round (July 1986-June 1987) focused attention on utilisation of public distribution system. These details were provided in *Sarvekshana* for All India and state-wise for rural and urban area separately. The details covered rice, wheat, bajra, jowar, other cereals, pulses, sugar, edible oil and standard cloth. Percentage distribution of persons using PDS only, using PDS and open market; and using open market only by fractile groups are provided state-wise. PDS is comprised of ration shops, fair price shops and control shops which get their supplies from Government and Government undertakings. Purchases made for household consumption in 30 days preceding the date of survey were considered in respect of all items except for standard cloth for which the last one year preceding the date of survey was considered.

We provide the findings of the survey for Andhra Pradesh and Orissa States for rural areas. In both Andhra Pradesh and Orissa, rice was the major commodity consumed among the cereals. Percentage of persons consuming rice is 80.88 in Andhra Pradesh rural and 60.32 in Orissa rural.

Estimated number of persons using only PDS rice as a percentage of total using rice is 22.22 per cent for rural Andhra Pradesh and another 51 per cent are using both PDS and open market rice. As against this, only 5.13 per cent are reported to be using PDS rice solely and another 45 per cent are using both PDS and open market rice in urban areas. Thus, no urban bias is reported in Andhra Pradesh. As against this, Orissa's position was deplorable. Only 0.24 per cent are using PDS rice in rural areas and 0.81 in urban areas of Orissa (Table 6.1). Percentage quantities of PDS rice purchase and quantity of purchase from PDS show a similar bad picture for Orissa. "Commodities not available in ration shops" is said to be the single major reason for not purchasing from PDS in Orissa State. While not available sufficient quantities is the major reason in Andhra Pradesh for both rural and urban areas (Table 6.2).

**Table 6.1: Distribution of Persons Using Rice by Different Sources : Rural and Urban**

| | Andhra Pradesh | | | | Orissa | | | |
|---|---|---|---|---|---|---|---|---|
| | Rural | % | Urban | % | Rural | % | Urban | % |
| Estimated No. of Persons using only PDS | 8,123,192 | 22.22 | 644,986 | 5.13 | 36,506 | 0.24 | 18,396 | 0.81 |
| Persons using other than PDS | 9,757,118 | 26.70 | 6,257,977 | 49.77 | 14,790,433 | 98.44 | 2,260,426 | 99.19 |
| Persons using both | 18,679,680 | 51.10 | 5,670,194 | 45.10 | 198,344 | 1.32 | — | — |
| Total | 36,559,990 | 100.00 | 12,573,157 | 100.00 | 15,025,283 | 100.00 | 2,278,822 | 100.00 |

**Table 6.2: Reasons for No Purchase/Part of Purchase from PDS**

| | Andhra Pradesh | | Orissa | |
|---|---|---|---|---|
| | Rural | Urban | Rural | Urban |
| Not entitled/No ration card | 19.80 | 42.69 | 1.95 | 11.82 |
| Not required | 13.00 | 3.00 | 28.25 | 0.54 |
| Not available in ration shop | 7.49 | 2.74 | 46.79 | 54.93 |
| Quantity not satisfactory | 2.26 | 5.07 | 0.86 | 5.90 |
| Not available sufficient quantity | 46.51 | 40.79 | 1.30 | 2.76 |
| Not available sufficient Small quantity | 0.05 | 0.33 | 0.15 | — |
| Credit purchase not possible | 1.71 | 0.19 | 0.70 | 0.39 |
| Others | 8.61 | 4.08 | 18.59 | 17.66 |
| Total | 100.00 | 100.00 | 100.00 | 100.00 |

## 6.2. PDS in Tribal Areas NSS 44th Round (July 1988–June 1989)

The preceding facts relate to both tribal and non-tribal areas. For tribal areas NSS survey of 44th Round (July 1988-June 1989) is useful. The detailed findings of this survey are available in *Sarvekshana*, April-June 1994. We compile the relevant data for rural Andhra Pradesh and rural Orissa. The percentage of tribal households purchasing rice at concession rates in rural areas of A.P. was 27.2 and 16.6 for rural areas of Orissa. The numbers purchasing at usual control rate were 33.5 in A.P. and 6.1 in Orissa. These figures suggest even within the tribal areas the performance of Andhra Pradesh is better than that of Orissa.[1]

## 6.3. Findings of Our Survey 1996-97 on PDS

As part of the household monthly consumption survey, we ask questions relating to purchase of rice from fair price shop. We also elicited details of rice bought from open market.

The questions asked are as follows :

1. What is the extent of benefit derived by the poor from PDS?
2. How is the subsidy distributed among expenditure/ income groups?

For answering the first question, we distributed the households in Andhra Pradesh as well as Orissa : (a) by per capita expenditure group, (b) by per capita cultivated area, (c) by occupational group, (d) by per capita consumption of rice purchased from fair price shops and (e) number of white/BPL and pink/APL card holders.

Number of white/BPL card holders as is to be expected in tribal areas was more in both A.P. and Orissa. In A.P., 191 out of 199 are white card holders and 8 pink card holders.[2] In Orissa, the corresponding numbers were 99 and 1. Estimation of household monthly per capita expenditure group for A.P. and Orissa is given in Table 6.3. The poverty of Orissa tribal areas as compared to poverty in Andhra Pradesh tribal area is seen from the data. The poverty is measured by taking Rs. 20 per month as a norm for 1960-61 prices. Applying CPIAL (Consumer Price Index for Agricultural Labourers) index for 1996-97 which was 1268, the per capita monthly consumption expenditure at 1996-97 prices will be of the order of Rs. 253. The households below poverty formed 86 per cent in Orissa, a comparative figure for Andhra Pradesh is 60.3 per cent.

## 6.4. Distribution of Households by Type of Purchase

The households are distributed by source of purchase *i.e.* (1) household purchasing PDS rice only, (2) purchasing from open market only and (3) purchasing from both PDS and open market. No household reported purchase from PDS only in A.P. and only 1 household reported purchase from PDS only in Orissa (Table 6.3). Similarly, purchase from open market only are rare. Only two households in A.P. and 1 household in Orissa reported purchase from open market only. Almost all households reported purchase of rice from both PDS and open market both in A.P. and Orissa. Even the poorest households is found to purchase from PDS. The availability of PDS is only cash purchases. There are very few leakages in PDS with regard to rice, though in A.P. the tribal household is found to purchase rice from PDS even if it means foregoing a day's wage.

Quantity purchase from PDS and open market for A.P. and Orissa by expenditure groups is shown in Table 6.4. The share of PDS purchases in the total purchases of rice as well as total cereals is also shown. For A.P. percentage of PDS purchase in total purchases of rice is almost same for every group. PDS share in total rice purchase was around 30 per cent in Andhra Pradesh. In Orissa, the corresponding figure was only 22 per cent. PDS rice purchase as a percentage of total cereal purchase was around 22 per cent for A.P. and around 18 per cent for Orissa.

Per capita quantity purchase for PDS and subsidy by expenditure group-wise shown in Table 6.5. Per capita consumption of rice from PDS was found to vary with the size of expenditure per capita. The poorest got less quantity per capita from PDS as compared to those above the poverty line. PDS price in Andhra Pradesh was revised upward with effect from 1996-97 from Rs. 2 per kg. to Rs. 3.50 per kg. The open market prices ranged around Rs. 7 per kg. Open market price paid by the poorer households was less than that paid by those above the poverty line because of the quality differences. The ceiling on PDS availability per household of 5 members is 20 kg. The ceiling of each individual with a household is 4 kg. Per capita consumption of rice from PDS in A.P. is maximum of 4 kg. But none of the groups reached this level of per capita consumption. Those above the poverty line were close to it. The poorest households could not buy the targetted quantity of 4 kgs. per head because of the non-availability of supplies in the fair price shop coupled with difficulties in mobilising cash when the stocks are available in the fair price shops. As a result, subsidy is regressive. Those above the poverty line got double the subsidy per capita obtained by the poorest households.

**Table 6.3: Distribution of Households by Source of Purchase and by MPCE Group in Orissa and Andhra Pradesh**

| | Andhra Pradesh | | | | | | Orissa | | | | | |
|---|---|---|---|---|---|---|---|---|---|---|---|---|
| MPCE (in Rs.) | Households purchasing PDS only | No. of persons | Purchasing from open market only | No. of persons | Purchasing from both PDS and open market | No. of persons | Household purchasing PDS only | No. of persons | Purchasing from open market | No. of persons | Purchasing from both PDS and open market | No. of persons |
| 1 | 2 | 3 | 4 | 5 | 6 | 7 | 8 | 9 | 10 | 11 | 12 | 13 |
| 0-65 | 0 | 0 | 0 | 0 | 0 | 0 | 1 | 1 | 0 | 0 | 8 | 38 (9.45) |
| 65-80 | 0 | 0 | 0 | 0 | 0 | 0 | 0 | 0 | 0 | 0 | 7 | 32 (7.96) |
| 80-95 | 0 | 0 | 0 | 0 | 0 | 0 | 0 | 0 | 0 | 0 | 4 | 14 (3.48) |
| 95-110 | 0 | 0 | 0 | 0 | 1 | 8 (0.87) | 0 | 0 | 1 | 3 | 7 | 29 (7.2) |
| 110-125 | 0 | 0 | 0 | 0 | 0 | 0 (0.00) | 0 | 0 | 0 | 0 | 13 | 55 (13.68) |

| | | | | | | | | | | | | |
|---|---|---|---|---|---|---|---|---|---|---|---|---|
| 125-140 | 0 | 0 | 0 | 0 | 4 | 30 (3.25) | 0 | 0 | 0 | 0 | 8 | 36 (8.96) |
| 140-160 | 0 | 0 | 0 | 0 | 10 | 66 (7.16) | 0 | 0 | 0 | 0 | 14 | 56 (13.93) |
| 160-180 | 0 | 0 | 0 | 0 | 9 | 56 (6.07) | 0 | 0 | 0 | 0 | 7 | 26 (6.47) |
| 180-215 | 0 | 0 | 1 | 8 | 48 | 267 (28.96) | 0 | 0 | 0 | 0 | 13 | 56 (13.93) |
| 215-253 | 0 | 0 | 0 | 0 | 47 | 295 (32.00) | 0 | 0 | 0 | 0 | 3 | 39 (9.70) |
| 253-280 | 0 | 0 | 0 | 0 | 19 | | 0 | 0 | 0 | 0 | 9 | |
| 280-385 | 0 | 0 | 1 | 7 | 48 | 172 (18.66) | 0 | 0 | 0 | 0 | 4 | 16 (3.98) |
| above 385 | 0 | 0 | 0 | 0 | 11 | 28 (3.04) | 0 | 0 | 0 | 0 | 1 | 5 (1.24) |

Figures in brackets relating to number of persons in that group as a percentage of total number of persons in the sample as a whole.

### Table 6.4: Quantity Purchased from PDS and Open Market for Andhra Pradesh and Orissa in 1996-97 by MPCE Group

| MPCE | Andhra Pradesh | | | | | | | Orissa | | | | | | |
|---|---|---|---|---|---|---|---|---|---|---|---|---|---|---|
| | Quantity of rice pur-chased from PDS (in kgs.) | Quantity of rice pur-chased from open market (in kgs.) | Other millets con-sumed (in kgs.) | Total rice (in kgs.) | Total cereals (in kgs.) | PDS rice as a % of total rice | PDS rice as a% of total cereals | Quantity of rice purchased from PDS (in kgs.) | Quantity of rice pur-chased from open market (in kgs.) | Other millets con-sumed (in kgs.) | Total rice | Total cereals | PDS rice as a % of total rice | PDS rice as a % of total cereals |
| 0-65 | 0 | 0 | 0 | 0 | 0 | 0 | 0 | 90.00 | 140.00 | 56.00 | 230.00 | 286.00 | 39.13 | 31.47 |
| 65-80 | 0 | 0 | 0 | 0 | 0 | 0 | 0 | 70.00 | 115.00 | 58.00 | 185.00 | 243.00 | 37.84 | 28.81 |
| 80-95 | 0 | 0 | 0 | 0 | 0 | 0 | 0 | 40.00 | 65.00 | 35.00 | 105.00 | 140.00 | 38.09 | 28.57 |
| 95-110 | 16.00 | 40.00 | 15.00 | 56.00 | 71.00 | 28.60 | 22.53 | 70.00 | 190.00 | 74.00 | 260.00 | 334.00 | 26.92 | 20.96 |
| 110-125 | 0 | 0 | 0 | 0 | 0 | 0 | 0 | 130.00 | 425.00 | 180.00 | 555.00 | 735.00 | 23.42 | 17.69 |
| 125-140 | 56.00 | 136.00 | 173.00 | 192.00 | 365.00 | 29.17 | 15.34 | 80.00 | 305.00 | 95.00 | 385.00 | 480.00 | 20.78 | 16.67 |
| 140-160 | 180.00 | 338.00 | 397.00 | 518.00 | 915.00 | 34.75 | 19.70 | 140.00 | 455.00 | 152.00 | 595.00 | 747.00 | 23.53 | 18.74 |
| 160-180 | 152.00 | 373.00 | 210.00 | 525.00 | 735.00 | 28.95 | 20.70 | 70.00 | 300.00 | 65.00 | 370.00 | 435.00 | 18.92 | 16.10 |
| 180-215 | 812.00 | 1706.00 | 155.00 | 2518.00 | 2673.00 | 32.25 | 30.40 | 130.00 | 710.00 | 155.00 | 840.00 | 995.00 | 15.48 | 13.10 |
| 215-280 | 1037.00 | 2328.00 | 2049.00 | 3365.00 | 5414.00 | 30.82 | 19.15 | 120.00 | 530.00 | 164.00 | 650.00 | 814.00 | 18.46 | 14.74 |
| 280-385 | 572.00 | 1741.00 | 723.00 | 2313.00 | 3036.00 | 24.73 | 18.84 | 40.00 | 270.00 | 70.00 | 310.00 | 380.00 | 12.90 | 10.53 |
| Above 385 | 108.00 | 272.00 | 35.00 | 380.00 | 415.00 | 28.43 | 26.02 | 10.00 | 10.00 | 10.00 | 20.00 | 30.00 | 50.00 | 33.33 |
| | 2933.00 | 6934.00 | 3757.00 | 9867.00 | 13624.00 | 29.73 | 21.53 | 990.00 | 3515.00 | 1114.00 | 4505.00 | 5619.00 | 21.97 | 17.62 |

**Table 6.5: Per Capita Consumption of PDS Rice and Subsidy Level by Expenditure Group**

| MPCE | Andhra Pradesh | | | | Orissa | | | |
|---|---|---|---|---|---|---|---|---|
| | Per capita constump-tion of rice from PDS in kgs. of rice (in Rs.) | Difference between PDS price to open market price | Subsidy per person | Subsidy per house-hold | Per capita consump-tion of rice from PDS in kgs. of rice (in Rs.) | Difference between PDS price to open market price | Subsidy per person | Subsidy per household |
| 0-65 | 0 | 0 | 0 | 0 | 2.31 | 5.20 | 12.00 | 52.00 |
| 65-80 | 0 | 0 | 0 | 0 | 2.20 | 6.00 | 13.20 | 60.00 |
| 80-95 | 0 | 0 | 0 | 0 | 2.90 | 5.00 | 14.50 | 50.00 |
| 95-110 | 2.00 | 3.5 | 7.00 | 56.00 | 2.20 | 5.10 | 11.20 | 46.90 |
| 110-125 | 0 | 0 | 0 | 0 | 2.36 | 5.45 | 12.90 | 54.50 |
| 125-140 | 1.87 | 3.40 | 6.40 | 47.50 | 2.22 | 5.55 | 12.30 | 55.50 |
| 140-160 | 2.73 | 3.35 | 9.15 | 60.30 | 2.50 | 6.60 | 16.50 | 66.00 |
| 160-180 | 2.71 | 3.40 | 9.30 | 57.33 | 2.70 | 5.40 | 14.58 | 54.00 |
| 180-215 | 3.04 | 3.3 | 10.03 | 54.67 | 2.32 | 5.50 | 12.76 | 55.00 |
| 215-280 | 3.52 | 3.4 | 11.97 | 53.41 | 3.10 | 5.50 | 17.10 | 55.00 |
| 280-385 | 3.33 | 3.7 | 12.32 | 43.20 | 2.50 | 5.50 | 13.75 | 55.00 |
| Above 385 | 3.85 | 3.8 | 14.63 | 37.30 | 2.00 | 5.00 | 10.00 | 50.00 |
| | 3.10 | 3.45 | 10.70 | 50.85 | 2.44 | 5.62 | 13.70 | 55.64 |

In Orissa, a household below poverty line is eligible to purchase only 10 kgs. of rice irrespective of the size of the household. PDS rice consumption per capita was 2.44 per kg. per month. The total rice purchased per capita per month was more in Orissa than in Andhra Pradesh. The difference between PDS price and open market price is much more because the PDS price continues to be lower in Orissa at around Rs. 2 per kg.[3] Unlike in Andhra Pradesh, subsidy per person is more among the poorer groups than those above the poverty line. Per capita purchase of PDS rice was higher among the poor groups and lower among the above poverty group because of the size of the family was larger than among the BPL.

### 6.5. Distribution of Households by Per Capita Cultivated Land

We also examined PDS purchased by size of cultivated land holding. We should expect the landless households to purchase more from the PDS than others who are cultivators and have home produce to consume. The facts for both Andhra Pradesh and Orissa suggest the contrary. Purchase from PDS by the landless and small holders below one acre are less than the corresponding purchases by households possessing more than one acre. Thus those who have more resources get more benefit from PDS than those with less resources.

Even by occupational groups, it is the poorly paid occupations such as agricultural labourers who get less benefit from PDS than others. Per capita purchase of PDS for rice is lowest for agricultural labourers in Andhra Pradesh. In Orissa per capita purchase for agricultural labour from PDS is found to be the highest. Among eight villages in Andhra Pradesh per capita consumption rice from PDS varies from 2.70 kgs. in Pedduru to 3.40 kgs. in Pothangi. Several factors account for the variations. These include the following :

1. Proximity of the fair price shop, whether located in the village or nearby or distantly located;
2. Whether supplies to fair price shop are regular and adequate;
3. Whether fair price shop operations are fair *i.e.* regularity

in opening the fair price shop, use of proper weights and measures etc.;

4. The difference between open market price and fair price shop price; and
5. The market dependence of the households in the village.

Open market price in the tribal villages of Andhra Pradesh ranged between Rs. 6.60 in Besupuram and Rs. 8.00 in Sumpangput.

In Orissa villages, range of variation is much less and the level of open market prices is also lower. The level ranges between Rs. 7.10 in Borikhal and Rs. 7.50 in Telengapodar. Surprisingly the village on road side in Orissa recorded higher prices than the interior villages, possibly, more than the cost factor, the demand factor is relevant to explain the variations in open market prices.

In Andhra Pradesh villages, the variations in open market prices are explainable in terms of market centres. For instance, the villages Pedduru and Kovelapalem are interior villages and in these, open market price of rice is found to be higher than the Cheruvuru and Veeravaram which are found to be closer to the market centres.

### 6.6. PDS other than Rice

Fair price shops, also distribute sugar and Kerosene in tribal villages. But in Orissa villages no sugar is consumed. In Andhra villages household consuming sugar vary from 0.00 percentage in Kovelapalem and 100 per cent in Kumaritham and Besupuram. Per capita sugar consumption from PDS is low ranges from 0.11 kgs. per month in Veeravaram village to 0.26 in Besupuram and Kumaritham villages (Table 6.6). Lighting requirements of tribals are limited for many tribal households. As in the case of other commodities, use of kerosene from PDS is much more limited in Orissa villages than Andhra villages.

### 6.7. Domestic Requirement of Tribals and the Role of PDS Summarised

It is important to meet the domestic requirements of tribals since the tribals are forced to borrow and sell their produce at throw away prices to the creditors. For this reason the GCC

**Table 6.6: Percentage of Persons Purchasing from PDS of Sugar and Kerosene and Per Capita Purchase of Sugar and Kerosene**

| Village | Sugar (%) | Kerosene (%) | Per capita Sugar purchased (in kgs.) | Per capita Kerosene purchased (in kgs.) |
|---|---|---|---|---|
| **Andhra Pradesh** | | | | |
| Kumaritham | 100.00 | 56.00 | 0.26 | 0.52 |
| Sumpangipur | 96.00 | 88.00 | 0.21 | 0.60 |
| Pothangi | 96.00 | 88.00 | 0.23 | 0.70 |
| Besupuram | 100.00 | 96.00 | 0.26 | 0.76 |
| Cheruvuru | 88.00 | 96.00 | 0.22 | 1.12 |
| Pedduru | 68.00 | 92.00 | 0.14 | 0.96 |
| Veeravaram | 16.00 | 100.00 | 0.11 | 1.28 |
| Kovelapalem | 0.00 | 100.00 | 0.00 | 1.32 |
| **Orissa** | | | | |
| Telengapodar | 0.00 | 56.00 | 0.00 | 0.46 |
| Borikhal | 0.00 | 76.00 | 0.00 | 0.54 |
| Minapai | 0.00 | 92.00 | 0.00 | 0.54 |

provides consumption credit to the landless tribals who are mainly dependent on collection of MFP for their sustenance during the lean season. It operates 850 fair price shops at important marketing centres. As against this TDCC in Orissa operates 74 fair price shops. All the household surveys bring out the better performance of PDS in Andhra Pradesh compared to Orissa. Even within A.P. only 30 per cent of the quantity is purchased from the PDS. Many reasons are attributed for this situation. The most important reason is "quantity not being available". This suggests the system has to be improved.

## SUMMARY

One of the objectives of GCC in Andhra Pradesh and TDCC in Orissa is supply of essential commodities under PDS through Domestic Requirement Depots to tribals at fair and reasonable prices. This chapter observed the relative performance of GCC and TDCC. Judged by the number of DR Depots and advances made, GCC perfomance in Andhra Pradesh is found to be better. This chapter also examined the findings of NSS 42 Round (July 1986-June 1987) and 44th Round (July 1988-June 1989) for Andhra Pradesh and Orissa. NSS 42nd Round refers to both tribals and non-tribals and this suggested that the performance of Andhra Pradesh was much better. 44th Round of NSS pertain only to tribals and even this suggested that the performance of PDS in tribal areas of Andhra Pradesh was much better than the performance of Orissa.

Finally the findings of our survey are brought together to throw light on two important issues : (1) extent of benefit derived by the poor from the PDS; (2) the subsidies distributed among expenditure/income groups.

The number of white card holders formed almost 100 per cent in both the areas. The households below poverty line formed 86 per cent in Orissa and 60 per cent in Andhra Pradesh tribal areas.

Almost every household is found to participate in PDS both in Orissa and Andhra Pradesh. Poorest households in Andhra Pradesh do not buy the targetted quantity of 4 kgs. per head because of non-availability of supplies in the fair price shops. Those above the poverty line were close to the targetted quantity. As a result, subsidy is regressive. In Orissa, which is under the Revamped Public Distribution System, the poorer people are found to purchase more than those above the poverty line from PDS. Distribution of households by per capita cultivated land and occupational group showed that landless and marginal farmers got less benefit from the PDS.

Several factors accounted for the variations in the extent of participation in PDS : (1) proximity of the fair price shop to beneficiaries; (2) regularity and adequacy of supply in fair price shops; (3) difference between fair price shop price and open market price; (4) use of proper weights and measures; (5) the market dependence of the households in the village.

The survey results suggested that more than the demand factor, supply factors are relevant to an explanation of proper functioning of fair price shops.

## NOTES

1. Government of India, NSSO (1994), *Sarvekshana*, Issue No. 59, Vol. No. XVII, No. 4, April-June, p. 44.
2. All those below Rs. 12,000.00 per household income per annum are considered to below poverty line in A.P.
3. The PDS was revamped in December 1996. As per revamped PDS, PDS is envisaged to serve a population of 2000. Under RPDS, the fair price shops are expected to provide other essential items such as : tea, soap, pulses and iodized salt etc. to households. States would identify households below poverty line (BPL). They would be issued 10 kgs. of foodgrains per month per family at prices less than the Central Issue Price (CIP). Supply of foodgrains for the BPL at 10 kgs. per month per family shall be guaranteed to States by Central. Additional quantities required by States would depend on the availability of stocks in the Central pool. Subsidised foodgrains will also be issued to all beneficiaries under the EAS/Jawahar Rojgar Yojana as per guidelines at the rate of 1 kg. per manday for which food coupons would be issued to beneficiaries for exchanging at FPS. Population above the poverty line (non-poor) now under PDS to continue to receive normal entitlement at the full CIP.

# 7

# Value Addition to Tribal Produce in GCC Area of Andhra Pradesh and in Orissa

## SECTION-I

### 7.1. Value Addition to Tribal Produce in GCC Area of Andhra Pradesh

Value addition to tribal produce is important for several reasons : firstly, it contributes to higher levels of employment and income; and secondly, the processing industry set-up in tribal areas could alter the tribal life patterns for better. Tribal will get a better price and their share will go up. Cost on transport is reduced if produce is sold after processing. Similarly cost on storage will be reduced.

Many commodities are sold without any processing at the tribal level. For instance, Gum is the most important MFP item constituting about 35.41 per cent of the total value of procurement of GCC during 1995-96. Volume of procurement and sale had increased multifold during the past 20 years. Tribals do not grade the Gum due to lack of awareness of the differential prices. The GCC staff grades the Gum at the purchasing point according to their specifications.

Gum is widely used in different industries. Finer varieties of Gum are used in classification of liquors, finishing of silk and preparation of water colours. Intermediate Gums are used in confectionaries, cosmetics, pharmaceuticals and printing inks in sizing and finishing textile fabrics and dyeing.

GCC engaged scientists as technical advisors to study the quality of gum collected and suggest suitable methods to improve the quality. It organised the gum pickers into small groups called Girijan Gum Pickers Association (GGPA) at the village level. It created a gum extension fund out of which all expenses towards training are met. It also increase the gum procurement prices, the increase in prices being higher for quality gums. Simultaneously, GCC also engaged scientists for research and development towards value addition of forest produce. To explain the benefits of research and development to the tribals, GCC decided to organise meetings of representatives of various GGPAs. In February, 1994 GGPAs unanimously decided to form a trust at the State level called Kovel Foundation, a trust by the indigenous people for research in sustainable technologies. Its major objectives are as follows :

(1) to realise higher prices for gum and other forest produce through value addition;

(2) to provide training and extension to forest produce collectors so as to enhance the quality and range of the forest produce collected thereby increasing the incomes realised and to protect the forest resources; and

(3) to voice the grievances of the tribals at appropriate fora and act as their spokesperson.

In addition to these efforts GCC has started a retail market department which serves 12 major cities in Andhra Pradesh. Above 15 products are being offered to consumers in various forms and pack sizes. Items such as tamarind, redgram, blackgram, greengram etc. purchased from the tribals are being supplied to houses and ashram schools after processing and converting into dhals. Wild Brooms are supplied after grading to Municipal Corporations of Hyderabad and Secunderabad and tamarind is being supplied to jail institutions throughout the State to obtain assured marketing and stable prices.

### 7.2. The Role of ITDAs and Voluntary Organisations in Value Addition to Tribal Produce

In addition to the marketing initiatives and research and development efforts to obtain better prices to the tribal products, the GCC has taken up processing some important commodities it has been procuring over years from the tribals to add value to the products. GCC has set-up new honey processing plant at

Rajahmundry duly revamping the age-old unit at Narasipatnam and shifting the machinery to Rajahmundry. Another most modern honey processing plant which is first of its kind in the country is installed at Araku. Shikakai and soapnut powder manufacturing unit is opened at Rajahmundry. Soap making units at Vizianagaram and Utnoor and soap base unit at Nirmal have also been set-up to add value to the non-edible oil seeds procured by the corporation.

In addition to the efforts of the GCC, some ITDAs and voluntary organisations have also taken up processing of some MFP items on a modest scale here and there involving the tribals to add value to the produce collected by the tribals in different parts of the State. A voluntary organisation called ARTIC, is operating in the Seethampeta Mandal area in Srikakulam district. It encourages value addition to tamarind procured individually and also common groves by the tribals in the area. Another note-worthy effort in the direction of value addition has been made by ITDA, Bhadrachalam in Khammam district. Similarly, ITDA, Parvathipuram organises training programme for tribal women who collect kendu leaves, to roll beedis. The Bhagavatula Charitable Trust is another voluntary organisation engaged in the value addition of MFP in Visakhapatnam district. The trust started adda leaf project in 1979 with rural women who make adda leaf plates.

### 7.3. Conclusion on Value Addition by GCC

So far the efforts at value addition by GCC, Government and voluntary agencies have touched only a fringe of the vast potential of MFP available in the forest tracts in the State. This is a very significant effort in the direction of raising the status of the tribal from MFP collector to the producer of finished goods out of MFP. Though some good work in the direction of value addition has been attempted in selected tribal pockets, these efforts need to be intensified in other tribal areas also.

Most of the industrial units established by the GCC are located in the urban areas far away from the tribal tracts and the tribal participation in the processing activities is very minimal because of its high technical orientation. The time has now come to project the tribal as the manufacturer of MFP based finished products specially those that do not require heavy machinery or sophisticated technology which the tribal at present cannot absorb and those that cannot be manufactured on a cottage or village industry basis. For this, better information is needed on the values of selected commodities in village, district, national and international markets.

**SECTION-II**

## 7.4. Value Addition to Tribal Produce in Orissa

In Orissa State a number of forest based industries have been set-up since the '60s. The Utkal Forest Products Ltd., a joint venture of the Government and private industry, was already referred to. The project envisages the systematic collection of MFP with processing on custom milling basis by existing expellers and solvent extraction units in the State. A publication of the Principal Chief Conservator of Forests lists 56 forest based industries operating in the Orissa State.[1] But the employment potential of these industries is limited, except the Orient Paper Mills, Brajrajnagar, Sambalpur, Titagarh Paper Mills, J.K. Paper Mills, which provide employment of more than 1000, in all other industries the employment creation is less than 100. They do not also add to the incomes of the tribals since most of the industries are located in towns like Cuttack.

With the nationalisation of kendu leaves in 1973, the Forest Department was entrusted with collection and processing of kendu leaves and the marketing responsibilities was with OFDC. Very little of kendu leaves is processed into beedi form within the State. As a result the value addition is minor.

In respect of sal seed, it was nationalised in 1983 and the OFDC and TDCC got the rights for sal seed trade. But due to mismanagement, both these Government organisations incurred losses. The Government handed over the right to procurement and processing of sal seed to four private oil entities. Sal seed collection provides sustenance to a number of people. On an average, one man collects upto 7 kg. a day and needs 2-3 days for primary processing. The private processing units, to which the OFDC and TDCC have entrusted the task, delay in appointing sub-agents to collect until the primary collectors are impatient to sell at whatever price is offered.

In respect of bamboo, division-wise lease was granted to four paper mills on the basis of royalties and further provision of rebate on royalties. In 1993 the Government allowed the private sector industry to get into the forest and start action in connection with the operation of bamboo coupes in advance.

By this notification the control of forests passed from OFDC to private paper mills. The mills are indulging in un-scientific cutting and are getting a piece at 15 paise, while the communities living on bamboo products have to pay Rs. 4.30 to Rs. 10.30 a piece at the time of auction. The labourers also get low wages.

Mohwa flower has customary uses in making country liquor. Private traders have been dominating Mohwa flower trade since long. TDCC got the agency right over procurement and marketing in 1980. In 1991 it became nationalised. It lost its market drastically following the ban on country liquor-making. TDCC also did not collect sufficient quantity. Lakhs of quintals of Mohwa flower collected by common people got wasted.

Recently tamarind in Rayagada division on which TDCC had an exclusive right has been taken away and handed over to M/s. Doki Satyanarayana China Guruvulu, a private trader. He does not have a processing plant. He collects tamarind at a price ranging from Rs. 2 to Rs. 2.25 per kg. and after removing kernel, sells the deseeded tamarind at Rs. 12 per kg. and seed at Rs. 3.50 per kg. mostly to one Mahindra International of Calcutta. Thus even the limited processing does not benefit the tribals.

Both OFDC and TDCC have deviated from their objectives of attaining scientific harvesting and management of forest produce as well as encouraging and establishing forest based industries. General impression from available literature does not support any appreciable industries utilising forest resources being established to cater to the needs of primary collectors.

Secondly, the performance of the corporation in training the tribals on the state of the art of technology in collecting/ harvesting the produce so as to minimise time and risk or maximise output or combination of both, is un-impressive. OFDC has done little to utilise the vast quantity of medicinal herbs and aromatic grass.

## 7.5. Conclusions : TDCC and OFDC Role in Adding to Value of Tribal Produce

MFP's like genduli gum and other gums, sal resins, lac, tanning and dyeing stuffs like myrobalans, tassar cocoons, tamarind seed cover, cleaning and marking nuts etc. require minor processing. Such processing techniques are simple enough to be learnt or oriented with by the primary collectors, tribals. Hence, the business of such items of MFP by TDCC or any private licensee exclusively is not proper when viewed from the tribals' income point of view. Cottage industries by the primary collectors need to be supported with both finance and techniques to produce certain finished items, value added items of course. It shall fetch better income to tribals. There should be no monopoly of TDCC in this process.

All along it has been the practice with the industrial policy planning to go for big industries. In most of the cases the results have been discouraging. This resulted in loss and wastage or blockade of capital and labour.

The best alternative can be area based small scale industries.

There is ample scope for small industrial units for :

- oil drilling and soap manufacturing;
- pharmaceutical and cosmetics manufacturing;
- rope, press board/straw board, fibre works etc.
- food products and animal food;
- starching material for textiles and cloth weaving and fibre processing;
- varnish (wood finish) and polish manufacturing.

Keeping pace with the spirit of the National Forest Policy and the repeated Government Policy of 'power to people' the management and control of kendu leaves and bamboo forest should be vested with the VSS (*Vana Samrakshana Samities*) under JFM (Joint Forest Management) or with the Gram Sabha.

OFDC has to correct and rectify in the conduct of its officials inasmuch as in its restructuring. Moreover, it ought to adhere to its objectives like scientific management of forest, facilitating and establishing forest based industries.

TDCC needs to be reorganised as only a promotional agency. Particularly, it should act as a catalytic body in supplying technology to the primary collectors and in marketing the processed product manufactured by these collectors.

NGOs have a challenging role to play in, forming a kind of producers associations, providing market information, establishing contact between technology seekers and technology givers, influencing policy making etc. And most important, the NGOs should not be involved in a haphazard way as the tribals will be looking towards them on a continuous basis on any particular issue.

As per the proceedings of the meeting held in the chamber of Chief Secretary on 13-3-1995 on collection and processing of MFP it was decided to entrust the processing of MFP to women groups and all possible support should be extended to these groups by the State Government.

**SUMMARY**

This chapter reviewed the value addition to tribal produce in the GCC area of Andhra Pradesh and in Orissa. In GCC area of Andhra Pradesh, several measures have been taken in recent years by GCC to enhance the value addition of tribal produce. So far the efforts at value addition by GCC, Government and voluntary organisations touched only a fringe of the problem. In Orissa, number of forest based industries have been set-up since 1960s, but these are mostly located in the towns like Cuttack and their impact on employment and income levels of tribals is negligible. For instance, very little of kendu leaves is processed into beedi from within the State. Similarly, in sal seed, the primary collectors did not benefit from the private processing unit. In respect of bamboo also, the mills indulge in unscientific cutting and get bamboo at a low price while the tribal communities pay several multiples of the price paid by the mills. In respect of mohawa flower, which is nationalised, TDCC did not collect sufficient quantity. The case of tamarind suggests that processing of tamarind by private individuals does not help the tribal in getting a better price. Further, both OFDC and TDCC have failed in providing training in the skills of processing to the tribals. OFDC has done very little to utilise medicinal herbs and aromatic grass. Finally, this chapter closes by providing an alternative to current practices in terms of area based small scale industries and a policy of "power to people". NGOs have a challenging role in forming a kind of producers association, providing marketing information, establishing contact between technology seekers and technology givers and influencing policy making bodies.

## NOTE

1. Government of Orissa, Office of the Principal Chief Conservator of Forests, Orissa, *A Decade of Forestry in Orissa, 1981-1990*, Bhubaneswar, pp. 84-87.

# 8

# Employment, Income and Quality of Life of Tribals in Andhra Pradesh and Orissa

## SECTION-I

### 8.1. Agro-Economic Research Centre's Study on MFP in the Tribal Economy of Andhra Pradesh : 1982-83

As part of the study, agro-economic research centre examined the significance of MFP in the employment and research income of the tribal households. This study was conducted in 1982-83 in three tribal regions of Andhra Pradesh : (1) Araku region of Visakhapatnam district; (2) Utnoor region of Adilabad district; and (3) Nallamalai region of Kurnool district. In each region 40 households were chosen. In Araku region, 4 villages around Sunkarimetta shandy were chosen for detailed study. The 40 sample households chosen in the four villages covered the major tribes Khond, Konda Dora, Parangi and Porja. The study of work participation rates revealed that among adult males and adult females more than 90 per cent are found to work. Among children 23 per cent are found to work. Work participation rates among adult females were higher than adult males. Relationship between landlessness and work participation rates had shown the work participation rates the highest for the landless groups both among males and females. The overall work participation rate was 65.67 per cent. Among 40 sample households in Araku division only three were landless. The operated area per cultivator is around 3 acres. Most of it was owned area under self-cultivation. Major portion of it is unirrigated area.

Podu land formed 43 per cent of the total evaluated land. All the 40 households are engaged in collection of MFP. One half of the households are engaged in forest labour besides collection of MFP. MFP accounted for 9 per cent of the total income and yielded much less as a percentage of total income as compared to cultivation, agricultural labour and forest labour. Collection of MFP accounted for the maximum in the first round of investigation *i.e.* January to May. It yielded very little in November to December. In the second round *i.e.* June to October it yielded roughly more than 1/3 of the income obtained in January to May.

Information on employment of individual worker was collected for the preceding week from the date of interview in each round. Adult males work for five days for a week, adult females work for 5.40 days and children work for 2.61 days. Employment of children was maximum in the first round. The distribution of employment between different types of avocations in which the tribal workers are engaged indicated that agriculture is the predominant avocation in which most of the workers are employed.

In Utnoor region, tribes studied are Nayakpod, Gond and Kalama of which Nayakpods formed the majority. The landless formed the majority of the households chosen; 25 out of 40 households are landless. Among the cultivating households, owner cultivators form the dominant majority. The average size of holding is 0.83 acres. Among the sample households, 2/3 of the land held is unirrigated. Agricultural labour and collection and sale of MFP were the main occupation for most of the households. 39 out of 40 households are engaged in sale and collection of MFP. It accounted for 73.68 per cent of the total income derived from different activities. Agricultural labour accounted for only 16.75 per cent of total income and cultivation 3.68 per cent. Gum formed 90 per cent of the MFP collected by the tribal households. Number of days employed (eight hours) per worker were 4.64 for adult males and 3.69 for adult females and 2.69 for children. Dependence on Forest on income is much higher in Utnoor region when compared to Araku region (Table 8.1).

In Nallamalai region, Chenchus are the major tribe. All the 4 villages in the sample are inhabited exclusively by the

Chenchus. Average size of the household of the Chenchus is much larger 5.57 against 5.02 in Araku and 4.80 in Utnoor region. Number of landless households are also much larger 32 out of 40. The information on occupational pattern indicated that collection and sale of various MFP items formed the main occupation of the 40 households. Number of eight-hour-day of employment per worker per week was the lowest in Nallamalai region 2.26 for adult males, 1.11 for adult females. Dependence on minor forest produce as a percentage of total employment is the highest in Nallamalai region.

One major inference of the study is the tribal households still depend heavily on the collection of MFP particularly in the areas in which agriculture has not developed. It constitutes the major occupation in all most all the sample tribal households in Telangana and Rayalaseema regions. In the coastal region of A.P., where cultivation of coffee and sericulture plantations, and allied activities have developed, and where also there have been a rapid degradation of forests in recent years. MFP has ceased to be a major occupation.

### 8.2. The Comprehensive Living Conditions of Tribals : NSS 44th Round (July 1988-June 1989)

The comprehensive living conditions of tribals was conducted by the NSSO in its 44th Round (July 1988-June 1989) with the objective of generating estimates on various characteristics for each major tribe separately as well as the tribal population as a whole. The tribal population covered in the survey consisted of the members of S.T. declared under the article 342 of the Constitution of India. The objective of the study was to examine the living conditions of tribals covering mainly the level of living and economic activities. The level of living was assessed in terms of household consumption, housing condition, social consumption, household assets and liabilities, education, morbidity etc. The economic activities of the tribes was studied through information from the enterprise accounts, agricultural operations, landholdings, alienation of land, marketing of produce, dependence on forest and employment and unemployment. Information was also collected on the disparity in living conditions between the tribals and

**Table 8.1: Employment Days Per Week within a Tribal Household — AERC Data (1982-83)**

| Region | Adult males | % of difference | Adult females | % of difference | Children | % of difference |
|---|---|---|---|---|---|---|
| **Araku** | | | | | | |
| Total | 5.07 | 5.33 | 5.39 | 9.46 | 2.61 | 4.59 |
| Collection of MFP | — | | — | | 0.12 | |
| Forest labour | 0.27 | | 0.43 | | 0.12 | |
| Collection of Firewood | 0.02 | | 0.08 | | — | |
| **Utnoor** | | | | | | |
| Total | 4.64 | 41.8 | 3.68 | 30.16 | 2.69 | 18.96 |
| Collection of MFP | 1.94 | | 1.11 | | 0.51 | |
| Forest labour | 0.21 | | 0.09 | | 0.42 | |
| Collection of Firewood | — | | — | | — | |
| **Nallamalai** | | | | | | |
| Total | 2.26 | 85.8 | 1.11 | 67.57 | 2.33 | 49.78 |
| Collection of MFP | 1.94 | | 0.75 | | 1.16 | |
| Forest labour | 0.26 | | — | | 0.28 | |
| Collection of Firewood | — | | — | | — | |

non-tribals and the problem stemming from migration to non-tribal areas in the rural sector.

The survey was conducted in whole of India except in Ladakh and Kargil districts in Jammu and Kashmir. We present in Table 8.2 the details compiled from the NSSO for Andhra Pradesh and Orissa.

Literacy and health care are critical variables for considering the levels of living. By these two variables, Andhra Pradesh's position is much worse than Orissa. But housing conditions are poorer in Orissa: one has to bend and crawl to get into the house. Houses are ill ventilated. Electrified houses form only 2 per cent of the total in Orissa. PDS provides a better access to tribals in A.P. The unemployment rate is lower in A.P. when compared to Orissa. Dependence on MFP for livelihood is much more in A.P. Shifting cultivation is of the same order both in A.P. and Orissa. Orissa records much more self-employment than A.P. Average value of assets per household, debt per household and percentage household reporting loans — all these record higher proportion in A.P.

If housing and poverty are considered indicators of levels of living, Orissa is in much worse position than A.P. But if literacy and health care are considered critical indicators, Orissa should said to be in a better position than A.P. But even here recent indicators like attendance rate of tribal children of age group 5-14 shows A.P. has caught-up with Orissa, since attendance ratios are same in both Orissa and A.P. Thus, several critical indicators suggest that A.P's. position is better than Orissa (Table 8.2).

### 8.3. Consumption Expenditure : Nabakrishna Chowdary Centre for Development Studies, 1992

Nabakrishna Chowdary Centre for Development Studies, Bhubaneswar, Orissa, throws some light on the quality of life, in their study on some MFP in Orissa undertaken in 1992. This study was conducted in undivided districts Kalahandi; Koraput; Mayurbhanj and Phulbani.

In total 7 sample villages were chosen and 207 households were investigated. Except in a couple of villages in all the other villages cultivators formed the majority. Collection of Forest produce was noted in all the villages. Scheduled Tribes formed the major ethnic group in all except one village. When households are distributed according to annual income, except 35 households all the rest were found to fall below Rs. 6000 annual income. Share of forest produce accounted for 70 per cent in one village and around 50 per cent in another. In all the other 5 villages share of forest produce as a percentage of annual income ranged between 24 per cent and 37 per cent. No income was recorded from remittances, agro-based industries, fisheries and crafts. Animal husbandry also accounted for a small proportion of income except in one village in which it accounted for 5 per cent. Major inference drawn from the study

## Table 8.2: Life and Economy of Scheduled Tribe in A.P. and Orissa : 1988-89

| S.No. | Variable | A.P. | | Orissa | |
|---|---|---|---|---|---|
| 1 | 2 | 3 | | 4 | |
| 1. | Tribal population NSS 44th Round (000') | 31,524 | | 60,508 | |
| 2. | % share in All India Tribal population | 5.58 | | 10.72 | |
| 3. | % Tribal population residing in tribal areas | 74.02 | | 78.08 | |
| 4. | Total No. of tribes | 33 | | 62 | |
| 5. | No. of major tribes | 5 | | 9 | |
| 6. | % share of major tribes in the tribal population of the State | 73.78 | | 73.92 | |
| 7. | Names of major tribes and their share in total tribal population of the State | Sugalia | 37.50 | Khond | 19.60 |
| | | Yanadi | 11.74 | Santal | 10.58 |
| | | Yerukula | 10.69 | Savara | 8.33 |
| | | Koya | 8.47 | Munda | 6.87 |
| | | Gond | 5.33 | Gond | 6.81 |
| | | | | Bhottada | 6.36 |
| | | | | Bhumij | 6.23 |
| | | | | Korba | 5.35 |
| | | | | Sabar | 3.78 |
| 8. | Average household size | 4.4 | | 4.7 | |
| 9. | Sex ratio | 985 | | 1011 | |
| 10. | Literacy : No. of literates per 1000 population aged 5 years and above | Male | 242 | 339 | |
| | | Female | 75 | 100 | |
| | | Persons | 161 | 217 | |
| 11. | Attendance ratio of tribal children in the age group 5-14 years | Male | 32.3 | 33.1 | |
| | | Female | 16.3 | 16.8 | |
| | | Persons | 24.9 | 24.87 | |
| 12. | Housing condition : | | | | |
| | (1) % of dwelling units by bending or crawling | 45.5 | | 52.3 | |
| | (2) No adequate ventilation and natural lighting | 19.9 | | 48.5 | |
| | (3) Living rooms shared with animals | 7.1 | | 16.0 | |

(*Contd.*)

**Table 8.2 (*Contd.*)**

| 1 | 2 | 3 | 4 | | |
|---|---|---|---|---|---|
| | (4) % of dwelling units by lighting arrangements : | | | | |
| | (i) None | 1.0 | 2.1 | | |
| | (ii) Electricity | 14.9 | 2.0 | | |
| | (iii) Others | 84.1 | 95.9 | | |
| 13. | (1) % of persons sick (during 30 days) | 9.6 | 10.6 | | |
| | (2) % of sick persons treated | 69.9 | 78.0 | | |
| | (3) % of Govt. agency treated persons | 18.6 | 37.0 | | |
| 14. | % of tribal population with MPCE less than Rs. 125 | 74.7 | 81.7 | | |
| 15. | % of persons purchasing wholly or partly from PDS : | Rice | Wheat | Rice | Wheat |
| | 1. At concessional rate | 27.2 | — | 16.6 | 2.5 |
| | 2. At usual control rate | 33.5 | 0.7 | 6.1 | 0.3 |
| 16. | Employment and unemployment : | | | | |
| | Male : | | | | |
| | 1. Work force participation rate | 61.8 | 64.3 | | |
| | 2. Unemployment rate | 8.0 | 6.0 | | |
| | Female : | | | | |
| | 1. Work force participation rate | 55.8 | 51.8 | | |
| | 2. Unemployment rate | 34.00 | 5.00 | | |
| 17. | Main source of livelihood of Tribal households : | | | | |
| | 1. Collection of MFP | 32.00 | 17.00 | | |
| | 2. Shifting cultivation | 29.00 | 30.00 | | |
| 18. | Percentage distribution of households : | | | | |
| | 1. Agriculture | 48.1 | 40.7 | | |
| | 2. Non-Agriculture | 2.7 | 5.6 | | |

(*Contd.*)

Table 8.2 (*Contd.*)

| 1 | 2 | 3 | 4 |
|---|---|---|---|
| 19. | % of households engaging in different economic activities in self-employment : | | |
| | 1. cultivation | 57.9 | 71.9 |
| | 2. other agricultural activities | 24.8 | 78.7 |
| | 3. manufacturing | 6.8 | 7.4 |
| | 4. any enterprises other than cultivation | 29.3 | 82.2 |
| | 5. any wage employment | 49.3 | 83.1 |
| 20. | % cultivation distribution of households by : | | |
| | 1. no cultivation | 42.1 | 28.1 |
| | 2. shifting cultivation only | 2.9 | 0.5 |
| | 3. settled cultivation only | 48.9 | 67.9 |
| | 4. both | 6.1 | 3.5 |
| 21. | % of cultivating households reporting shifting cultivation | 15.5 | 5.6 |
| 22. | Cultivated area per household (in hect.) | 0.87 | 0.87 |
| 23. | % cultivated land under shifting cultivation | 3.0 | 1.00 |
| 24. | % cultivation of household reporting : | | |
| | 1. leasing out | 3.1 | 2.9 |
| | 2. leasing in | 12.00 | 19.5 |
| 25. | Average value in assets per household (in Rs.) | 18,000.00 | 16,400.00 |
| 26. | Average amount of dues outstanding (Rs.) | 1,330.00 | 361.00 |
| 27. | % cultivation of households reporting outstanding dues | 43.5 | 21.6 |
| 28. | % of households reporting loans : | | |
| | 1. in cash | 41.2 | 15.2 |
| | 2. in kind | 3.4 | 7.9 |
| 29. | % of household reporting institutional loans | 12.9 | 13.9 |
| 30. | % share of institutional loans | 23.2 | 72.1 |

is that the MFP plays a significant role in meeting the basic subsistence needs of a large segment of tribal population directly or indirectly. Household size does not account for the variations in MFP proportions across households but the location of the household and the accessibility of MFP to household is an important factor. Person-day employment from MFP varied from 133.4 days in Koraput to 457 days in Mayurbhanj for a household. Dependence of forest dwellers on forests and its produce is still crucial to households. In Kalahandi, landless households show more employment in Forest activities than other activities. The situation in Koraput is a little different. In Mayurbhanj dependence of landless households is more than average but in Phulbani district landless households are found to have greater dependence on forest and its produce. Female labour days of employment in collection of forest produce are found to be greater than for males in almost all categories of income.

Illiteracy among tribal population has been rampant. In three villages illiterates formed around 80 per cent, in two villages illiterates formed more than 90 per cent. In one village illiterates formed more than 60 per cent. In one of the seven villages illiterates formed less than 60 per cent.

## SECTION-II

In this section we present the findings of our field survey relating to employment, income and quality of life. Survey covered 12 villages, 8 villages in A.P. and 4 villages in Orissa and a sample of 300 households *i.e.* 25 households in each village, comprising all the major tribes *viz.*, Khonds in Orissa State and Konda Reddy, Gonds in Andhra Pradesh.

### 8.4. Work Force Participation Rate: Andhra Pradesh and Orissa

Average size of the tribal households in Andhra Pradesh is 4.71 and 4.06 in Orissa. Average No. of workers per household is 3.20 in Andhra Pradesh while in Orissa 2.41.

Among the tribal population generally all adult women are found to participate in work. Those who do not report participation in work are found among land owning families. In some cases adult women aged above 15 are found to be studying in residential schools. The cases of non-participation of adult women in work are found to be more in Orissa than in A.P. In general 90 per cent of the adult women are found to participate in work while the corresponding figure in Orissa is 80 per cent. Even among adult men we find differences in work participation rates between A.P. and Orissa. 95 per cent of adult men are found to work in A.P. while only 89 per cent are found to work in Orissa (Table 8.3). These differences could be explained by the participation rates of men in schools and colleges. Participation rates of men studying are much higher in Orissa when compare to A.P. This is also reflected in the percentage of child workers to total child population. In A.P. while 16 per cent of the male children are found to work and only 10 per cent of male children are found to work in Orissa. Among female children differences between two States are much higher. In 3 out of the 4 villages in Orissa, no child worker is reported. Possibly this does not however mean that no child is working. Our observations in villages suggests during some seasons even children participate in work. What it implies is that this contribution to income is not significant. We also examined whether children who are reported to be not working are found in school. This is not the situation in all the cases even in Orissa. Most children do not work and also do not go to school. Even if they go to school it is for the purpose of taking noon-meal which is supplied free by the Government. Our observations in the village suggest that the noon-meal scheme is not functioning well in the Orissa State. In one of the villages which we visited, the attendance in school is very thin. Though many children are found at the time of noon-meal (Table 8.4).

### 8.5. Sector-wise Participation Rates: Andhra Pradesh and Orissa

Sector-wise participation rates are judged by the main occupation as well as the secondary occupation pursued by the worker. The criterion for judging the main occupation is the income. In the tribal areas agriculture and forestry continued to be the main occupation in several villages. More than 90 per cent of the members interviewed reported agriculture and forestry as main occupation. In almost all villages in Rampachodavaram and Addateegala villages no other occupation

**Table 8.3: Percentage of Adult Workers in Total Adult Population (Adult Workers)**

| Village | Male | | | Female | | |
|---|---|---|---|---|---|---|
| | Total | Workers | Percentage | Total | Workers | Percentage |
| Kumaritham | 53 | 51 | 96.22 | 45 | 42 | 93.33 |
| Sumpangiput | 57 | 50 | 87.71 | 49 | 42 | 85.71 |
| Pothangi | 38 | 38 | 100 | 39 | 39 | 100 |
| Besupuram | 39 | 38 | 97.43 | 42 | 40 | 95.23 |
| Cheruvuru | 29 | 29 | 100 | 35 | 31 | 88.57 |
| Pedduru | 33 | 29 | 87.87 | 34 | 33 | 88.57 |
| Veeravaram | 31 | 31 | 100 | 29 | 29 | 100 |
| Kovelapalem | 30 | 28 | 93.33 | 25 | 24 | 96 |
| A.P. Total | 310 | 294 | 94.84 | 298 | 280 | 93.95 |
| Telangapodar | 36 | 29 | 80.55 | 34 | 21 | 61.76 |
| Borikhal | 36 | 28 | 77.77 | 32 | 24 | 75 |
| Minapai | 34 | 34 | 100 | 35 | 31 | 88.57 |
| K. Gursi | 36 | 36 | 100 | 35 | 33 | 94.28 |
| Orissa Total | 142 | 127 | 89.43 | 136 | 109 | 80.14 |

**Table 8.4: Percentage of Child Workers in Total Child Population**

| Village | Male | | | Female | | |
|---|---|---|---|---|---|---|
| | Total | Workers | Percentage | Total | Workers | Percentage |
| Kumaritham | 14 | 2 | 14.28 | 21 | 7 | 33.33 |
| Sumpangiput | 18 | 6 | 33.33 | 26 | 3 | 11.53 |
| Pothangi | 19 | 5 | 26.31 | 21 | 6 | 28.57 |
| Besupuram | 19 | 1 | 5.26 | 19 | 1 | 5.26 |
| Cheruvuru | 28 | 6 | 21.42 | 18 | 2 | 11.11 |
| Pedduru | 27 | 3 | 11.11 | 25 | 7 | 28 |
| Veeravaram | 18 | 3 | 16.67 | 20 | 2 | 10.11 |
| Kovelapalem | 23 | 4 | 17.39 | 13 | 0 | 0 |
| A.P. Total | 166 | 27 | 16.26 | 163 | 28 | 17.17 |
| Telangapodar | 14 | 0 | 0 | 12 | 0 | 0 |
| Borikhal | 14 | 4 | 28.57 | 18 | 0 | 0 |
| Minapai | 25 | 1 | 4 | 13 | 0 | 0 |
| K. Gursi | 18 | 2 | 11.11 | 14 | 1 | 7.14 |
| Orissa Total | 71 | 7 | 9.85 | 57 | 1 | 1.75 |

reported as main occupation. Even in one of the Orissa villages agriculture and forestry is the sole occupation.

Among females in some villages number reporting other than agricultural sector was more than the corresponding number for males. Overall, the percentage reporting in other sectors among females is higher both in A.P. and Orissa. Women in tribal areas are engaged in crafts occupation pursued at home.

### 8.6. Occupational Distribution in Andhra Pradesh and Orissa

Occupational distribution was judged in terms of four occupational categories namely cultivation, agricultural labour, MFP and others. Details are shown for males and females separately (Table 8.5). Within agriculture, cultivators among men exceeded the female cultivators by large proportion in Pedduru and Araku villages. Similarly, agricultural labourers among males exceeded corresponding number for females in Araku villages, while in Pedduru villages agricultural labourers among females exceeded the corresponding number for males. In Rampachodavaram and Addateegala tribal villages of A.P. cultivators both among men and women exceeded the number for agricultural labourers. Very few reported manufacturing or service as main occupation. MFP was reported by a fewer males as compared to women. Its significance as a main occupation for both men and women is low as compared to cultivation in A.P.

In Orissa there are wide variations across the villages in the significance of each of the occupations. Cultivation, agricultural labour and others are not recorded as main occupations in one of the villages of Rayagada district. In another village of Rayagada district, agricultural labour and others are recorded nil while cultivation is recorded in a few. In both these Rayagada villages MFP is more significant. However, in Koraput villages MFP ceases to be significant as main occupation. In these villages cultivation and agricultural labour are much more prominent.

### 8.7. Significance of MFP Income in Household Income

Household income is a better measure for judging the distribution of income by source in a situation in which an individual is pursuing multiple occupations.

**Table 8.5: Occupational Distribution**

| | Cultivation | | MFP | | Agricultural Labour | | Others | |
|---|---|---|---|---|---|---|---|---|
| | M | F | M | F | M | F | M | F |
| Kumaritham | 32 | 23 | 8 | 9 | 11 | 14 | 2 | 3 |
| Sumpangiput | 37 | 28 | 7 | 11 | 5 | 7 | 5 | 0 |
| Pothangi | 31 | 8 | 7 | 16 | 19 | 4 | 0 | 0 |
| Besupuram | 26 | 11 | 4 | 12 | 14 | 8 | 3 | 1 |
| Cheruvuru | 37 | 35 | 0 | 0 | 0 | 0 | 1 | 2 |
| Pedduru | 32 | 40 | 1 | 0 | 0 | 0 | 0 | 0 |
| Verravaram | 32 | 20 | 0 | 0 | 0 | 0 | 0 | 0 |
| Kovelapalem | 32 | 24 | 0 | 0 | 0 | 0 | 0 | 0 |
| A.P. Total | 259 | 198 | 27 | 48 | 49 | 33 | 11 | 6 |
| Telangapodar | 0 | 0 | 30 | 16 | 0 | 0 | 0 | 0 |
| Borikhal | 3 | 2 | 22 | 15 | 0 | 0 | 0 | 0 |
| Minapai | 19 | 13 | 1 | 2 | 14 | 13 | 1 | 1 |
| K. Gursi | 35 | 9 | 0 | 1 | 0 | 12 | 0 | 12 |
| Orissa Total | 57 | 24 | 53 | 34 | 14 | 25 | 1 | 13 |

An examination of village-wise income shows that there is a little of diversification of occupation in tribal villages. Tribal villages continue to depend upon agriculture and forestry for their sustenance. In Andhra Pradesh tribal villages 75 per cent of the household income is derived from these two sources. When agricultural labour is also added 93 per cent of the household income is derived from agriculture and forestry. In Orissa a tribal village's 73 per cent of the income is derived from the agriculture and forestry. It appears that there is more diversification in Orissa villages. It is because of two villages in which significant source of income is derived from transport and two other villages in which significant source of income is derived from non-agricultural wages. Such diversification is however not a sign of progress but a sign of its backwardness in agriculture which pushes people to pursue non-remunerative non-agricultural occupations (Table 8.6).

### 8.8. Per Household and Per Capita Income from MFP

Per household income in A.P. is roughly double the income obtained in Orissa villages. Per Capita Income is also more in

## Table 8.6: Percentage Distribution of Household Income by Source

| Village | Cultivation | Agricultural Labour | Livestock | Fishing | Mining | Household Industry | Business | Construction | Transport | Services | Other wages | Migrants | Others | MFP | Total |
|---|---|---|---|---|---|---|---|---|---|---|---|---|---|---|---|
| ANDHRA PRADESH | | | | | | | | | | | | | | | |
| Kumaritham | 49.86 | 10.17 | 0.78 | 0.34 | 0.00 | 0.00 | 0.00 | 0.00 | 2.24 | 0.00 | 1.45 | 0.56 | 4.52 | 30.09 | 100.00 |
| Sumpangiput | 71.81 | 1.89 | 0.00 | 0.00 | 0.00 | 0.00 | 0.00 | 0.00 | 0.00 | 0.00 | 2.92 | 0.00 | 2.07 | 21.30 | 100.00 |
| Pothangi | 40.12 | 13.50 | 0.00 | 0.35 | 10.93 | 2.43 | 0.00 | 0.00 | 0.00 | 0.83 | 0.45 | 0.17 | 0.42 | 30.80 | 100.00 |
| Besupuram | 42.45 | 3.80 | 0.00 | 0.00 | 0.00 | 0.00 | 0.00 | 1.56 | 0.00 | 0.00 | 0.52 | 0.00 | 6.64 | 45.04 | 100.00 |
| Cheruvuru | 40.71 | 36.62 | 2.47 | 0.00 | 0.00 | 0.55 | 0.00 | 0.00 | 0.00 | 1.99 | 0.00 | 0.00 | 2.27 | 15.41 | 100.00 |
| Pedduru | 40.79 | 35.51 | 0.00 | 0.00 | 0.00 | 0.45 | 0.00 | 0.00 | 0.00 | 0.00 | 0.00 | 0.00 | 0.00 | 23.25 | 100.00 |
| Veeravaram | 44.35 | 34.66 | 0.00 | 0.00 | 0.00 | 0.00 | 0.00 | 0.00 | 0.00 | 0.00 | 1.36 | 0.00 | 0.00 | 19.64 | 100.00 |
| Kovelapalem | 25.81 | 30.95 | 3.22 | 0.00 | 0.00 | 0.00 | 2.50 | 0.00 | 0.00 | 0.64 | 0.04 | 0.00 | 0.00 | 36.84 | 100.00 |
| A.P. Total | 45.10 | 18.13 | 0.71 | 0.08 | 1.07 | 0.32 | 0.32 | 0.25 | 0.34 | 0.31 | 1.02 | 0.10 | 2.32 | 28.93 | 100.00 |
| ORISSA | | | | | | | | | | | | | | | |
| Telangapodar | 17.87 | 0.00 | 0.00 | 0.00 | 0.00 | 0.00 | 0.00 | 0.00 | 30.09 | 0.00 | 0.01 | 0.00 | 0.98 | 51.06 | 100.00 |
| Borikhal | 36.03 | 0.00 | 0.00 | 0.00 | 0.00 | 0.00 | 0.00 | 0.00 | 23.27 | 0.00 | 0.00 | 0.00 | 3.38 | 37.31 | 100.00 |
| Minapai | 25.19 | 32.07 | 3.51 | 0.00 | 0.00 | 9.12 | 0.21 | 0.00 | 0.00 | 0.00 | 15.12 | 1.75 | 0.00 | 13.02 | 100.00 |
| K. Gursi | 57.57 | 15.85 | 1.34 | 0.42 | 0.00 | 0.00 | 0.00 | 0.83 | 0.00 | 0.00 | 8.80 | 0.33 | 0.92 | 13.94 | 100.00 |
| Orissa Total | 31.75 | 9.08 | 0.93 | 0.07 | 0.00 | 1.82 | 0.04 | 0.14 | 16.86 | 0.00 | 4.50 | 0.41 | 1.53 | 32.87 | 100.00 |
| Grand Total | 43.31 | 16.37 | 0.75 | 0.08 | 0.86 | 0.61 | 0.26 | 0.23 | 3.55 | 0.25 | 1.69 | 0.16 | 2.17 | 29.70 | 100.00 |

Andhra Pradesh villages. But per capita income is less than twice, because Andhra Pradesh villages have larger household size compared to Orissa villages. Per capita MFP income in Andhra Pradesh villages is also higher compared to Orissa villages. In Andhra Pradesh for purpose of issue of white card the income fixed was form only Rs. 6,000. It was later revised to Rs. 11,000. Based on this in Cheruvuru and Pedduru alone the average income is below the poverty line. In Orissa, in all the villages, the average income per household is below the poverty line.

We constructed a poverty line for the year of survey *i.e.* 1996-97 based on the estimate of Rs. 20 per capita per month at 1960-61 prices for the rural areas. 1996-97 agricultural labour price index is 1,268. Applying this index we derive a poverty line of Rs. 3,043 per capita per year. All the Orissa villages are below the poverty line while Pothangi, Cheruvuru and Pedduru alone in A.P. are below the poverty line (Table 8.7).

### 8.9. Quality of Life : Andhra Pradesh and Orissa

The value of consumption of food expenditure gives a measure of food security. The lower the value, lower the food security. By this measure Pothangi in Andhra Pradesh and Minapai village in Orissa have the least food security. While relatively highest food security is achieved in Kovelapalem in Andhra Pradesh and Telangapodar in Orissa. In villages with least food security expenditure on foodgrains forms the major proportion. The people in these villages spend most of the resources on foodgrains and are left with very little to spend on other nutritive items of food. In Pothangi foodgrains consumption formed 72 per cent of the total food consumption while in Minapai 81 per cent is spent on foodgrains (Table 8.8).

### 8.10. Per capita Consumption of Different Items of Food : Andhra Pradesh and Orissa

In tribal villages, consumption is most difficult to capture. Much of the expenditure on food items is not in cash and is not purchased. Most of it is home produced. Some of them like fruits are got free from forests. Such limitations should be recognised in interpreting the data on food expenditure.

## Table 8.7: Per Household and Per Capita Income : Village-wise

| Village | Per Household Income | | Per Capita Income | | Household |
|---|---|---|---|---|---|
| | MFP | Total | MFP | Total | Size |
| Kumaritham | 5,379.8 | 17,879.8 | 1,011.2 | 3,360.86 | 5.32 |
| Sumpangiput | 4,196.8 | 19,700.8 | 699.47 | 3,283.47 | 6.00 |
| Pothangi | 3,549.6 | 11,525.6 | 758.46 | 2,462.74 | 4.68 |
| Besupuram | 8,683.2 | 19,279.2 | 1,824.20 | 4,050.25 | 4.76 |
| Cheruvuru | 1,347.8 | 8,748.24 | 306.32 | 1,988.24 | 4.00 |
| Pedduru | 2,544.00 | 10,947.56 | 534.64 | 2,299.90 | 4.76 |
| Veeravaram | 2,956.00 | 15,050.4 | 754.10 | 3,839.40 | 3.92 |
| Kovelapalem | 5,712.9 | 15,508.75 | 1,506.7 . | 4,090.22 | 3.79 |
| A.P. Total | 4,289.25 | 14,826.63 | 910.S5 | 3,148.88 | 4.70 |
| Telangapodar | 4,602.56 | 9,013.64 | 1,198.58 | 2,347.30 | 3.84 |
| Borikhal | 3,360.28 | 9.005.44 | 840.07 | 2.251.36 | 4.00 |
| Minapai | 742.28 | 5,700.28 | 173.43 | 1,331.8 | 4.28 |
| K. Gursi | 668.68 | 4,795.8 | 162.31 | 1,164.03 | 4.10 |
| Orissa Total | 2,343.46 | 7,128.8 | 577.21 | 1,755.86 | 4.06 |
| Grand Total | 3,628.48 | 12,252.12 | 810.05 | 2.727.75 | |

## Table 8.8: Total Value of Food Consumption, Foodgrain Consumption Per Capita Per Month

| Village | Per Capita Exp. of food | Per Capita Exp. of food-grains | Foodgrains Expenses % of food exp. | Per Capita total expenses Ratio (4) | Per Capita food expenses 1 % of (4) | Per Capita Foodgrains expenses as % of (4) |
|---|---|---|---|---|---|---|
| (1) | (2) | (3) | (4) | (5) | (6) | (7) |
| **Andhra Pradesh** | | | | | | |
| Kumaritham | 161.18 | 111.13 | 68.95 | 234.44 | 68.75 | 47.40 |
| Sumpangiput | 155.16 | 110.92 | 71.49 | 208.94 | 74.26 | 53.08 |
| Pothangi | 130.23 | 93.99 | 72.17 | 186.33 | 60.89 | 50.44 |
| Besupuram | 165.07 | 120.97 | 73.28 | 233.30 | 70.75 | 51.85 |
| Cheruvuru | 180.88 | 103.91 | 57.45 | 246.76 | 73.30 | 42.10 |
| Pedduru | 222.40 | 122.64 | 55.14 | 281.9 | 78.80 | 43.50 |
| Veeravaram | 225.79 | 104.59 | 46.32 | 303.89 | 74.30 | 34.42 |
| Kovelapalem | 235.66 | 102.49 | 43.53 | 312.71 | 75.36 | 32.77 |
| **Orissa** | | | | | | |
| Telengapodar | 143.63 | 119.36 | 83.10 | 192.03 | 74.80 | 62.20 |
| Borikhal | 136.88 | 108.33 | 79.14 | 190.03 | 72.03 | 57.01 |
| Minapai | 82.62 | 66.68 | 80.71 | 114.59 | 72.10 | 58.19 |
| K. Gursi | 137.31 | 121.47 | 88.46 | 150.91 | 90.98 | 80.50 |

Among the cereals rice is the most prominent item consumed by everybody. Millets are generally not purchased; they are grown by the tribals on their farms. Millet consumption is found in those villages where millets are grown. In Orissa villages and two villages in A.P. of Addateegala block, very little millets are grown. Pulses are grown as a catch crop in paddy lands. Consumption of pulses is not high in most villages. Even for a sedentary person the norm set for consumption of pulses per day is 50 grams. None of the villages reach the standard of 50 grams. In the case of oils only one of the villages namely Veeravaram reaches the norm of 20 grams. Norm for vegetables and green leaf vegetables together set for a sedentary person per day is 250 grams. Maximum consumption in any of the villages is only 96 grams. The consumption in Orissa villages is much less. The norm for sugar consumption is 20 grams per day. Except in two villages *viz.*, Veeravaram and Kovelapalem in A.P. and none of the other villages reach the norm. Orissa villages record hopelessly low consumption of sugar. Milk consumption is known to be poor in tribal areas. None of the villages is close to the target of milk consumption of 300 grams per day. In fact in three villages in Orissa no milk consumption is recorded (Table 8.9).

## 8.11. Determinants of Per Capita Expenditure of Tribal Households

The earlier analysis implicates that the number of socio-economic and demographic variables govern the per capita expenditure of the tribal households. As is known that per capita expenditure indicates the level of living of the household. It is viewed that an increase in the income derived from the MFP items in a family would rise the per capita expenditure. Similarly the per capita cultivated land as a proxy to the agricultural income would be positively related to the per capita expenditure. However, higher the family size, higher would be the household income as children in the tribal households be treated as income earning assets. This would possibly rise the per capita expenditure. For testing the above hypotheses, a linear multiple regression models are fitted. The best fitted models for Andhra Pradesh and Orissa are presented.

## Table 8.9: Per Capita Monthly Consumption of Different Items of Food in A.P. and Orissa in 1996-97

| Village | Branch | Per Capita Consumption of Rice | Millets | Pulses | Oil Qty. | Meat | Vegetable | Sugar | Salt | Milk | Spices | Fruit | Beverages |
|---|---|---|---|---|---|---|---|---|---|---|---|---|---|
| **Andhra Pradesh** | | | | | | | | | | | | | |
| 1. Kumaritham | Paderu | 9.97 | 10.46 | 0.29 | 0.33 | 0.176 | 1.97 | 0.25 | 1.025 | 0.00 | 0.92 | 0.08 | 0.423 |
| 2. Sumpangiput | Paderu | 10.20 | 6.04 | 0.26 | 0.30 | 0.17 | 2.13 | 0.28 | 0.31 | 0.095 | 0.93 | 0.025 | 0.404 |
| 3. Pothangi | Araku | 7.91 | 10.21 | 0.30 | 0.25 | 0.15 | 1.66 | 0.23 | 0.34 | 0.16 | 0.895 | 0.02 | 0.328 |
| 4. Besupuram | Araku | 9.69 | 12.27 | 0.25 | 0.31 | 0.18 | 2.28 | 0.26 | 0.32 | 0.00 | 1.06 | 0.00 | 0.375 |
| 5. Cheruvuru | R. Chodavaram | 10.69 | 3.56 | 0.85 | 0.51 | 0.41 | 2.33 | 0.38 | 0.28 | 0.05 | 0.78 | 0.04 | 0.00 |
| 6. Pedduru | R. Chodavaram | 12.54 | 4.23 | 1.31 | 0.66 | 0.65 | 2.35 | 0.33 | 2.01 | 0.16 | 1.75 | 0.013 | 0.00 |
| 7. Veeravaram | Addateegala | 11.51 | 0.00 | 1.19 | 0.72 | 0.72 | 2.30 | 1.78 | 0.82 | 0.14 | 1.71 | 0.00 | 0.00 |
| 8. Kovelapalem | Addateegala | 11.07 | 0.00 | 0.95 | 0.65 | 0.80 | 2.90 | 1.79 | 0.98 | 0.006 | 2.07 | 0.00 | 0.00 |
| **Orissa** | | | | | | | | | | | | | |
| 9. Telangapodar | Muniguda | 15.20 | 2.93 | 0.30 | 0.19 | 0.26 | 0.78 | 0.006 | 0.87 | 0.03 | 0.27 | 0.00 | 0.09 |
| 10. Borikhal | Muniguda | 13.65 | 2.89 | 0.31 | 0.18 | 0.28 | 1.30 | 0.008 | 0.93 | 0.00 | 0.035 | 0.00 | 0.00 |
| 11. Minapai | Sunabeda | 8.83 | 3.27 | 0.20 | 0.15 | 0.0026 | 0.84 | 0.004 | 0.67 | 0.00 | 2.19 | 0.00 | 0.197 |
| 12. K. Gursi | Sunabeda | 7.09 | 1.93 | 0.01 | 0.04 | 0.23 | 0.102 | 0.0 | 0.61 | 0.00 | 0.26 | 0.00 | 0.072 |

**Andhra Pradesh**

$$PCE = 2769.5 - \underset{(3.27)}{170.13\ FS^*} + \underset{(0.44)}{64.32\ PCCA} + \underset{(4.59)}{0.63\ MFPI^*}$$

$R^2 = 0.1368$; F (295,4) = 15.58*

* Indicates 1 per cent level of significance.

Figures in brackets under the coefficients refer to 't' value.

From the model, it is found, based on the significant variables that the income from MFP (MFPI) contributes positively to the per capita annual expenditure on (PCE) in Andhra Pradesh. However, the higher the family size seems to result in lower the per capita expenditures, thereby, rejecting the proposed hypothesis. This may be because of higher the dependency ratio or non-work participation rate among the tribal families causes low family income and low per capita expenditure.

**Orissa**

$$PCE = 3819.8 - \underset{(6.27)}{272.65\ FS^*} - \underset{(0.26)}{34.71\ PCCA} + \underset{(3.62)}{0.39\ MFPI^*}$$

$R^2 = 0.2815$; F (195,4) = 25.47*

Similar, to Andhra Pradesh, the causation is found to be the same in Orissa. However, the contribution of higher MFP income to per capita expenditure is relatively at the lower magnitude in Orissa (Rs. 39 PCE per every Rs. 100 MFP income) compared to that in Andhra Pradesh (Rs. 63 PCE per Rs. 100 MFPI). The negative impact of family size is also higher in Orissa compared to that in Andhra Pradesh. This again indicates that the work participation is relatively lower in Orissa tribals that in their counterparts in Andhra Pradesh.

## 8.12. Calorie Requirement *Vs.* Calorie Intake

Intake of calories is estimated based on the physical quantities and their calorie content as reported in "Nutritive Value of Indian Foods" by Gopalan and others.[1] The calorie content per day per capita is found to fall below the norm of 2435 calories in rural areas prescribed by the task force on projection of minimum needs and effective consumption demand of the Planning Commission[2] in all the Orissa villages and 5 out of 8 Andhra villages. Calories obtained from food grains as a percentage of total calories exceeded 90 per cent in all the Orissa villages and in one half of the Andhra Pradesh villages. This is an index of poor quality of life in tribal villages (Table 8.10).

### 8.13. Age Distribution: Andhra Pradesh and Orissa

Age distribution of tribal population of selected villages of A.P. and Orissa are given in Table 8.11. For purpose of comparison we have chosen to present NSSO data 43rd Round 1987-88 in the absence of readily available census data for 1991 (Table 8.12). The comparison with the 43rd Round data shows that old people are far less in numbers in tribal villages when compare to entire rural areas. It is seen from the data that the percentage in A.P. for the group above 60 is much less when compared to Orissa. Partly, this is due to difficulty in estimating the age and partly it reflects higher mortality rates for tribals among old people in Andhra Pradesh.

We try to capture infant mortality in tribal villages by asking a question relating to deaths of infants during past one year and also births during the past one year. Total births recorded were 10 in A.P. and 8 in Orissa and deaths recorded among infants were only 1 in A.P. and none in Orissa. Quite obviously births and deaths are not captured well in our schedules.

### 8.14. Deaths by Causes: Andhra Pradesh and Orissa

It is difficult to capture deaths in the tribal villages. Only 5 out of 12 villages deaths were recorded. The causes of deaths were as follows :

| Cause of deaths | No. of deaths recorded | |
|---|---|---|
| | Male | Femal |
| Fever | 4 | 3 |
| Murder | 2 | nil |
| Jaundice | 1 | nil |
| T.B. | 1 | nil |

### 8.15. Morbidity and Hospitalisation : Andhra Pradesh and Orissa

Even while mortality rates have declined morbidity has increased and the levels of morbidity are much higher than the levels of mortality. A number of diseases are recorded during

## Table 8.10: Per Capita Daily Intake of K. Cal. Average Per 25 Tribal Households in Each Village

| Village | Rice | Millets | Pulses | Oil | Meat | Vegetables | Jaggery and Sugar | Milk | Fruits | Species | Total | Calories obtained from Food-grains | Calories obtained from Food-grains as a % of Total calories |
|---|---|---|---|---|---|---|---|---|---|---|---|---|---|
| 1. Kumaritham | 1143.22 | 1199.40 | 33.06 | 99 | 7.68 | 33.05 | 32.54 | 0.00 | 2.16 | 10.26 | 2560.42 | 2375.68 | 92.78 |
| 2. Sumpangiput | 1169.60 | 692.57 | 29.64 | 90 | 7.42 | 35.74 | 36.44 | 2.69 | 0.66 | 7.03 | 2071.78 | 1891.81 | 91.31 |
| 3. Pothangi | 907.00 | 1170.75 | 34.20 | 75 | 6.55 | 27.85 | 29.93 | 4.53 | 0.53 | 4.43 | 2260.77 | 2111.95 | 93.41 |
| 4. Besupuram | 1111.12 | 1406.96 | 28.50 | 93 | 7.86 | 38.25 | 33.84 | 0.00 | 0.00 | 6.18 | 2725.71 | 2546.58 | 93.42 |
| 5. Cheruvuru | 1225.79 | 408.20 | 96.90 | 153 | 17.90 | 39.09 | 49.46 | 1.41 | 1.05 | 18.35 | 2011.06 | 1730.89 | 86.07 |
| 6. Pedduru | 1437.92 | 485.04 | 149.34 | 196 | 28.38 | 39.42 | 42.95 | 4.50 | 0.34 | 21.05 | 2406.94 | 2072.30 | 86.10 |
| 7. Veeravarm | 1319.60 | 0.00 | 135.66 | 216 | 31.44 | 38.58 | 231.69 | 3.90 | 0.00 | 29.78 | 2006.20 | 1455.46 | 72.55 |
| 8. Kovelapalem | 1341.60 | 0.00 | 108.30 | 195 | 34.93 | 48.65 | 233.00 | 0.17 | 0.00 | 28.88 | 1990.53 | 1449.90 | 72.83 |
| 9. T. Podar | 1742.90 | 335.97 | 34.20 | 57 | 11.35 | 13.08 | 0.78 | 0.85 | 0.00 | 2.61 | 2198.70 | 2113.07 | 96.10 |
| 10. Borikhal | 1565.20 | 331.39 | 35.34 | 54 | 12.23 | 21.80 | 1.04 | 0.00 | 0.00 | 6.96 | 2027.96 | 1931.93 | 95.26 |
| 11. Minapai | 1012.50 | 374.96 | 11.40 | 45 | 0.11 | 14.09 | 0.52 | 0.00 | 0.00 | 1.94 | 1460.52 | 1398.86 | 95.77 |
| 12. K. Gursi | 812.98 | 221.31 | 1.14 | 12 | 10.04 | 1.71 | 0.00 | 0.00 | 0.00 | 0.26 | 1049.40 | 1035.43 | 98.66 |

**Table 8.11: Age Distribution for Selected Villages in Percentages**

| | Andhra Pradesh | Orissa |
|---|---|---|
| 0-5 | 12.2 | 16.5 |
| 6-14 | 23.2 | 16.5 |
| 15-30 | 33.50 | 36.2 |
| 31-45 | 18.8 | 16.3 |
| 45-60 | 11.9 | 10.1 |
| above 60 | 0.5 | 4.4 |
| Total | 100.00 | 100.00 |

**Table 8.12: Distribution of Population by Age-Group 1987-88 NSS 43rd Round**

| Age Group | Percentage of Population | |
|---|---|---|
| | Orissa | Andhra Pradesh |
| 0-4 | 12.01 | 13.33 |
| 5-9 | 13.20 | 13.70 |
| 10-14 | 11.60 | 11.14 |
| 15-19 | 10.00 | 8.70 |
| 20-24 | 9.24 | 8.60 |
| 25-29 | 8.20 | 8.55 |
| 30-34 | 6.50 | 6.50 |
| 35-39 | 5.63 | 5.73 |
| 40-44 | 4.74 | 5.00 |
| 45-49 | 4.97 | 4.72 |
| 50-54 | 4.10 | 4.10 |
| 55-59 | 3.10 | 3.10 |
| 60 and above | 6.71 | 6.80 |

*Reference* : Govt. of India, NSSO, Department of Statistics, Ministry of Planning, *Sarvekshana, 54th Issue.* Vol. XVI, No. 3. Jan.-Mar. 1993, NSS 43rd Round (July 1987-June 1988), p. 333.

the past one year both in A.P. as well as tribal villages of Orissa. The diseases recorded are of chronic nature. In Andhra Pradesh around 22 per cent of the households reported chronic diseases while in Orissa the corresponding number is 80 per cent. As regards number of persons reporting diseases, in Orissa where malaria fever is more prevalent, 51 per cent of people reported chronic diseases while in A.P. the corresponding figure was only 4.8 per cent. As regards the distribution of diseases both in Orissa and A.P. malaria fever claimed the maximum proportion, it is followed by cardiovascular diseases. Only in two villages we do not find cardiovascular diseases. There is one case of T.B. in Orissa village namely K. Gursi. Around 3/4th of those reported diseases are hospitalised both in A.P. and Orissa (Table 8.13).

Average period of illness per person is reported to be 1.51 months in A.P. and 1.13 months in Orissa. Expenditure per person hospitalised in A.P. is much more Rs. 793 as against in Rs. 120 in Orissa. As against this, non-hospitalised people spent less than 1/6th of the hospitalised persons in A.P. and around 1/4th to 1/5th in Orissa. Per household hospital expenditure is found to be around 5 per cent of the income in A.P. and only 2 per cent in Orissa (Table 8.14). We classified the hospitalised cases into two categories *viz.*, those who are admitted in private hospitals and others who are admitted in Government hospitals. In A.P. one half of the cases are admitted in private hospitals and in Orissa cases admitted in private hospitals formed a small proportion *i.e.*, around 12 per cent. The closeness of two villages in Orissa to Muniguda hospital was a factor accounting for high proportion of those admitted in Government hospitals. The expenditure per capita hospitalised in A.P. it was seen earlier is higher by 6.6 times as compared to Orissa. Expenditure incurred by individual household on Government hospitals varied largely from Rs. 100 to Rs. 5,000 while as expenditure on private hospitals varied from Rs. 300 to Rs. 2,000. The expenditure per capita incurred by individual on Government hospitals is Rs. 1,108 and Rs. 867.86 on private hospitals. This variation is mainly due to the period of hospitalisation. Though the Government charges should be less than the private charges as a result of bribes paid to the doctors, the expenditure incurred by the patients is found to be more in Government hospitals.

**Table 8.13: Number Reported Chronic Diseases, Number of Hospitalised**

| Village | Number Reported Chronic Diseases | Number of Households Hospitalised | % of Persons Hospitalised in the total diseased |
|---|---|---|---|
| **Andhra Pradesh** | | | |
| Kumaritham | 7 | 5 | 71.43 |
| Sumpangiput | 4 | 4 | 100.00 |
| Pothangi | 2 | Nil | 0.00 |
| Besupuram | 3 | 3 | 100.00 |
| Cheruvuru | 7 | 5 | 71.43 |
| Pedduru | 6 | 5 | 83.33 |
| Veeravaram | 6 | 6 | 100.00 |
| Kovelapalem | 10 | 7 | 70.00 |
| A.P. Total | 45 | 35 | 77.78 |
| **Orissa** | | | |
| T. Podar | 80 | 75 | 93.75 |
| Borikhal | 73 | 53 | 72.60 |
| Minapai | 37 | 24 | 64.86 |
| K. Gursi | 18 | 8 | 44.44 |
| Orissa | 208 | 160 | 76.92 |

## 8.16. Health Status of Tribal Areas of A.P. in Recent Years

K. Sujatha Rao[3] brings out unexceptionally adverse differentials in health indicators between tribal and non-tribal areas of A.P. Meternal mortality is 8 per thousand going up to 25 among tribal groups as against 4 per thousand for the State. Infant mortality rate is 120 to 150 per thousand compared to 72 for the State. Longevity of life is lower. Under T.B. and malaria the tribals suffer disproportionately to the population. There has been a impressive spread of basic health care services in tribal areas in recent years. The positive aspects, however, are negatived by the highly dispersed nature of population. The siting of the facilities on poor communications has resulted in making distance and access a major barrier for utilisation of health care services, as per the detailed survey of the Department of Family Welfare in 1994. None of the 29 NMU's is functioning.

**Table 8.14: Average Period of Illness, Average Expenditure per Person**

| Village | Average Period of illness hospitalised (in months) | Not Hospitalised (in months) | Income per household | Average expenditure per person hospitalised (in Rs.) | Not hostpitalised (in Rs.) |
|---|---|---|---|---|---|
| **Andhra Pradesh** | | | | | |
| Kumaritham | 3.00 | 4.00 | 17879 | 1140.00 | 100.00 |
| Sumpangiput | 1.25 | Nil | 19700 | 400.00 | Nil |
| Pothangi | Nil | 3.5 | 11525 | Nil | 150.00 |
| Besupuram | 1.3 | Nil | 19279 | 1433.33 | Nil |
| Cheruvuru | 2.00 | 1.00 | 8748 | 710.00 | 550.00 |
| Pedduru | 1.60 | 1.00 | 10947 | 1130.00 | 100.00 |
| Verravaram | 1.50 | Nil | 15050 | 516.67 | Nil |
| Kovelapalem | 1.43 | 1.00 | 15508 | 1014.29 | 66.67 |
| A.P. Total | 1.51 | 1.31 | 14826 | 793.0 | 120.83 |
| **Orissa** | | | | | |
| Telangapodar | 0.78 | 0.2 | 9013 | 118.00 | 26.00 |
| Borikhal | 1.25 | 1.27 | 9005 | 159.00 | 83.25 |
| Minapai | 2.10 | 3.44 | 5700 | 4.79 | 0.00 |
| K. Gursi | 0.38 | 0.4 | 4795 | 200.00 | 0.00 |
| Orissa Total | 1.13 | 1.33 | 7128 | 120.44 | 27.31 |

66 per cent of the PHC's require repairs to make them usable; 30 per cent have no electricity (affecting vaccine potency); 62 per cent have no labour rooms or water supply (making institutional deliveries impossible); 19 per cent are located in thatched huts; 53 per cent of PHC's have no operational theatres and of the remaining, in 22 per cent of the theatres no equipment and therefore are unutilised. Manpower availability in tribal areas is equally bad. The treatment in PHCs is casual and unsympathetic if not hostile and exploitative. Unable to efford being sick for long, the tribals find it less expensive to seek private care. It is a measure of certainty, prompt services, better quality of medicines etc. A base line survey conducted in 12 road side villages of Maredumilli Mandal of East Godavari district showed among 405 households interviewed there are 420

morbidities observed. Of these 420, only 270 were treated and 95 cured. The failure of Government institutions to provide effective health care services is the main reason for the large out of pocket expenses being incurred by the tribals and a minimum of almost Rs. 200 for a episode of illness — towards transport, professional fees, days and tests. It is easy to assume that a family spends on health care between Rs. 100 to Rs. 2000 amounting to a maximum of 20 per cent of its income. The money required for health care is raised by taking loans at high rates of interest ranging from 5 to 10 per cent per month and on condition of preferential sale of produce at 70 per cent of the prevailing price of the market.

## 8.17. Tribal Health Project for a New Approach for the Health Care of Tribals : Andhra Pradesh

The positive aspect of the Tribal Health Project is that for the first time an attempt has been made to build on the concept of people's participation. A community approach is proposed to be achieved in two ways : (a) providing for a Community Health Worker (CHW), a married woman resident of the village for providing prevention and curative services at the village level and as a liaison between the community and medical officer of the PHC. She is given training for two months in Malaria, Scabies, diarrhea, preparation of nutritional charts and undertaking of health education activities and (b) constitution of village health committee covering MCH, environmental health, education, reproductive tract, infection control etc.

## 8.18. A Critique of Tribal Health Plan : Andhra Pradesh

The Tribal Health Plan is a statement of good intentions. In the absence of a tightly knit health delivery systems there will be little utility. A serious shortcoming of the health policy of the tribals is the routine compartmental approach. Despite evidence of the adverse impact of malaria and T.B., the implementation of these programmes has not been incorporated. The existing system of T.B. treatment requires the patient to visit the hospital at the district headquarter which is 200 km. away, obtain a referral and keep visiting the PHC for medication. This system has been found to be expensive and time consuming and fairly unaffordable. Further physical access, quality of care and information have been inadequately addressed. There is a need for new development paradigm. Development paradigm will need to make health at the centre stage in the overall development strategy. Strategies to reduce morbidities and mortalities among tribals need to contain specific directions establishing the inter connectivity between improving incomes through female literacy and better utilisation of health facilities at the PHC level based on micro planning. More cost effective systems of health care need to be urgently examined. In tribal areas, GCC and the Department of Ayurveda have done commandable work in listing and identification of herbal medicinal plants. This R and D work needs to be continued.

## SECTION-III

## LITERACY AND EDUCATION

### 8.19. Survey of NSSO on Participation of Education 42nd Round 1986-87 :

The enquiry on utilisation of public educational facilities and services in general by population formed an integral part of social consumption carried out in 42 Round (July 1986 - June 1987) of NSS. The results of this enquiry for all India are released in *Sarvekshana*, issue No. 46, Jan.-Mar. 1991. State-wise tables are presented in two volumes, one volume covering 8 major states including Orissa and another volume covering other 8 major states including A.P. We present the results of A.P. and Orissa from NSSO studies in the section that follows.

Illiterates in rural Orissa formed a higher proportion as compared to rural Andhra. Both in Orissa and Andhra, female illiteracy is much more than male illiteracy. These details are for the entire population. For the tribal population, NSS 44th Round (July 1988-June 1989) provides figures of illiteracy. Illiteracy among the tribal males in A.P. is 81.9 per cent, while in Orissa the tribal males record less illiteracy 72.4 per cent. Rural female illiteracy among tribals is maximum both in Andhra Pradesh (94.3 per cent) and Orissa (91.8 per cent), (Table 8.15).

NSS data also provides details of distribution of students by class. We compile the figures for A.P. and Orissa from Classes I

**Table 8.15: Percentage Distribution of Highest Level of Education Attained for Tribals and Non-tribals in Tribal Areas**

| | Andhra Pradesh | | | | Orissa | | | |
|---|---|---|---|---|---|---|---|---|
| | Rural Males | | Rural Females | | Rural Males | | Rural Females | |
| | Tribal | Non-Tribal | Tribal | Non-Tribal | Tribal | Non-Tribal | Tribal | Non-Tribal |
| 1. Not literate | 81.9 | 61.9 | 94.3 | 78.9 | 72.4 | 41.1 | 91.8 | 67.7 |
| 2. Literate without formal education | 1.1 | 3.3 | 3.4 | 1.6 | 3.5 | 7.5 | 1.1 | 3.3 |
| 3. Literate below primary | 9.8 | 13.8 | 3.3 | 9.0 | 12.2 | 20.2 | 4.0 | 13.9 |
| 4. Primary | 3.7 | 8.0 | 0.6 | 4.9 | 4.6 | 12.2 | 1.2 | 8.2 |
| 5. Middle | 2.4 | 6.9 | 0.4 | 3.3 | 5.7 | 12.7 | 1.6 | 5.2 |
| 6. Secondary | 0.6 | 1.5 | 0.2 | 1.5 | 1.1 | 3.7 | 0.2 | 0.8 |
| 7. Higher Secondary | 0.6 | 1.5 | — | 0.7 | 0.2 | 1.2 | 0.0 | 0.6 |
| 8. Certificate of Diploma | 0.1 | 0.4 | — | — | — | 0.3 | — | — |
| 9. Graduation and above | — | 0.8 | — | 0.1 | 0.1 | 1.1 | 0.0 | 0.1 |
| 10. Not recorded | 0.2 | — | 0.3 | 0.1 | 0.1 | — | — | — |

*Source* : Government of India, Ministry of Planning, Department of Statistics, NSSO, *Sarvekshna 59th Issue*, Vol. XVII, No. 4, April-June 1994, NSS 44th Round (July 1988-June 1989), pp. S-303 and S-305.

to Classes IX for rural areas. Among males in A.P. for every 100 people in Class I, there are only 22 pupil in Class IX. Among the females this position is much worse. For every 100 pupil in Class I are only 10 pupil in Class IX. Most children drop out by Class V. In Orissa the position is slightly better than Andhra Pradesh for both males and females (Table 8.16). NSSO also provides details of reasons for discontinuance by sex and social groups. These details are compiled for Orissa and Andhra rural areas. There are differences between males and females among tribals. As regards reasons for discontinuance, while economic reasons and failures accounted for the major discontinuance among males, the females indicate not interested in education/further studies and participation in household economic activity as the major reason (Table 8.17). In Andhra Pradesh economic reasons were equally applicable for both males and females. 3/4th of the females who discontinued in Andhra Pradesh were not interested

**Table 8.16: Percentage Distribution of Students by Sex and Class in which Currently Enrolled**

| | Andhra Pradesh Rural | | Orissa Rural | |
|---|---|---|---|---|
| | Male | Female | Male | Female |
| Class I | 756587 (100.00) | 567017 (100.00) | 329512 (100.00) | 249286 (100.00) |
| Class II | 566981 (74.94) | 410771 (72.44) | 229213 (69.56) | 190214 (76.30) |
| Class III | 525089 (69.40) | 270146 (47.64) | 166948 (50.67) | 137869 (55.31) |
| Class IV | 276280 (36.52) | 198929 (35.10) | 170144 (51.64) | 104503 (41.92) |
| Class V | 299403 (39.57) | 140802 (24.83) | 171518 (52.05) | 105935 (42.50) |
| Class VI | 324565 (42.90) | 129511 (22.84) | 161843 (49.12) | 75219 (30.17) |
| Class VII | 274247 (36.25) | 116196 (20.50) | 143944 (43.68) | 87019 (34.91) |
| Class VIII | 161058 (21.30) | 68067 (12.00) | 123840 (37.58) | 56846 (22.80) |
| Class IX | 164319 (21.72) | 56897 (10.03) | 107441 (32.61) | 58000 (23.27) |

*Source* : For A.P. — Government of India, Ministry of Planning, Department of Statistics, NSSO, *Sarvekshna 55th Issue,* Vol. XVI, No. 4, April-June 1993, 42nd Round.

For Orissa — *Sarvekshana 56th Issue,* Vol. XVII, No. 1 July-Sept., 1993, NSS 42nd Round.

in education/further studies while the corresponding figure for Orissa is only 30 per cent (Table 8.18).

## 8.20. Survey Results on Illiteracy and Education : 1996-97

The percentage of illiteracy by village is quite high in all the villages. Illiteracy is higher in Orissa villages as compared to Andhra Pradesh villages. NSSO Data studied earlier showed the tribal Orissa record the less illiteracy as compared to tribal areas

**Table 8.17: Percentage Distribution of Drop-outs over Reasons for Discontinuance by Sex and Social Group (Orissa), 1988-89**

RURAL

| Reason | Social Group | | | | | | | | |
|---|---|---|---|---|---|---|---|---|---|
| | Scheduled Tribe | | | Scheduled Caste | | | Others | | |
| | Male | Female | Person | Male | Female | Person | Male | Female | Person |
| Not interested in education/ Further studies | 21.30 | 30.00 | 23.23 | 19.03 | 26.80 | 21.01 | 25.76 | 40.98 | 31.14 |
| For participation in household economic activity | 15.93 | 22.53 | 17.34 | 10.02 | 1.24 | 7.79 | 16.60 | 4.39 | 12.26 |
| For other economic reason | 28.89 | 14.82 | 25.88 | 40.07 | 26.63 | 36.64 | 28.97 | 19.40 | 25.55 |
| Busy in attending domestic chores | 2.31 | 9.13 | 3.77 | 1.12 | 5.33 | 2.20 | 1.88 | 11.55 | 5.31 |
| Failure | 13.69 | 11.91 | 13.31 | 24.71 | 26.56 | 25.18 | 20.82 | 15.52 | 19.00 |
| Others | 17.88 | 11.28 | 16.47 | 5.04 | 13.43 | 7.18 | 5.97 | 8.16 | 5.74 |
| All | 100.00 | 100.00 | 100.00 | 100.00 | 100.00 | 100.00 | 100.00 | 100.00 | 100.00 |
| Estimated No. of persons who discontinued studies | 385321 | 104795 | 490116 | 299508 | 102426 | 401934 | 1499958 | 825247 | 2326975 |

*Source* : Govt. of India, Ministry of Planning, Department of Statistics, *NSSO, Sarvekshana, 56th Issue*, Vol. XVII, No. 1, July-Sept. 1993, NSS 42nd Round.

of Andhra Pradesh. This suggests that the selected villages in Andhra Pradesh are in a better position compared to generality of villages in A.P. Even then, villages in Paderu and Araku have only single teacher schools namely Maabadi (our school). In Addateegala and Rampachodavaram area some of the primary schools do not have teachers since primary teachers are reluctant to work in tribal village. In one village namely Veeravaram, there is an Ashram School (residential type). In this village the number of children enrolled as a percentage of children in the school going age 0-14 is the highest. We sought to know whether enrolment in school is related to the significance of MFP in the total income. No relationship is observed between MFP values and enrolment in schools. Enrolment is also not related to the percentage of workers among child population. For instance, in

**Table 8.18: Percentage Distribution of Drop-outs over Reasons for Discontinuance by Sex and Social Group (Andhra Pradesh), 1988-89**

RURAL

| Reason | Social Group | | | | | | | | |
|---|---|---|---|---|---|---|---|---|---|
| | Scheduled Tribe | | | Scheduled Caste | | | Others | | |
| | Male | Female | Person | Male | Female | Person | Male | Female | Person |
| Not interested in education/ Further studies | 23.50 | 74.65 | 31.55 | 29.94 | 28.82 | 29.95 | 28.39 | 36.38 | 31.18 |
| For participation in household economic activity | 33.53 | 1.83 | 28.55 | — | 14.80 | 20.48 | 32.42 | 12.85 | 26.58 |
| For other Economic reason | 26.55 | 23.52 | 26.07 | 24.25 | 21.10 | 23.13 | 17.57 | 12.65 | 15.92 |
| Busy in attending domestic chores | — | — | — | 1.05 | 12.31 | 5.04 | 0.51 | 11.40 | 4.31 |
| Failure | 6.79 | — | 5.72 | 10.25 | 6.78 | 9.02 | 14.37 | 7.65 | 12.35 |
| Others | 9.63 | — | 8.11 | 10.91 | 16.19 | 12.78 | 6.13 | 19.08 | 10.66 |
| All | 100.00 | 100.00 | 100.00 | 100.00 | 100.00 | 100.00 | 100.00 | 100.00 | 100.00 |
| Estimated No. of persons who discontinued studies | 130804 | 24418 | 155222 | 582720 | 318450 | 901170 | 3188753 | 1713229 | 4901982 |

*Source* : Govt. of India, Ministry of Planning, Department of Statistics, *NSSO, Sarvekshana, 55th Issue*, Vol. XVI, No. 4, April-June 1993, 42nd Round.

Orissa villages there are less workers among children as compared to A.P. villages. The enrolment ratios in Orissa are far less as compared to Andhra Pradesh villages (Table 8.19).

## 8.21. Per Capita Income and Expenditure : Andhra Pradesh and Orissa

Per capita expenditure is seen to range from Rs. 3753 in Kovelapalem village to Rs. 2236 in Pothangi village in Andhra Pradesh (Table 8.20). Such expenditure variations are closely related to income variations. In Orissa villages, income per capita is seen to be very low. Per capita expenditure also is low in three out of the four villages. Per capita expenditure exceeded the per capita income in three out of the four villages in Orissa. In one village the income from MFP is the least, dissaving was

**Table 8.19: Children Enrolled in Schools and Number of Children School Going Age Group 0-14**

| Village | No. of Children Enrolled in School | | | No. of Children in the Age Group 0-14 | | | No. of Children Enrolled in School as a % of No. of Children in the Age Group 0-14 | | |
|---|---|---|---|---|---|---|---|---|---|
| | M | F | T | M | F | T | M | F | T |
| **Andhra Pradesh** | | | | | | | | | |
| Kumaritham | 9 | 7 | 16 | 14 | 21 | 35 | 64.28 | 33.33 | 45.71 |
| Sumpangiput | 10 | 8 | 18 | 19 | 25 | 44 | 52.63 | 32.00 | 40.91 |
| Pothangi | 4 | 3 | 7 | 19 | 21 | 40 | 21.05 | 14.28 | 17.50 |
| Besupuram | 10 | 4 | 14 | 19 | 19 | 38 | 52.63 | 21.05 | 36.84 |
| Cheruvuru | 2 | 1 | 3 | 28 | 18 | 46 | 7.14 | 5.56 | 6.52 |
| Pedduru | 4 | 7 | 11 | 27 | 25 | 52 | 14.81 | 28.00 | 21.15 |
| Veeravaram | 10 | 8 | 18 | 17 | 18 | 35 | 58.82 | 44.44 | 51.43 |
| Kovelapalem | 3 | 3 | 6 | 23 | 13 | 36 | 13.04 | 23.08 | 16.67 |
| Total | 52 | 41 | 93 | 166 | 160 | 326 | 31.33 | 25.63 | 28.53 |
| **Orissa** | | | | | | | | | |
| Telengapodar | 1 | 0 | 1 | 15 | 14 | 29 | 6.67 | 0.00 | 3.45 |
| Borikhal | 3 | 3 | 6 | 14 | 18 | 32 | 21.43 | 16.67 | 18.75 |
| Minapai | 10 | 1 | 11 | 25 | 13 | 38 | 40.00 | 7.69 | 28.95 |
| K. Gursi | 7 | 2 | 9 | 18 | 14 | 32 | 38.89 | 14.29 | 28.13 |
| Total | 21 | 6 | 27 | 72 | 59 | 131 | 29.17 | 10.17 | 20.61 |

the highest. In two villages of Rayagada block in which per capita expenditure is close to per capita income. Per capita income is high because of the high value MFP per household. Food security is very much effected as a result of low income caused by low values of MFP in villages of Sunabeda Branch of Koraput district. In Andhra Pradesh villages, particularly in Addateegala block, MFP collection is high. This contributed to high incomes and better food security.

## SUMMARY

This chapter made a comparative study of employment, income and quality of life of tribals in A.P. and Orissa. As in the preceding chapter, this chapter also made a review of earlier

**Table 8.20: Per Capita Expenditure, Per Capita Income, Savings and Deficit Per Annum : Village-wise**

| Village | Per Capita Income | Per Capita Expenditure | Savings/ Deficit | Saving or Deficit as a % of Per capita Income |
|---|---|---|---|---|
| **Andhra Pradesh** | | | | |
| Kumaritham | 3360.90 | 2813.28 | +547.62 | 16.29 |
| Sumpangiput | 3283.47 | 2507.28 | +776.19 | 23.63 |
| Pothangi | 2462.74 | 2235.96 | +226.78 | 9.21 |
| Besupuram | 4050.25 | 2799.60 | +1250.65 | 30.90 |
| Cheruvuru | 1988.24 | 2961.12 | -972.88 | -48.93 |
| Pedduru | 2299.90 | 3382.08 | -1082.90 | -47.10 |
| Veeravaram | 3839.40 | 3636.68 | +192.72 | 5.02 |
| Kovelapalem | 4090.20 | 3752.52 | +337.68 | 8.25 |
| A.P. Total | 3148.90 | 3012.41 | 136.50 | 4.33 |
| **Orissa** | | | | |
| Telengapodar | 2347.30 | 2307.60 | +39.07 | 1.70 |
| Borikhal | 2251.40 | 2280.36 | -28.96 | -1.30 |
| Minapai | 1331.80 | 1375.08 | -43.28 | -3.25 |
| K. Gursi | 1164.10 | 1810.92 | -646.82 | -55.56 |
| Orissa Total | 1755.80 | 1942.68 | -186.88 | 10.64 |

studies *i.e.*, the study of Agro-Economic Research Centre, Andhra University, Waltair, in 1982-83, the comprehensive living conditions of tribals, NSS 44th Round, 1988-89, survey, findings of consumption expenditure of Nabakrishna Chowdary Centre for Development Studies, 1992. These reviews are followed by findings of field survey conducted by us in 8 villages in Andhra Pradesh and 4 villages in Orissa, covering a total of 300 households.

The Agro-Economic Centre's study brought out that the MFP collection accounted for around two days in a week, both in Nallamoli and Utnoor, while in Araku Valley, MFP collection accounted for least number of days. NSS data on living conditions of tribals showed that the position of Andhra Pradesh is much worse than Orissa in respect of literacy. But the housing conditions are poorer among Orissa tribals. Percentage of persons below poverty line is also higher among tribals in Orissa.

Nabakrishna Chowdary Centre's study in Orissa, in 1992, confirms the findings on poverty by the NSS 1988-89. Percentage employment from MFP per household varied from 133 days in Koraput to 457 days in Mayurbhanj. This study showed that the highest dependence of forest dwellers is on MFP. Landless households are found to have a greater dependence on forest. It also brought out the high rates of illiteracy among tribals.

Finally, the review of our field survey in 8 villages in Andhra Pradesh and in 4 villages in Orissa, threw light on several aspects including work participation, occupational distribution, significance of MFP income in household income, and quality of life covering particularly different items of consumption of food, calorie requirement *vis-a-vis* calorie intake, morbidity and mortality levels.

Work participation rates are found to be high for tribals in both Andhra Pradesh and Orissa. In Andhra Pradesh villages, cultivation accounted for the highest proportion of workers. Orissa villages show a wide divergence. In two of them, MFP accounted for major proportion, while in the other two villages, cultivation and agricultural labour accounted for major proportion. What is glaring is the absence of diversification of occupations in the tribal villages. Distribution of income of households showed that MFP accounted for around 30 per cent of total income in both Orissa and A.P. villages. Cultivation accounted for a higher proportion of total income in A.P. 46 per cent, as against 32 per cent in Orissa villages. Similarly, agricultural labour also accounted for higher proportion in A.P. 18 per cent as against 9 per cent in Orissa. In Orissa villages, income from transport accounted for a very high proportion particularly in two villages of Muniguda TDCC branch area. Annual Per Capita Income in Andhra villages for MFP ranged between Rs. 306 in Cheruvuru to Rs. 1824 in Besupuram, while in Orissa State, per capita for MFP is ranged between Rs. 162 and Rs. 1198. The per capita income from MFP in A.P. for all villages together was Rs. 911, while in Orissa it is only Rs. 577.

The per capita income from all sources also found to be little more than the one half in Orissa as compared to Andhra Pradesh.

Food security as measured by per capita expenditure on foodgrains is less in Orissa villages as compared to Andhra Pradesh villages. However, food security in Orissa villages in which MFP income is high, is found to be better. Calories obtained from foodgrains in general are found to form a higher proportion in Orissa villages. Consumption of pulses, oil and vegetables, jaggery, sugar is much less in Orissa villages. Health status is also poorer in Orissa villages when compared to Andhra Pradesh villages. Children enrolled in schools as a percentage of number of children in the age group is found to be more in selected villages of Andhra Pradesh as compared to selected villages in Orissa. But this picture could not be generalised. NSS data for whole of the state Orissa and Andhra Pradesh shows that illiteracy is much higher among Andhra Pradesh tribal areas as compared to Orissa tribal areas. What is striking is the difference between tribal and non-tribal areas in Orissa in literacy levels.

## NOTES

1. Gopalan C., Rama Sastri B.V. and others (1995), *Nutritive Value of Indian Foods,* National Institute of Nutrition, Indian Council of Medical Research, Hyderabad.
2. Planning Commission, *Report of the Expert Group on Estimation of Proportion and Number of Poor,* Government of India, New Delhi, July 1993, p. 4.
3. Sujatha Rao K. (1998), "Health Care Services in Tribal Areas of Andhra Pradesh — *A Public Policy Perspective, Economic and Political Weekly,* February 28, pp. 481-86.

# 9

# Summary and Conclusion

## 9.1. Highlights of the Major Differences between Framework for Marketing of MFP in Orissa and in Andhra Pradesh

It may be noted at the outset, the objectives of the TDCC of Orissa and GCC of Andhra Pradesh are similar. Both the institutions are interested in promoting the incomes of the tribals :

(a) by ensuring a fair price for tribal seller;

(b) by providing adequate production and marketing credit for the seller; and

(c) by meeting the domestic requirements of the tribals.

Though the objectives are similar, the institutional framework for ensuring achievement of the objectives is found to be different. In Orissa, TDCC has to pay royalty and establishment charges to the Government, while in Andhra Pradesh, GCC is exempted from payment of these. As a result the tribal seller gets a lesser price in Orissa.

The TDCC of Orissa does not have autonomy in fixing the price or choosing the time schedule of the procurement while GCC exercises the monopoly in fixing the price and is more autonomous in choosing the time schedule of procurement. Due to the arrears of royalty payment to the government, the TDCC is much constrained insofar as the Forest Department does not give the work order until the arrears are cleared.

The second major difference relates to recent trends of privatisation of procurement in Orissa State. Many of the activities which were hitherto performed by TDCC are now entrusted to the private agencies.

The third major difference relates to credit flow to the tribals. Credit flow is weak in Orissa State because of the bad functioning of apex cooperative institutions and equally bad functioning of the cooperatives like LAMPS at the grass-roots level.

Domestic Requirement Depots are also functioning badly in Orissa State as compared to GCC.

## 9.2. A Critical Appraisal of GCC

The Corporation had many ups and downs during the course of the 42 years of its operation. During this period, organisational reforms were introduced with a view to streamlining the administration. One very important step that was taken was in respect of its pricing policy. It was revised and reoriented to offer a 'support price' instead of a 'fair price'. One of the important problems that the Corporation faced was the provision of adequate storage facilities. In many cases, this was a contributory cause for the loss that the primary society had sustained.

The forest rentals and establishment charges had been a serious drain on the resources of the Corporation. These two together took a lion's share of the total funds made available to the Corporation. Had the Government not subsidised the Corporation in respect of forest-rentals and establishment charges, the Corporation would have been in doldrums.

The Corporation and its activities are exposed to the following criticisms :

1. In spite of the monopoly it enjoyed in respect of the purchase of minor forest produce, the Corporation failed to make much headway. A few might, however, question its monopoly power.
2. The Corporation which was started to replace the middlemen for marketing the produce collected by the tribals and supplying domestic requirements to them did not prove very effective in the beginning as it failed to provide a price-incentive. At a later stage the Government realised the loopholes and tried to set things

right by adopting a more helpful attitude towards retail prices and domestic requirements; and

3. It is an over protected infant, inasmuch as its rentals and establishment charges to the tune of 35 per cent are borne by the Government which also gives financial aid and provides godowns, etc. It is doubtful whether such an over-protected infant can develop into an adult with the necessary strength to stand up to any crisis, especially, in the event of the assistance being withdrawn.

### 9.3. Measures for Improvement of Functioning of GCC

Some measure of monopoly power might be desirable in a situation such as the present one where a few merchants could play havoc with the economy of tribals. In the past, it was only a seller's market as the tribals did not have much choice. The monopoly power of the Corporation can be justified on grounds of social welfare. This may not be motivated by any desire for mere profit.

1. The periodicity fixed in by-laws for convening the meetings of the Board and General Body should be scrupulously followed. The attendance of official and non-official directors at the Board meetings should be improved to ensure their effective participation in the affairs of the committee.

2. Creation of a separate cell at the head office is necessary for prompt follow-up action on the decisions taken by the Board. Constitution of a business advisory committee and a loan advisory committee has to be explored.

3. The primary societies should be made to work as independent bodies instead of as branches of the Corporation. There is a need to take action by the Corporation authorities for payment of commission to the primaries as prescribed in the by-laws of the Corporation. A suitable provision should be incorporated into the by-laws of the primary societies authorities by authorising laws of the primary societies from the Corporation.

4. Measure should be taken for streamlining the procedures of procurement and eliminating all chances of misappropriation and deficits in stocks. The existing practice of advancing funds

to the shandy inspectors should be discontinued. Instead, the manager or the accountant of the primary society should arrange to effect payments to the tribals. For the stocks purchased or procured, the Branch Manager should be directed to send purchase abstracts soon after the completion of transaction at the shandy to the society office. An advisory committee consisting of at least 5 local tribals should be constituted for each shandy and at other purchasing points to exercise vigilance over the instances of malpractices like under-weighments and short payments, etc. Immediate transport arrangements should be provided by the manager for transportation of stocks from the purchase centre to the main godowns to minimise the deficits.

5. There is a need for a change in the existing system with regard to the fixation of prices for purchase and sale of commodities. The manager must be vested with some discretionary powers in adopting the local market rate for the procurement and disposal of the stocks wherever there is any variation in relation to the prices fixed by the authorities of the Corporation.

6. The Andhra Pradesh Legislative Assembly Committee which enquired into the working of the Girijan Cooperation strongly recommended that the quick disposal of the crops should be the main policy and guiding principle for the corporation to achieve the following results :

(a) for avoiding heavy and frequent borrowings as a consequence of prolonged storage of stocks;

(b) to minimise deficits;

(c) to reduce overhead charges like payment of interest and godown rents etc.;

(d) to avert the deterioration in the conditions and quality of the stocks.

7. The Legislative Committee found that the extraction of the gum by the tribals was mainly confined to the Telangana region and the techniques adopted for it were found to be crude and destructive to the plants and therefore, needed a change and improvement.

8. Regarding the Domestic Requirement, necessary measures should be taken to streamline the functioning of the Domestic Requirement Depots and ensure proper distribution of the stocks to the tribals at a fair price. Only popular and quick-moving commodities are to be supplied to the Domestic Requirement Depots to avoid deficits due to accumulation of unwanted stocks. Improved methods in storage and package should be adopted to prevent deterioration in the condition of stocks and to reduce the magnitude of deficits. Whenever any revision of prices is effected, the managers must first obtain the stock position of the commodities in Domestic Requirements Depots before communicating the revised prices.

9. The Civil Supplies Department should allow the Corporation to undertake the operation of procurement of paddy under 'producer levy' for the purpose of supply of rice to the tribals in adequate quantities. This arrangement will go a long way in supplying rice at a fair price and in sufficient quantities to the tribal population.

10. The Corporation should undertake wholesale purchase of commodities in Hyderabad and other important marketing centres during the peak season to ensure direct supplies to the different societies.

11. Regarding agricultural credit, the Corporation should undertake a survey of credit requirements of the tribals with reference to their holdings and the quantum of finances required for raising different crops. The present scale of finance should be revised providing maximum cash component with a minimum fertilizer component as the tribals are yet to be motivated for taking up improved methods of cultivation.

12. The time for the utilisation of the kind component should last a few weeks in the off-season to enable and induce the tribals to avail the kind component fully. There is every need and justification for the Corporation to be made the sole credit agency for all tribal cultivators residing in the area of its operation.

13. To intensify the procurement operations with regard to minor forest produce and agricultural produce the purchase

points should be widespread so as to cover as many tribal villages as possible and reduce the distance between the tribal villages and the procurement centres.

### 9.4. Critical Appraisal of TDCC and OFDC

TDCC has been continuously incurring losses thereby leading to the complete erosion of its capital base. Consequently, it has been increasingly depending on loans from bank and other institutions as well as on budgetary support from State Government. The major reasons for the losses are : low business turnover; heavy interest burden on borrowings; high overheads; payment of heavy amount of royalty to the Forest Department for procurement of MFP; market fluctuations; and the compulsion for passing higher rate on procurement. Since 1991, the involvement of LAMPS in procurement has been decreasing. For example, the number has decreased from 50 in 1991-92 to 36 in 1992-93 and to 8 in 1993-94. The tie-up arrangements of TDCC, although has the virtue of assuring the state market, denies it the best available price in the market. TDCC maintains excess staff. The functioning of its storage department has been found to be inadequate. The most important reason for the failure of TDCC is lack of autonomy. The procurement prices for MFP items are fixed by the Price Fixation Committee headed by the District Collector and the TDCC has no say in price fixation. Further, TDCC has to wait the work orders from the Government for starting procurement. The work orders of the Government are being issued much after the season commences. The issue of work order is contingent upon clearance of all earlier royalties to the government. The lease agreement will be renewed every year. Further, sales tax clearance certificate should be submitted by the TDCC before starting procurement. For some of the commodities, parallel lease is given to private traders.

The practice of giving monopoly procurement rights to TDCC etc. was aimed at eliminating the commission agents. However, the situation has come to such a sorry state of affairs that TDCC is found to have employed the same commission agents for collection of MFPs. All other lease holders also in varying degrees trade through local sub-agents/traders.

Therefore, the primary collectors only get a fraction of the fixed prices. The revenue oriented policy has also created a host of distortions. For example, in case of hill broom, TDCC in some divisions pays only Rs. 3.00 per kg. to the primary collectors but a higher amount, Rs. 7.00—9.00 per kg. to the Government as royalty. The price calculation, according to the Agragamee Report, "are made using the official prices as determined by the district level Price Fixation Committee. The actual price paid to the primary collectors is much lower considering that TDCC rarely collects hill brooms directly; rather it appoints, unofficially sub-agents on a commission basis. These sub-agents are often the same traders—moneylenders from whose clutches the TDCC was supposed to save the tribals. The price received by the tribals is a fraction of the administered prices."

The procurement price/minimum support price announced in advance by OFDC is, by its very nature, oriented more towards protecting the interest of the buyers. The procurement price for some items bears little relationship with the market conditions which may witness up swing or down swing in prices. In case of MFP, there is a possibility of depressing trend in prices or conversely, the market is at most of the time upbeat largely due to the limited source of supply of and greater and diversified demand for these products. So the increased prices of MFP greatly fail to be devolved to the primary collectors.

MFP collection involves rigorous labour in identifying, drying, sorting, grading, decorticating of the products and in this chain of activities, the collector carries out some processing necessities—the processing involves labour and almost no use of capital. However, they obviously use certain basic tools and equipment. The irony is that the price fixing authorities do not recognise this primary level processing because of the non-involvement of capital and, therefore, fix price in such way as to treat the produce merely non-processed.

The State continues to treat the MFP as falling in the domain of its exclusive rights and consequently the people directly dependent on forest are granted a few customary rights. Issuance of permits and licences and the Orissa Forest Produce (control of trade) Act, 1981 establishing state monopoly, therefore, put a ceiling on the production capacity.

The creation of monopolistic conditions in the market by authorising a few public undertakings, or even private ventures, for purchase of and trade in MFP, has in no way served better the interest of forest dwellers. The deep inefficiency and large scale corruption in public enterprises are well-known and it would not be inappropriate to say that these undertakings have managed to thrive on the interest of forest dwellers and on budgetary support which is the tax-payers money. Also it does not seem well to allow outside private business of industrial houses where profit is the sole motive.

The Orissa Forest Produce (control of trade) Rules, 1983 confers preferential treatment on people's bodies like gram panchayats and public institutions like Orissa Tribal Development Co-operative Corporation, in the appointment as agents. However, these matters little when, co-operatives are mismanaged and not fully representative, and the corporation in question is inefficient in addressing the issues of tribal people. Even when the co-operatives are well-structured and representative, their treatment at par with the corporation on a horizontal scale while making preferential provision, is less favourable to these grass-root organisations compared to their upper level counterpart—the corporation. Therefore, the more the institution approximates to the grass-roots level, the more the chances of unequal treatment.

With the nationalisation of kendu leaves, there has arisen a situation today in which for every Re. 1 paid to the grower/ collector, the state appropriates a profit ranging from Rs. 2.50 (1993-94) to Rs. 9.00 (1989-90). There has been no attempt to sharing the profit with the growers/collectors.

### 9.5. Measures for Improvement of Functioning of TDCC

There is a need for improving the procedures of price fixation. The Orissa Forest Produce (control of trade) Act, 1981 provides for the creation of an Advisory Committee at revenue Divisional Commissioner's level for fixing the price of specified forest produce. However, the prices are not binding on the part of the government to accept. Secondly, the Committee does not have a representation from among the primary collectors. Thirdly, the fixation procedure seem to forget the important criteria like bringing a parity between the income of primary collectors and other income earners, forecasting demand conditions for these products, indexation to the general price increase; etc.

The practice of giving monopoly rights to a private trader, UFP Ltd., raises eyebrows. To agree with N.C. Saxena, "there is no check on the price paid by this private company to the tribals. The orders creating private monopolies are *ad-hoc*, arbitrary and against the principle of natural justice, as no tenders or offers have been invited before bestowing monopolistic powers to a private agency. These orders smack of favouritism, and lack of probity and openness".[1] Also, leasing of land under the grab of leasing of forest produce as in the case of bamboo, goes against the spirit of Forest Conservation Act.

The OFDC and TDCC pay huge royalties to state; and for kendu leaves alone the royalty realised as in 1990 was Rs. 77 crores.[2] TDCC pays royalty on hill brooms, siali leaves, tamarind, nuxvomica, honey and wax, soap nuts, marking and cleaning nuts and myrobalans. Such huge royalties to the state meant that the tribal could not be paid a fair price. Besides TDCC also pays purchase tax. Due to the heavy burden of royalty, purchase tax and establishment cost TDCC is unable to pay fair price to the tribals. Orissa Legislative Assembly Committee of SC/ST in its report has suggested for complete exemption of forest royalty to TDCC to enable them to pay better prices to the tribals, for their MFP items.

Finally the functions of LAMPS needs to be improved to enable the TDCC to give credit to the tribals for marketing.

## 9.6. Weekly Markets in the Development of Tribal Marketing

An analysis of primary markets shows both in Orissa and A.P. that they are undeveloped.[3] They are small in size without any infrastructural facilities and any kind of amenities. The method of sale is purely by mutual agreement between buyer and seller. Most of the produce are brought by cycles or by bullock carts. The study of market arrivals by the market committees of Orissa State in the rural primary markets indicated that MFP forms only a small proportion of the total arrivals. It is possible that most of the MFP is sold by the tribals locally in the villages concerned. Since most of the primary markets do not have infrastructural facilities.

The Orissa State has undertaken the development of rural tribal markets with partial assistance from the Central Government. One hundred and thirty haats are located in 89 blocks are selected for development in the first phase of the project. The objective of the project is to identify the facilities available and harness for betterment and all-round development of tribal people. The work of preparing project profiles is entrusted to various agricultural produce market committees. The following facilities are proposed for multi-commodity haats : (1) auction platform, (2) office-cum-godown, (3) trader shops, (4) water supply and sanitary arrangements, (5) fencing, (6) watchmen's quarter, (7) electrification, wherever desired and feasible, (8) resting shed for buyers and visitors, (9) water troughs. In addition to the above components multi-commodities-cum-cattle markets are to be provided with : (1) veterinary dispensary, (2) additional water trough and (3) cattle sheds. The estimated cost for development of 130 multi-commodities in Orissa State-cum-cattle haats works out to Rs. 10.09 crores.

The study of the market committee in Orissa State revealed that 84 tribal haats out of 130 are owned and managed by regulated market committees; 41 by Panchayat Samitis; and 5 by private bodies. The market board while providing physical facilities in the haat area may consider the following points before construction :

(i) Foodgrain sellers prefer closed premises as they generally maintain a certain stock which requires protection from moisture and pests.

(ii) Fruit and vegetable sellers and also petty traders are often satisfied with accommodation in open sheds since they provide better ventilation.

(iii) Sellers of manufactured products generally require

closed premises to protect their goods from rains, theft etc.

(iv) Small traders often sell by mobile hand carts and take their stocks home after the market hours.

But development of the primary market may provide a necessary but not a sufficient condition for attracting the tribal produce to the market. First, tribals must be freed from the shackle of the village moneylender and village trader. Secondly, the infrastructure facilities for taking his produce to the market must be developed. In the absence of these, the cost of taking produce to the market will be higher than the benefits derived.

## SUMMARY

This chapter highlighted the major differences between the framework for marketing of MFP both in Orissa and Andhra Pradesh. It undertook a critical appraisal of GCC followed by a similar appraisal of TDCC in Orissa. A number of recommendations are made for improving the functioning of GCC in Andhra Pradesh and TDCC in Orissa. Finally, the role of primary markets in development of tribal marketing is examined and a number of suggestions are made for the development of primary markets. It concludes by saying the development of primary markets provides a necessary but not a sufficient condition for attracting the tribal produce to the market.

## NOTES

1. Orissa Drought Action Forum — Advocacy Cell, *Forest Dwellers and Non-Timber Forest Produce Marketing in Orissa — A Study and Policy Analysis*, Bhubaneswar, 15 August, 1996, p. 44.
2. Government of Orissa, Office of the Principal Chief Conservator of Forests, Orissa, *A Decade of Forestry in Orissa, 1981-1990*, Bhubaneswar, p. 63.
3. Ministry of Rural Development, Directorate of Marketing and Inspection Branch, *Project Report for Development of Tribal Haats in Orissa State, Part I*, Nagpur, 1991.

# Bibliography


Agro-Economic Research Centre, Andhra University, *MFP in the Tribal Economy of Andhra Pradesh*, Waltair, August, 1985.

Agro-Economic Research Centre, Andhra University, *Prospects of Value Addition to Tribal Produce (A Study of Selected Commodities in Tribal Areas of Andhra Pradesh)*, Visakhapatnam, November, 1996.

Chief Planning Officer, *Statistical Abstract—Visakhapatnam District*, Visakhapatnam, 1988-89.

Chief Planning Officer, *Statistical Abstract—East Godavari District*, Kakinada, 1991-92.

Council of Professional Social Workers, *Forest Dwellers and Non-Timber Forest Marketing on Orissa—A Study and Policy Analysis*, Bhubaneswar, Orissa, 1996.

Directorate of Economics and Statistics, *District Statistical Hand Book 1993, Koraput*, Orissa Bhubaneswar.

Directorate of Economics and Statistics, *Statistical Abstract of Orissa, 1996*, Bhubaneswar.

Govt. of Orissa, Department of Forestry and Animal Husbandry, Work Order given by the DFO, Rayagada.

GCC, *Statement Showing the Particulars of Division-wise, Unit-wise and Commodity-wise Procurement of Minor Forest Produce/Agricultural Produce for the Last Five Years i.e., from 1989-90 to 1993-94*, Visakhapatnam.

Govt. of Orissa, Statistical Branch, Office of the Principal Chief Conservator of Forests, Orissa, *A Decade of Forestry in Orissa, 1981-90*, Bhubaneswar.

Girijan Cooperative Corporation Limited, *Note on Activities*, Visakhapatnam, April, 1995.

Govt. of Andhra Pradesh, Directorate of Economics and Statistics, *Andhra Pradesh Statistical Abstract, 1992-93*, Hyderabad.

Govt. of Orissa, *Economic Survey, 1995-96*, Bhubaneswar.

Govt. of Andhra Pradesh, Finance and Planning (Planning Wing) Department, Directorate of Economics and Statistics, *Andhra Pradesh Four Decades of Development*, Hyderabad, 1997.

Govt. of Orissa, Department of Agriculture and Cooperation, Ministry of Agriculture, *Commission for Agricultural Costs and Prices for Corps Sown in 1995-96 Season and 1996-97 Season*, New Delhi.

Govt. of Orissa, Directorate of Agriculture and Food Corporation, *Agricultural Statistics of Orissa—at a Glance*, Bhubaneswar.

Govt. of India, NSSO, *Sarvekshana Issue No. 59, Vol. No. XVII, No. 4*, April-June 1994, 44th Round.

Govt. of Andhra Pradesh, *A.P. District Gazetteers*, Hyderabad, 1979.

Govt. of Andhra Pradesh, *Committee of the House Report on the GCC*, A.P. Legislative Assembly, Govt. of Andhra Pradesh Publications, Hyderabad, 1976.

Govt. of Orissa, Planning and Coordination Department, *Long-term Action Plant for K.B.K. Districts, 1995-96 to 2001-2002*, 1995.

Institute of Applied Manpower Research, *Pricing of Minor Forest Products Procured by the Girijan Cooperative Corporation, Government of Andhra Pradesh*, New Delhi, September, 1997.

Kansal, A.P., *Success Story of the AMCS, Tikabali in Rainbow*, Bhubaneswar, Orissa Cooperative Union, Ph.D. Thesis submitted to the Berhampur University, 1982.

Ministry of Rural Development, Directorate of Marketing and Inspection, *Project Report for Development of Tribal Haats in Orissa*, Part-I, Nagpur, 1991.

NABARD, *Expost Evaluation Study*, Evaluation Series No. 5, Regional Office, Bhubaneswar.

Radhamohan Malik, *Study of Some Minor Forest Produce in Orissa: An Empirical Investigation,* Nabakrishna Chowdary Centre for Development Studies, Orissa, Bhubaneswar, 1994.

R.P. Sarma and N.C. Sahu, *Tribal Indebtedness in Koraput District,* Orissa, 1973.

Sagrieya, K.P., *Forests and Forestry,* National Book Trust India, 1967.

### THE OTHER BOOKS/ARTICLES REFERRED IN THE STUDY

Anonymous, "Brief History of Forest Legislation in India," *Perspectives,* Document File No. 37, Legal Resources for Social Action (LRSA), Chengalpattu, Tamil Nadu, 1996, pp. 12-15.

Ashwini Chhatre, "A Summary and Critique of the Draft Forest Bill, 1994," *Perspectives,* Document File No. 37, Tamil Nadu, 1996, pp. 16-20.

Anonymous, "Amendments Proposed by NGOs," *Perspectives,* No. 37, Tamil Nadu, 1996, pp. 35-36.

Agarwal, Anil, "Ecological Destruction and the Emerging Patterns of Poverty and People's Protests in Rural India," *Social Action,* Vol. 35, No. 1, Jan.-March, 1985, pp. 54-80.

Ayyappan, A., *Report on the Socio-Economic Conditions of the Aboriginal Tribes of the Province of Madras,* 1948.

Agnihotri, S.K., "*Poor Man's Smoke (Beedi) and Tendu Leaves,*" Paper presented at the Second Forestry Conference, Forest Research Institute and Colleges, Dehradun (mimeo), 1980.

Awastha, "Availability of Mohwa Flowers and Seeds in Dandakaranya and Prospects of Mohwa Oil Industry," *Indian Forester,* 1971, 97(1).

Chowdhary, R.L., *Estimates of Income and Employment Generated through Forestry Sector in Chandrapur District of Maharashtra State,* Indian Forester, 1975.

Elwin, Vernier, *Tribal Myths of Orissa,* Oxford University Press, Bombay, 1954.

Fernandes, W. and Geeta Menon, *Tribal Women and Forest Economy: Deforestation, Exploitation and Status Change,* Indian Social Institute, 1987.

Gadgil, "Forestry with a Social Purpose" in Walter Fernandes and Shaarad Kulkarni (eds.), *Towards a New Forest Policy: People's Rights and Environmental Needs,* Indian Social Institute, 1983.

Govt. of India, *Report of the Committee for Review of Rights and Concessions in the Forest Areas of India* (*Chaudhary Report*), 1984.

Gupta Tirath and Guleria Amar, *Non-wood Forest Products in India: Economic Potentials,* Centre for Management in Agriculture, Indian Institute of Management, Ahmedabad, Published by Oxford and IBH Publishing Co., New Delhi, 1982.

International Fund for Agricultural Development, *A.P. Tribal Development Project—Preparation Report,* Asia Division, Project Management Department, June 1990.

Jagannadha Rao, V., *Forest Laws in Andhra Pradesh,* Asia Law House, Hyderabad, 1983-84.

Murali Manohar, K., P. Ramaiah and C. Sivaramakrishna Rao, *Political Economy of Tribal Development,* Indian Institute of Public Administration, Warangal, 1985.

Nadkarni, M.V., Syed Ajmal Pasha and L.S. Prabhakar, *The Political Economy of Forest Use and Management,* Sage Publications, New Delhi, 1989.

Raghavaiah, *Tribal Revolts,* Andhra Rashtra Adimajati Sevak Sangh, Nellore, Andhra Pradesh, 1971.

Ramamani, *Tribal Economy : Problems & Prospects,* Chugh Publications, Allahabad, 1988.

Ramaiah, P., *Tribal Economy of India: A Case Study of Koyas of Andhra Pradesh,* Light & Life Publishers, New Delhi, 1981.

Govt. of India, Ministry of Agriculture and Irrigation, *Report of the National Commission on Agriculture,* Part IX, Forestry, New Delhi, 1976.

Saxena, N.C., "Forest and the Poor in India," *Management in Government,* Vol. XXVIII, Nos. 3-4, October, 1996-March, 1997.

Tirath Gupta and Amar Guleria, *Some Economic and Management Aspects of a Non-Wood Forest Product in India: Tendu Leaves*, Oxford & IBH, New Delhi, 1982.

Tirath Gupta and Amar Guleria, *Non-wood Forest Products in India*, Oxford & IBH, New Delhi, 1982.

Vyasulu, Vinod, "Alternative Development Strategies for Koraput," Paper presented at the Seminar on Alternative Development Strategies: Their Relevance to India (Lucknow, February 21-22, 1981).

# Index